CUENTOS TEJANOS

Intriguing and Historical Tales of the Wild Horse Desert
An Anthology

CUENTOS TEJANOS

Intriguing and Historical Tales of the Wild Horse Desert

An Anthology

Revised Edition

Dr. Manuel C. Flores

CITIOFBOOKS, INC.
3736 Eubank NE Suite A1
Albuquerque, NM 87111-3579
www.citiofbooks.com
Hotline: 1 (877) 389-2759
Fax: 1 (505) 930-7244

Ordering Information:
Quantity sales. Special discounts are available on quantity purchases by corporations, associations, and others. For details, contact the publisher at the address above.

Printed in the United States of America.

ISBN-13:   Softcover   979-8-89391-613-3
                    eBook   979-8-89391-614-0

Library of Congress Control Number: 2025905561

Table of Contents

Dedicated to My Ancestors

(Dedicado a Mis Antepasados)

Thank you for clearing the way for our family to succeed and prosper in this wonderful land we call Texas.

(Gracias por abrir los caminos para que nuestra familia lograra éxito y prosperidad en esta maravillosa tierra que llamamos Tejas).

For you, here are these "Tejano Tales."
(Para ustedes aquí están estos "Cuentos Tejanos.")

Family photo at ranch in Oilton, Texas, circa 1888

Wedding Photo for Pedro G. Chapa and Maria Marta Saenz in Laredo's
San Agustin Cathederal, March 23, 1923.

Foreword

Cuentos are a family tradition

It's late in the afternoon.

Transito Sáenz is arriving in his ranch house after a hard day of working cattle, tending fences and inspecting crops. It's 1894.

His little *ranchito* is doing well, he thinks. The family is healthy, the cattle and horses are safe and there is plenty of food, *"Gracias a Dios* (Thanks be to God)."

His wife Francisca greets him with an *"abrazo* (hug)" and a kiss.

"¿Como te fue, Viejo? (How did it go, old man), she asks lovingly.

Transito goes into an explanation of how one of the cows is going to have a calve soon and he has to make arrangements at the barn to make sure she will survive and he replies that the barbed wire fence on the south pasture seems to have been torn down by something or someone. He rambles as if making a report to the *caporal* to the ranch foreman.

Francisca hands him a cup of coffee and a piece of sweet cornbread as he sits down on an rickety rocker on the front porch and looks toward the orange trees that have sprung in the middle of the mesquite grove.

"No, pos, todo está bien, pero ay huellas que alguien o algo anda en el pasto, (All looks Good but there are signs that something or someone has been in the pasture)."

A soft and warm breeze blows in from Gulf of Mexico and rustles the leaves of the nearby trees and brush, lifting up a *"remolino* (whirlwind)" sending mourning doves scurrying into the blue South Texas sky.

Transito asks where his daughter María is. *"¿Y la sobrina, nuestra hija, ¿en dónde anda?* (And, our niece, our daughter, where is she?)"

"Anda en el naranjal de los Barreras con su amigas, colectando la cosecha. Creo que les van a pagar. (She's in the Barrera's orange grove with her friends helping with the harvest. I believe they're going to pay them).

Francisca and Transito took over caring for María when her mother, their daughter, died giving birth. They are María's aunt and uncle but they are raising her as their own daughter. María is 12 now and is as active as humming bird seeking the nectar from the blooms on the orange trees.

"Ay, esa niña se va a comer más naranjas que las que va a colectar (That girl is going to eat more oranges than what they're going to collect," Transito says, causing Francisca to give him a harsh glare.

"*No seas malo con ella,*" she says scolding him. "*Es niña, todavía* (She is still a little girl)"

But Transito realizes she's growing up too fast. He worries about her education. The ranch is in the Brush Country, *"El Chaparral"* he calls it. Laredo is the biggest down and is almost 40 miles due west. It takes the family 5 days on horse wagon to get there. Trips are usually every other month to stock up with food for the family and livestock and just things to live on. He can't remember the last time he bought María nice shoes. *"Esta creciendo muy pronto. Va necesitar un par de zapatos nuevos muy pronto.* (She's getting older. She's going to need a new pair os shoes soon)," he thinks.

He looks out at his ranch. It has a nice garden and a couple of good fruit trees, orange and lemon. The fences are up, now that he fixed them. He considers the ranch, bought by his father in the 1870s after saving money from one of the many cattle drives heading up to Kansas one spring. It was a blessing for the family who was accostumed to travel from ranch-to-ranch seeking work, the men as vaqueros and the women as maids or cooks. Now the 60 acres make it look like a big ranch. He compared it to *"La Parrita"* (The Kenedy Ranch near Baffin Bay) and *"La Kineña"* of King Ranch fame. It wasn't close to those big ranchos but this, *"El Rancho Los Sáenz" was his. "Gracias a Dios que tenemos agua aquí.* (Thank goodness there is plenty of water here)," he reflects. Water came from underground wells and a strong southeast breeze from the Gulf of Mexico that kept *"El Papalote* (windmill)" humming every day.

"Nos bendijo Dios, Francisca, (God blessed us Francisca)," he says to his wife. Francisca tears up. She never got over losing her daughter but thanked god every day for letting them raise Maria. *"Si, mi amor. Nuestro Rancho es una bendición.*(Yes my love, the ranch is a blessing)." She remembers the travelling priest who rode from the Rio Grande Valley on horseback to offer mass to the Catholic faithful maybe every 2-3 months was due soon.

She would light vigil candles for him and to give thanks for her family's health.

Transito and Francisca worry about María's future. The ranch school only goes through the 6th grade and most of the instruction is in Spanish. English is quickly becoming the main language of the area.

At the distance they see María and her friend running toward the ranch house, a sack full or oranges in each girl's back bopping up and down as they skip through the tall buffel grass.

They stop to catch their breath and the burlap bags hang loosely behind them.

"Cuidado con las víboras! (Watch out for snakes!)" Francisca hollers at the top of her lungs.

But the girls are having too much fun and start their hurried trek again, their laughter getting closer as Transito gets off the patio chair and starts walking toward them. María jumps on Transito and gives him an adoring hug saying, *"Papa Transito nos pagaron con un costal lleno de naranjas, mira* (They paid us with a sack full of oranges, look), taking an orange that barely fits in her hand and shoving it into his face.

"¿Y el dinero? (And the money?" Transito asks.

María looks down at her shoes. They are full of burrs, grass and other weeds she picked up while running through the pasture.

"Y mira esas manos (and look at those hands," Francisca retorts, seeing María's hands covered with dust from the orange trees. It looks, too, as if she has a scratch. *"Anda y lávate* (go clean up)," she orders.

María heads inside the house and her friend excuses herself and takes off running toward her ranch, about a ½ mile away. As María struts into the house, Transito tells her to hurry up and come back. He has something to tell her, he explains.

Francisca looks at him quizzically.

"Ay Transito, ya vas a comenzar con tus cuentos (Oh, Transito, you're going to start with your tales.)

Transito smiles, take a sip of his now lukewarm coffee and munches into the cornbread which is still warm and covered with mesquite honey.

He's about to tell his niece another story of the history of the area and South Texas. Word-of-mouth was the only way to keep the stories alive back then. Family time involved sitting outdoors under the shade of the tree or a porch of patio as the Gulf breeze caressed your face. Here, details about important people and events in life would be told and retold. Some chats were like history lessons. Transito was going to make sure María knew all about them.

"*Ven María, vamos a platicar* (Come Maria, let's chat)," he implores. María sits down on the patio floor next to where he is sitting, her long legs dangling from the floor. There is still good light, and the birds are making their final sweep for food, cackling and buzzing to and fro enthusiastically. In the distance, the plaintive wail of a coyote can be heard and the trees are busting with the cries of the cicadas. Night is approaching. It's the perfect time for a "*cuento* (tale)."

"*¿María, estas lista para otro cuento Tejano?*" (María are you ready for another Texas tale)," Transito asked with a whimsical look on his fase.

"*Si Papa Transito* (Yes Papa Transito), she replied excitedly. "*¿Es leyenda?* (Is it a legend?), she asks.

Transito starts, "*María, en aquel entonces había una muchacha, como tu, que le gustaba cantar . . .* (Maria, in those days there was a girl, like you, who liked to sing. . ."

Transito would continue his story. He had a dozens of them. Sometimes he would repeat a story. He didn't want *María* to forget who she was, who her ancestors were or where she came from.

The stories had to survive.

Some were exciting legends or stories of heroism and survival. Others just funny stories he had experienced or lived. Many were just family stories handed down to him by his parents or *tíos* (aunts or uncles) or *primos* (cousins). He told her, some day she would have cuentos too and would tell them to her children and others.

And so the story-telling tradition in our family continues. In 2025, I am the story-teller. Generation-to-generation the stories are told and continue. New ones emerge as each years pass by and some have lasting power that become almost like heirlooms of our memories. They are engrained in the circuits of our brains like a spring shower that wets the dry earth and becomes part of the soil that will bring life to vegetation and the world around us.

Our stories are our life. They help us understand the past and maybe even see into the future.

I've heard countless stories from my elders, *mi familia,* and my friends and even teachers and professors. They have become part of me, my memory, and have helped me become the person I am. I, as Transito predicted, heard them from my mom and now I'm passing them down to my children and grandchildren.

They are stories that must survive.

But, today's society is different. There is little time to sit and chat and youngsters tend to be in a rush too, well, be on the cell phone.

So will stories survive?

I hope so. I love books and so I will use that medium to convey the stories I've heard and kept throughout my life.

What better way to do that than by putting them in a book which can be stored and retrieved anytime you want to find out something? Why, you could even start a conversation and talk. . . .

Let's start. Please enjoy "Cuentos Tejanos/Tejano Tales" and see if you recognize any them. Like my great uncle Transito, I have dozens to tell.

Prologue

The Wild Horse Desert, a.k.a. The Nueces Strip

By Dr. Manuel Flores

It has been described in many ways both in folklore and historical documents.

It has been called "no man's land", the "disputed territory" and "the land where no one lives."

Well, most of them are wrong. Historically, "disputed" is the most accurate.

The Wild Horse Desert has been part of Texas history since various indigenous tribes lived in it for many years. It was just land, back then.

Today it has been described as the South Texas Triangle, but at first there were no defined boundaries. One of the best descriptions of the area was penned in a blog by songmao327 who described it as: "The Wild Horse Desert is a slice of Texas generally south of the Nueces River often referred to as the Nueces Strip. Boundaries are not defined, but I consider the Wild Horse Desert boundaries to be from the mouth of the Rio Grande River then northwest following the Rio Grande River to an area around Laredo, and east along the Nueces River to Corpus Christi and south along the Gulf coast to the mouth of the Rio Grande." Agreed. The northern edge however rolls up to the Uvalde-Del Rio area, in my view.

It was the Indigenous tribes of Texas who first tamed this land. But there were no horses, or cattle for that matter. But then came the Spanish settlers meandering through the Texas prairies and coastal plains. They brought horses and cows with them. Many stayed with the settlers. Horses were valuable beasts of burden and war and were nurtured to multiply. Some horses were tamed and corralled at way stations so that new Spanish explorers could find fresh mounts and continue their journey to explore Texas and what is now the United States. Other horses spread into the Brush Country and started the wild herds that would roam the area for nearly a century.

One way station was Rancho Santa Petrolina, located 18 miles southeast of what is now Corpus Christi. That became the largest cattle and horse ranch in the hemisphere now ruled by Spain, primarily, all the way to Tierra del Fuego in South America. It is in the Petronila area there where the Spanish first mention the wild mustangs roaming the land freely. Captain Blas María de la Garza Falcón (sent to the area by colonizer José de Escandón), let his horses – *Los Mesteños* in Spanish -roam freely in the area from the Gulf of Mexico's sand dunes to the myriad of mesquite groves and chaparral of South Texas down to banks the Rio Grande. Nearby was what is now Mustang Island near Port Aransas. The wild mustangs found fresh water to drink there as dew formed in the tall grass near the dunes and lingered there for hours before the Texas sun evaporated the moisture. At the time the Spanish were here, the site was known as *"La Isla de Los Mesteños,"* thus Mustang Island, today.

Wild horses, estimated by some at one million, roamed throughout South Texas. They would be the fresh mounts for Spanish explorers, and later the local Indian tribes, the armies of Texas and Mexico, the Confederates, and the Union. Some historians claim they even helped George Washington during the American Revolution.

Regardless, south of the Nueces River there were horses, wild horses, by the tens of thousands. But then came the Texas War of Independence from Mexico, the Battles of the Alamo and Goliad and many others would change the area as Texas staked its claim to be free of Santa Anna's despotic rule. After San Houston's victory at the Battle of San Jacinto, for the first time, boundary lines were drawn. The area known for the free-roaming wild mustangs would now have boundaries. Politics was now involved, and more wars would follow.

Toward the end of the 1850s, many of the wild mustangs had become beasts of burden for ranchers and farmers and tools of war for soldier and Indians. Hunting, too, to rid the area of the pesky horses thinned the herds considerably.

After its loss to Texas and Sam Houston's troops, Mexico refused to concede the area south of the Nueces River and continued to claim it as part of Mexico. Texas, now a republic, insisted that its boundaries extended south to the Rio Grande. Now, the parcel of land between the Nueces River and the Rio Grande was disputed territory recognized officially as the Wild Horse Desert. Politicians called it "The Nueces Strip."

Tejanos, descendants of the 17th century Spanish explorers and settlers, now dominated the area. The Indian tribes were minimal, and many had mixed with the Spanish. Municipalities like Laredo and those in the Rio Grande Valley provided much of the order and bandits from both sides of the Rio Grande and the Nueces were the real controllers of the land. Neither the Mexican government nor the Republic of Texas had clear control. The United States, meanwhile, eyed the parcel of land and Texas, for that matter, as being crucial for its quest for expansion and the mantra of Manifest Destiny. Some Texas politicians contacted U.S. President James K. Polk. He saw the disputed area as an opportunity to expand the United States and embellish his legacy as President.

In 1845, Texas joined the Union, becoming the 28th state of the United States. Soon after, President Polk sent Gen. Zachary Taylor to Port Isabel by the mouth of the Rio Grande on the U.S.-Mexico border to reaffirm the now United States' claim to the disputed land called "The Nueces Strip." War ensued in 1846 and lasted two years with a decisive United States victory. In 1848 all the "Mexican" residents of the disputed area were given one year to declare their citizenship, under the rules of the Treaty of Guadalupe Hidalgo. Ironically, they were already residents of Texas and one would think that once Texas became a state of the United States all its residents then became citizens of the United States. Again, ironically, it seems some of the Texas residents of Spanish and Mexican descent are still struggling to gain the rights of full citizenship in the United States. Historically speaking, when the Mexican War ended the United States increased its size by one third with lands taken from Mexico.

This was the final legacy of the Wild Horse Desert, a.k.a. the Nueces Strip. After this, life went on with a sea of local disputes. Land owned by Spanish and Mexican settlers and Tejanos was soon lost to the encroaching new Anglo settlers. Cultures would clash, some would survive. The Tejano and former residents of Mexico became second class citizens in what was once their own land. The Indigenous tribes disappeared or were absorbed into the general Spanish-speaking population.

Stories of struggle and survival and perseverance would arise. A new history was evolving aligned with the ranching and cattle industry developed by the Spanish and now central to the survival of the area. Tejanos lost their land, their jobs and some say their dignity but never their pride. They would have stories to tell that sprang from the Wild Horse Desert and the history of the Nueces Strip.

In this book, we have captured some of those stories. This book, then, focuses on tales of the Wild Horse Desert. They are legends of people who helped tames this land, historical anecdotes often left out of the history books, and family tales that deserved to be shared with others.

They are *"Cuentos Tejanos* – Tejano Tales."

Cuentos Tejanos

Episode 1

Irma Lerma Rangel – A South Texas Giant

There is a defining moment in the life and legacy of former Texas State Representative Irma Lerma Rangel and she was not even alive to enjoy the moment.

On a sunlit but cold and blustery February 16 morning in 2007on the campus of Texas A&M University-Kingsville (TAMUK), a statue of her likeness was unveiled and dedicated on the back plaza of the Texas A&M University Health System College of Pharmacy named in her honor. There, facing the TAMUK Student Recreation Center and in the shadows of fabled Javelina Stadium where the university's football team has won seven national championships, came to rest a statue in her honor.

The location was appropriate, for she too was a champion for the people of Kingsville, the university, South Texas and the State. The moment was bittersweet, however. Yes, she would be honored with a statue in front of a building in her alma mater, but in a strange twist of fate and politics the building did not actually belong to her beloved alma mater – Texas A&I University now Texas A&M University-Kingsville.

It was "the System's" building. Rangel would not have liked that.[2]

During her more than 26 years as a state legislator, she championed many causes for education, including the landmark legislation in 1997 known as the "Top Ten Percent Rule," which required state colleges and universities to automatically admit all students who graduate in the top 10 percent of their high school class.[3]

Now, here was a statue of her resting solidly as a reminder of her legacy as an alumna of Texas A&I, a citizen of Kingsville, a politician and a woman. She would have liked that . . . . She would have been proud.[4]

A crowd of more than 200 – mostly family and Texas A&M-Kingsville university administrators, politicians and A&M System representatives -

joined the somber yet exciting unveiling of the statue that cold February day.

Rangel served as state representative for District 43 in South Texas – presenting Kleberg and Kenedy counties and parts of several counties in the Rio Grande Valley - for more than 26 years and had been instrumental in securing the College of Pharmacy. In her last legislative session, Representative Rangel passed the bill creating South Texas' first professional school—the school of pharmacy at Texas A&M University-Kingsville.[5]

That the pharmacy school and her statue had come to rest in Kingsville and on the campus of her beloved university was not lost in the moment for those present, that February Friday. Rangel had passed away March 17, 2003, after a valiant fight with cancer. Her once stoic and fiery stance portrayed on the floor of the Texas legislature for more than a quarter-century while she fought and lobbied for an array of legislation that would impact the people of South Texas and state for years to come, however, was never lost the statue inflected that. Now, her statue was there for all to see, a striking pose on top of a solid granite pedestal looking beyond the northern horizon - toward Austin - with her right hand outstretched and perched as if to start a lecture on the reasons she was backing yet another piece of social legislation. The statue seems to come to life as the noon sun casts a giant shadow toward the building named in her honor. On her left hand she holds two folders, laden with papers explaining the latest law she is supporting. Her face is bedazzled with her trademark big earrings and a necklace representing her culture (it must be topaz) hanging from her neck.

The dedication seemed magical, especially for family and friends present. While the voices of the speakers at the dedication echoed off the buildings, past College Hall on University Boulevard and through the storied buildings of South Texas' oldest university, a reverent attitude reserved for wakes prevailed. The statue would become a source of inspiration and to this date, the pharmacy students drop pennies at her feet to get good luck for the tough exams they face.[6]

After the customary dedication speeches and commemorative words, her sister – Minnie Rangel-Henderson – stepped up to the statue and slowly reached out her white-glove covered and shaking left hand, touching the left hand of her sister's statue that was clutching the ledgers of law she seemed about to speak on that day. Tears welled from Minnie Rangel-Henderson's face, which was covered in a traditional lace shawl reminiscent of the family's religious ties. She turned, speaking to no one and everyone. The group gave her room.

"It's a beautiful statue," she said in soft voice. A nearby reporter for the college student newspaper nodded affirmatively as he clicked picture after picture of the scene. "It looks like her, (it's) like she was."[7]

Yes, but much taller. Rangel was 5-foot-4 and the statue was more than 6-foot tall.

Then – with a wry smile and a tear streaming down her left cheek - she turned to the reporter and said, "She is bigger in the statue than she was in real life."[8]

Indeed, Irma Rangel was bigger in real life than her 5-foot-4 height showed, and now the statue would show that phenomena. She is portrayed as almost 6-feet tall in the statue, appropriate for this South Texas giant who never took the back seat when it came to lobbying for legislation that would help her district. In the Texas legislature, she would be strong voice for the powerless and for her beloved Kingsville. Armed with a bachelor's degree in education from Texas A&I and a law degree from St. Mary's University, this woman became a trailblazer and role model for women, Hispanics and everyone who feels the need to fight for justice.

Dr. Mauro Castro, a regents professor of chemistry at Texas A&M University-Kingsville, recalled Rangel's passion with great admiration. Castro was a strong proponent for the pharmacy school and served associate dean of the school of pharmacy from 2001-05.[9] "She was a caring person, always championing the cause of education for the citizens of South Texas," Castro said in an interview in October 2013. "She grew up in an environment of 'the wrong or other side of the tracks' and was always wanting to equalize things."[10] While the phrase "wrong side of the tracks" is familiar to Mexican-Americans growing up in 20th century Texas, it has a universal use that the Cambridge Dictionary identifies or defines simply by saying the wrong side of the tracks is "a part of a town that is considered poor and dangerous."[11] "She was always fighting for people to have equal opportunity – especially in education – in all of Texas,"[12] he said. Castro worked for 15 years with Rangel on a number of educational initiatives, especially the pharmacy college for South Texas, and called her "a champion for education . . . . She felt that if more educational and professional programs were brought to South Texas, it would give the opportunity for students to stay in (South Texas). The pharmacy school was the last part of her legacy."[13]

On that blustery 40-degree sun-lit day, Minnie Lerma-Henderson was well aware of the irony the statue of her sister brought not only to the university she championed, but also to the City of Kingsville and, indeed, South Texas and the State.

"I am very proud of Irma," she said that day. "I remember my parents when they told (us) 'go further in your education because it is the only thing you take with you when you die'."[14]

It is not surprising that the Rangel sisters grew up with fervor for education. Growing up in the depression era of the 1930s, the family worked hard to survive not only economic pressure but also discrimination suffered in their hometown. The family survived in spite of many obstacles and, in the 1950s, made a move that would impact their lives – and that of the citizens of Kingsville - forever. They moved from the Mexican side of town to house just southwest of the then Texas A&I college campus on Santa Gertrudis Ave. It was "the other side of the tracks" where the more affluent Anglo community lived.

Rangel-Henderson admitted her family were trailblazers when it came to housing for Mexican Americans and remembered the struggles well.

"As a family, we were faced with discrimination in a segregated community and we never accepted it. We were taught by our parents to fight injustices and stand up for the poor and oppressed. We never acted (as if) women were not equal to men and that Mexican-Americans could not be successful," Rangel-Henderson said.[15]

In 1947, the Rangel parents bought some land near then Texas College of Arts and Industry (later A&I and A&M-Kingsville). They later decided to build a home in the western part of Santa Gertrudis Ave., close to the King Ranch gate. But the land was in the "Anglo-White" area of Kingsville, Rangel-Henderson recalled. One of the neighbors organized a petition collecting signatures against the Rangel family because he believed that to have a Mexican American family in the area would be bad for the neighborhood.[16]

The family did not move. It resolved to stay and eventually build a 2-story Spanish colonial style stucco and brick house. With the college now across the block, the concept of education was reinforced for the three Rangel sisters. Minnie would go on to become a pharmacist. Olga would get her master's in education. Irma would be a lawyer, a politician and a trendsetter and a heroine for many.

Irma Rangel credits their parents for helping them survive and persevere because of the lesson they taught their girls. "I never really had any problems (growing up) because we were raised with the idea that, you know, that I had to do more work than the other person because I was Mexican American, my parents would say."[17]

Their father was Presiliano M. Rangel, but was known as "P.M." He was born in 1903 near La Rosita in Duval County. Her father was orphaned at the age of 5 and was raised by his sisters. He would go from family member to family member on *"un caballito* (a little horse)" about 1918 and jump from job to job to survive. He would pick cotton in the Kingsville area and finally settled there. He had no education.

Her mother was Herminia Lerma and was born in Los Arrieros, a ranch community in what is now Starr County. She and her father and brothers came to Los Hogos, a ranch community in Nueces County near Corpus Christi, in the 1920s. Known as "Minnie" and later "Big Minnie" because she would name one of her daughters after her, the Rangel's mom had a grade school education. The two were married "about 1926" she said in a 1996 interview for "Tejano Voices." [18]

That interview also revealed more about the family's encounter with discrimination. From stories her mother told her, she reconstructed the scene of her mother going to school in Kingsville. The Lermas lived in a ranch house west of what is now Texas A&M University-Kingsville. They used the rental property to farm the area near the King Ranch. It would eventually become the site of their home. From that farmhouse, the nearest school was Flato Elementary, but her mom could not attend that school. Instead, she would have to go another mile to the school she was assigned to attend. "The Flato School was used for the Anglo students only and so (my mother) had to go like another mile or so to go to what as called the Mexican Ward at that time."[19]

That lease would become an important part of the Rangel family legacy. When P.M. and Herminia Rangel saw the old lease property the Lermas used to farm go up for sale, they hurried up and bought the lot in the late 1940s.[20]

" . . .(W)hen she saw that this (lease) property was being sold, both she and my father went and bought it. And, as soon as they bought it, well, there were no Mexican Americans here in the neighborhood and so they wanted to buy it back from them and they offered five times more than they (her mother and father) had paid for it."[21] The Rangels did not budge.

"We were the only Mexican Americans. But there was only one very good person here that just told them that, you know, you are crazy." The house on Santa Gertrudis St., just a half-mile from the King Ranch gate to the west, still stands. The family moved in to the new house on December 1951. Irma Rangel remembered the neighbors kept to themselves and that the Rangels went on make a living and raising a family.[22]

P.M. Rangel was a respected member of the Kingsville and South Texas community. Rangel-Henderson remembers her father as a "hard-working" man who worked in farming, ranching, construction and business. He became a merchant, owning an appliance store, a furniture store, a plumbing service two barbershops and a bar. He also helped his wife develop a successful dress shop located just off the main street of Kingsville and not restricted to the Mexican side of town.[23] Irma credited her family upbringing for teaching valuable lessons that lasted a lifetime and, in the final analysis, impacted South Texas as the State. "And my father had no education and my mother went to the fifth grade and that was it because she, of course, was Mexican (American), and when she came to Kingsville" that was all she was allowed, she said in the 1996 interview.[24]

The family would travel to surrounding ranch towns and would sell her mom's dresses while the girls would sell candy to help the family make a living. Her father would say it was important to share in the prosperity one enjoyed. This is where Irma Rangel said she learned her next lesson about life and her first about politics- helping others and being politically active is important in life. "(My parents) were hard-working people. So they wanted to help other people . . . .they wanted to share what they had been able to achieve for themselves. So they were always trying to help . . . .(A)nd a lot of people would come to him when elections would come around because he was very active and he wanted to better the community. And they trusted him. They trusted that he was going to select the best candidate for the benefit of the community and (the Mexican Americans in Kingsville) would look to him (for guidance)."[25]

P.M. Rangel was keenly aware of the obstacles Mexican Americans faced to vote. As detailed in Evan Anders book "Boss Rule in South Texas," those obstacles included a poll tax, permission from their boss, voting for whom the boss or "patron" asked for, facing armed gunmen at the polls and just finding time to vote.[26] For these reasons he – and the family – became active, in the 1940s, in the Good Government League which would assist politicians to stage political rallies and campaign for office with support from progressive citizens who wanted every one to have a fair chance to participate in the political process.[27] The Rangel family was active in city, county and school elections, but few Mexican Americans were elected to any of these posts until the 1980s. Later, "Little Minnie," – Irma's sister, was elected to the Kingsville ISD school board and served as president.[28] She was the first Mexican American woman to serve on the board and the first Mexican American to serve as president.[29]

Armed and inspired with the lessons learned from her father and family, Irma Rangel set out on trail-blazing career. It started modestly: a college education at neighboring Texas A&I with a bachelor's degree in business administration in1951, a job as a teacher in Venezuela and in South Texas at Robstown and Alice for 14 years. She later enroll at St. Mary's University School of Law in San Antonio, to pursue a career as a prosecutor and finally politics.[30]

At the root of her legacy is the fact that Irma Rangel was raised in Kingsville, Texas, where her parents were the first Mexican Americans to build their home in a traditionally Anglo-American neighborhood. When she returned to the U.S. to attend St. Mary's University, to obtain her law degree in 1969, she embarked on a storied and historic politics career. She was the first woman to work as an assistant district attorney in Corpus Christi and, in 1973; she was the first Mexican American woman to open a law office in Kingsville. She was the first woman elected as chairman of the Mexican American Legislative Caucus and, in 1974, the first Mexican American woman elected as chairman of the Kleberg County Democratic Party. Rangel devoted herself to her career in law and politics. In 1976, she became the first Mexican American woman to be elected to the Texas Legislature and continuously represented the her legislative district in the Texas House of Representatives for 26 years, also serving as chairman of the House Higher Education Committee. Among other honors, she was inducted into the Texas Women's Hall of Fame in 1994.[31]

Rangel's venture into law was the turning point in her life. After graduating from St. Mary's she served as a clerk for Federal Judge Adrian Spears in San Antonio. She then moved to Corpus Christi where she served as assistant district attorney for three years. She went into public practice in 1972 with Corpus Christi attor. Tony Canales and Rudy Garza. In 1973, she finally returned to Kingsville to set up a law practice with Hector García. She took over the law practice in 1983 after Garcia's death and kept it until 1993 (even when she was in the legislature), when she closed the office and decided to become "a full-time legislator."[32]

Her venture into politics came after she was invited to attend the Texas Women's Political Caucus convention in Austin. Lady Bird Johnson and Liz Carpenter spearheaded the TWPC gathering. It was there she noticed the lack of Mexican American women in politics. At the urging of other Mexican American women leaders present she was asked to consider running for the state legislature. "Because the incumbent house representative in Rangel's district, Greg Montoya, was under federal investigation he was considered vulnerable. The Latinas at the conference, who were also members of the Women's Texas Political Caucus, felt the time was right for someone to run against Montoya, and they specifically encouraged Rangel to run against Montoya. . . Finally, after talking it over with her parents, she decided to 'take a crack at'." [33]

With the support of her parents and the backing of Mexican American women leaders, she ventured off into politics. It wasn't easy, she recalls in her 1996 interview. She hadn't been in Kingsville for several years. All she had was her education, her family's good name and reputation and a sincere passion to serve the people of South Texas. She was facing the incumbent Greg Montoya and two other candidates in the Democratic Primary. There were no Republican opponents as Texas was essentially a one-party state at the time. [34] "Rangel had several things going against her when she ran for office the first time. First, she had been back in the Kingsville area for only a short period after being away 17 years. Many people did not know her or remembered her only as a little girl." [35]

Rangel would use her family roots to gain a foothold in the race. Her family was well known not only in Kingsville, but also in South Texas. Her sister Minnie, with the exception of going to college and becoming a pharmacist, had also never left Kingsville. "(My parents) had always been loved and respected and so I remembered going to a Bingo and saying, you know, 'I am Irma Rangel, you know, P.M.'s daughter and la *hermana* (sister) of Minnie." [36]

This tactic had worked a year earlier when professors (Jim Hobbs, Cecilia Hunter and Leslie Hunter) at Texas A&I encouraged her to run for Kleberg County Democratic Chair. [37] But, now, she was running for the state legislature and she admitted she "had never been to the Capital" in Austin. [38]

"Rangel frequently took her parents with her on the campaign trail, even having them sit with her when she attended a televised candidate forum for station KGBT in Harlingen. Her sister (Minnie) went door-to-door with her in Kingsville and also rode with her in a car caravan through the entire district."[39]

There were other issues, too. Rangel's status as a single woman came into play and there were even rumors she was a lesbian. In Elsa in the Rio Grande Valley, she had to visit with community leaders, including the mayor, to proclaim to them she was not a lesbian. " …I am not going to go to bed (with you) to prove it to you …" she told the men.[40] In her interview in 1996 she eloquently defended herself and described that encounter by saying, "(E)ven if I was (a lesbian), you know, I am still very qualified, if I was a lesbian because I am an attorney, and I know how to work hard. And that wouldn't make me any less capable, but I am not. I am sure there are lesbians; they must be wonderful people. They pay taxes and they get an education and they are no different."[41]

Her marital status was a point of contention, at first. Few knew that in 1954 she had a relationship with a Navy jet fighter pilot from San Jose, California, named Alfredo Carrillo. The two were engaged. Carrillo was killed in a jet crash in California that year.[42]

> "That's true, yeah. I almost got married several times, you know, but it is somewhat personal because there were deaths, you know. He (Carrillo) was killed and all that and then the older you become, the more particular you get, so you are trying to put all the good things you have met in other men, and I have never been able to find that guy, and then I was always very independent. And I got the taste of men who were overly possessive, and who wanted to tell me what to do, when to do it and I didn't like that and I said, 'If this is what marriage is going to be all about, I don't know that I want to get married because I wanted to do my own thing.' And I have not yet met the guy that is going to let me do whatever I want, whenever I want to, without permission because I am not used to that. My father encouraged us to do and do whatever we wanted to."[43]

Gaining financial support from power players and prominent lawyers was hard because she was not married. By confronting the "lesbian" issue and her marital status head-on, it soon became a non-issue. The issue died down because "it wasn't important to them any more."[44]

But, she ran a "very good grassroots campaign" and "great support" from women in her district, especially the farm workers' wives.[45] She had a very small campaign chest, using her personal finances mainly to finance a campaign that cost her almost $10,000. She had a hot dog sale to raise money and received a contribution from the TWPC of $1,850. With that, she bought some radio ads, yard signs and candidate cards.[46]

But mainly, Rangel's first campaign was personal. She recalls going door-to-door with her sister Minnie, asking for votes and support. In her 1996 interview, she said, "And so I went to this house and I knocked on the house and I will never forget that. An elderly woman, *era una viejita* (she was an old lady), she came out *y le dije, 'Mire Señora, soy Irma Rangel'* (and I said, 'Look, lady I am Irma Rangel.' (and she said) *'Ah si, yo la e oido en la radio y me gusta mucho la voz, esperese un momento.* (Ah, yes, I have heard you on the radio and I like your voice a lot, wait just a moment.' She came back with a dollar for my contribution. Oh, that was wonderful. I will never forget that."[47] Irma found that contributions from her supporters came from the heart. In one instance, the women farm workers she visited in the hamlets of LaSara and McCook in the Rio Grande Valley were so impressed with her leadership and campaign style that they asked her to visit them in one of their houses after they got back from working in the fields. It was about 6 or 7 in the evening, she recalled. They wanted to give her something. They presented her with a handmade red-white-and-blue tablecloth. It was their way of supporting Rangel. It read "IRMA For Representative." It was, Irma Rangel said, *"Muy, muy humilde* (Very, very humble) you know. And it was so beautiful . . ." Rangel credits her victory in the primary to the knowledge she gained from her father about working with rural citizens. "(I)n a rural area, the people want to see you . . . you know, you go in and they offer you coffee, tamales, *pan dulce* (sweet bread), and all this. And you sit down and, you know, they just pass (their thoughts about your conversation) on to the others, you know."[48]

In the four-person race, Rangel managed to pull in enough votes to advance to a runoff with Jean Hines, a native from Riviera just south of Kingsville on U.S. 77. "Hines was from a well-known political family, her father having been Kleberg County commissioner for many years."[49] She would need help. State representative Gonzalo Barrientos came down from Austin to help Irma Rangel with her campaign. She would hold her first political rally and did the traditional South Texas politician scene of standing on top of an old flatbed truck and urging people to vote. Hundreds of enthusiasts would come to show support. A friend gave her office space for the campaign headquarters. Neighbors, friends and part of the Mexican American extended family cooked and donated money for food for volunteers. Word-of-mouth became her calling card as she and her campaign workers spread the word about the run-off election.[50, 51]

Rangel's campaign gained momentum and she won by more than a 2-to-1 margin. With no Republican foe in the general election, she was heading for Austin. In 1977 she became the first Mexican-American woman state legislator in history.[52] She would hold that distinction – the only Mexican American woman state legislator – until 1985 when Lena Guerrero from the Austin area got elected to serve in the legislature.[53]

"I didn't know I was going to be the first one," she told reporters after she got elected. "I felt like I was really going to have to deliver. If I didn't succeed they were going to say 'All Mexican women were failures'."[54] Rangel did not falter. She would serve for more than a quarter century and become the "Dean of Tejana Legislators." In 2000, she became the chair of House Higher Education Committee, becoming first Mexican American and woman to hold that post.[55] In between, she sponsored a myriad of social legislation that would earn her an impeccable reputation on the floor of the Texas house.

"People who knew Irma will remember her for her unmistakable voice," said Minnie Rangel. "She pronounced her words, syllable by syllable . . . she was very precise."[56] Jeremy Brown, a *Corpus Christi Caller-Times* reporter who covered Irma during her terms in the legislature said it best, according to the special edition published by the Texas A&M University-Kingsville student newspaper, *The South Texan*. Detailing Irma's mannerism as a state representative, Brown said, "She spoke with the precision of an experienced orator. Her pitch rose and fell, rhythmically, as if she invests a steady but hefty dose of emotion in every sentence. Then there is that accent, which some have said sounds British, or at least European, but which Rangel said . . . might come from speaking Spanish and English syntax when she was a little girl, in a childish attempt to sound like she actually knew English."[57, 58]

When she arrived in Austin and walked into the Capitol and the House Chambers, she was determined to make a difference and to represent her people and the women of Texas with dignity and grace. When she finally closed her law office in Kingsville in 1993, she became, in her mind, a full-time politician. That decision came when she started lobbying for the chair of the Mexican American caucus. "And that is when I started, you know, closing up my files and closing my law office because if I am going to be chair, I had better be 100 percent for the legislature, full-time legislator."[59] She must have done well, she never lost a re-election bid.[60]

Her legislation was social, to say the least, and it started in her first year.

During her first legislative session, she sponsored and passed House Bill 1755 that provided education and employment programs for mothers with dependent children.[61] Her presentation on the floor was memorable and the stuff of legend for the first Mexican American woman to serve on the Texas house. As a first-term legislator, respect doesn't always come easy. As she recalls, it was late at night and some of the legislators were starting to pack up, including herself. But then the Speaker (Bill Clayton, a Democrat like Rangel) called her bill up, at the last minute, about 9:30 or 10 p.m. She was surprised. Rangel picked up the memos on her bill and went up to the front marker where legislators stand and said, simply, "All right guys, you want us to have babies, then help us support them . . . Let us help those who cannot help themselves and make them self-supporting." Again, there was silence. "I think that is all I said and poof, the bill passed."[62] But she wasn't over. The bill was good and it had passed but her legislation needed money. When the appropriations bill came on the floor, Rangel, the first-term politician, was at it again. Appropriations are not an easy thing to obtain on the Texas House. All the members are scrambling to get deals done to fund their legislation. She recalled, in her 1996 interview, there was a lot of smoke and a lot of noise." I wanted them all to hear me and I said, ' This is a good amendment, we need the moneys for that bill'," hollering over the noise. But the noise continued. Then it happened, the attention-getter she needed came as if a sign from above. To the day she did her interview for Tejano Voices 1996, she believed she got help from above. "I am practically shouting on the mike and then all of a sudden, bang! What was that? A light bulb *de alli arriba* (from up there in the ceiling). All the glass came on down on and it hit . . . Smith Gilley (D-Greenville). Smith Gilley was the one that got all the glass on his head and everybody was very quiet. Everybody got scared. You could've heard a pin drop." In the confusion and ensuing quiet, Garcia went up to the mike and said, "All right members, someone up there is trying to tell you something. I respectfully request vote for my amendment (for funding)." It passed.[63]

But it wasn't that easy for her. She soon discovered she had little in common with the male dominated legislature. She knew she had to earn respect and be cooperative to succeed, but how do you work with an all-male crew who often put women on a different and lower pedestal than man? Mexican American legislators, for example, like to go out and have a beer with the guys to get things accomplished, she said. Rangel would have none of that. "You know, you have to be over-protected. I know how to hold my own (when it comes to drinking) guys, so don't worry. And so when they found out how I would, you know, talk to them, you know, *pero yo les decia asi como me decian ellos porque soy mujer, ultimamente se mas que ustedes.* (I would say to them like they said to me because I was a woman, ultimately I know more than you all). (Eventually) I was one of them. But not to go drink beer, not to do this, no, uh huh."[64]

In Austin, however, half the battle is listening to lobbyists, many of whom come bearing gifts and are constantly asking state representatives to go out to dinner or a drink, she recalled in her 1996 interview. "But, I didn't look for that . . . I didn't hang out with the lobbyists either. I was living with these friends of mine. They were a married couple who were very . . . I didn't socialize that much with the lobbyists or anybody, (I) just went up there and did my business."[65]

Rangel was a hard-worker and somewhat of a perfectionist, the result of the expectations her parents had of the Rangel sisters and also her own expectations of not failing her constituency, the Mexican Americans and women in general. When the Texas House was trying to pass a bill criminalizing abortion, Rangel again stood up for what she felt was right. "I am very strong pro-choice and I had been an assistant district attorney (in 1971) . . . I was the only woman prosecutor (in Nueces County). And so all the rapes and the incest were coming to me."[66] Her experience of having to tell women that having an abortion was not legal in Texas solidified her believe on being pro choice, but she was still against abortion. Before a hushed House membership, Rangel spoke with vigor on the issue when the House and Senate were trying to pass a law that would be criminalize abortion. She recalled in her 1996 interview: "So, I went and I told them 'I do not condemn nor do I condone abortion'. I wanted (them) to know why this amendment has to go on. I told them that I had been a prosecutor. (I told them) it was not right that we, and you men here, be telling a woman whether or not she has the right to her privacy, to her own body . . . (E)verybody was quiet where you could've hear(d) a pin drop . . . ."[67]

She returned to her next session, having earned the respect of fellow house members, but still learning. She would get key committee appointments that she felt made her more powerful in her quest to serve her constituency. During her more than quarter-century of service to the Texas legislature she served on more than 50 committees, chairing or vice chairing several. Here is a list of her service during the Regular Sessions (R.S.) she served in the Texas House:

78th R.S. 2003

Border and International Affairs

Higher Education (Vice Chair)

77th R.S. - 2001

Higher Education (Chair)

Higher Education Excellence Funding

Pensions and Investments

Return-to-Work, House Joint

76th R.S. - 1999

Higher Education (Chair)

Rural Development, Select

75th R.S. - 1997

Higher Education (Chair)

Pensions and Investments

TRS-Care, House Joint

74th R.S. - 1995

Higher Education (Chair)

Pensions and Investments

Pensions and Investments Subcommittee on Optional Retirement Program

Pensions and Investments Subcommittee Teacher Retirement Insurance (Chair)

State Investment Policy, House Joint

73rd R.S. - 1993

General Investigating

Higher Education (Vice Chair)

Historically Underutilized Businesses, Select

International and Cultural Relations (Vice Chair)

NAFTA and GATT, Special Select (Vice Chair)

72nd R.S. - 1991

Higher Education

Higher Education Subcommittee on Professional Schools (Chair)

Higher Education Subcommittee on Student Financial Aid

Higher Education Subcommittee on Texas State Technical Institute

Higher Education Subcommittee on Tuition and Fees

Judicial Affairs (Vice Chair)

Judicial Affairs Subcommittee on Budget and Oversight

Judicial Affairs Subcommittee on Domestic Relations

Judicial Affairs Subcommittee on Judicial Selection

Judicial Affairs Subcommittee on Surrogate Parentage Contracts

71st R.S. - 1989

Higher Education (Vice Chair)

Higher Education Subcommittee on Continuing Education (Chair)

Higher Education Subcommittee on Upper Level Centers

House Administration

Judicial Affairs

Judicial Affairs Subcommittee on Juvenile Matters

Judicial Affairs Subcommittee on Spousal Maintenance

Texas Catastrophic Property Insurance Pool, Special

70th R.S. - 1987

Businesses Owned by Women or Minorities, Special

Child Abuse and Pornography, Select

Higher Education

Higher Education in South Texas

Higher Education Subcommittee on Budget and Oversight

House Administration

Judicial Affairs (Vice Chair)

69th R.S. - 1985

Advisory Committee to Study Viable Alternatives to the House Study Group

Higher Education

House Administration

Urban Affairs (Vice Chair)

Urban Affairs Subcommittee on Budget and Oversight (Vice Chair)

68th R.S. - 1983

Higher Education

Judicial Affairs (Vice Chair)

67th R.S. - 1981

Committee to Study Texas Dept. of Mental Health and Mental Retardation, Special

Judiciary Subcommittee on Venue (Chair)

Texas Department of Mental Health and Mental Retardation, Special

Special, Subcommittee on Citizen Complaints Regarding Operating Procedures

Texas Department of Mental Health and Mental Retardation, Special, Subcommittee on Study Revisions of State Mental Health Code

Transportation

Transportation Subcommittee on Rail Safety

66th R.S. - 1979

Judiciary

Judiciary Subcommittee on Concurrent Resolutions (Chair)

Security and Sanctions

65th R.S. - 1977

Business and Industry

Business and Industry Subcommittee on Consumer Protection

Business and Industry Subcommittee on Fire Prevention

Business and Industry Subcommittee on Professional Licensing

Business and Industry Subcommittee on Rural Industrial Development Act

Illegal Immigration, House Joint

Social Services

Social Services Subcommittee on Appropriative Matters Social Services Subcommittee on Rehabilitation[68]

Her service on these committees and mentorship of new legislators, in particular Mexican American women who followed her trail-blazing path to Austin, brought her much respect. By the end of her legislative career, she was characterized as "our den mother"[69] of Mexican American lawmakers. State legislator Paul Moreno (D-El Paso) who was the longest-serving Hispanic elected official in the USA, and presided as the Dean of the Texas House until his defeat in 2008,[70] knew and respected Irma Rangel's techniques and influence in Austin. "She never tired of telling me, 'Vote your conscience, you won't go wrong',"[71]

> "Rangel initially earned the confidence and trust (of her fellow legislators) with her strong professionalism and considerable knowledge of the legislative process. For these reasons she was asked several times to run for chair of the Mexican American Legislative Caucus, but she declined, primarily due to other Commitments associated with her law practice in Kingsville. In 1995, however, she finally consented to run and, with little opposition, was elected as the caucus's first (Mexican American Woman) chair. At that time she closed her law office and devoted 100 percent of her time to her responsibilities to Austin."[72]

As chair of the Mexican American Legislative Caucus and as a member of the Higher Education Committee of the House, she had new-found power. Always a strong proponent of social legislation and always a strong voice on the house floor, she had extra ammunition now to push her agenda to help South Texas and her constituency. Armed with new confidence, she set out to get a law school for South Texas to be located at Texas A&I. She proposed the bill in 1991. Because of the respect she had in the House with her fellow legislators, the bill passed. However, it failed in the Texas Senate and died. "I will never forget Lt. Governor Bill Hobby saying that it was ludicrous to have a law school here in South Texas. But it wasn't ludicrous to have three law schools in Houston, you know? And so I sent the message to him and I told him, I said, 'How can you say that? You have got three law schools in Houston and that is not ludicrous, you know?' So, I couldn't get it passed'."[73] The fact that they turned down a request for a law school at her alma mater in Kingsville offended her but did not deter her. She blamed the loss to politics and the inability for the Democratic Party and the Mexican American caucus to work together.[74] However, the plan continued. A decision that was reached by more than 150 Mexican American professionals during a meeting in San Antonio that was moderated by former Secretary of Housing and Urban Development and former San Antonio Mayor Henry Cisneros in 1990 had solidified a plan to develop higher education institutions in South Texas and along the border region with Mexico.[75] Her fight, however, had been well documented and appreciated. Cecilia Hunter and Leslie Hunter, authors of the book on the history of the university, remembered the legislative battle.

> "In 1991, Rangel and (State Senator Carlos) Truan introduced legislation to establish a law school at Texas A&I University. (Texas A&I) President (Manuel) Ibanez wrote a letter to the (university's student newspaper) *The South Texan* stating that a law school at Texas A&I 'would be one of the finest things ever to happen to the entire state.' It would have long-lasting benefits . . . and probably spawn other high-level programs (for South Texas)."[76]

Alas, the bill did not make it through both houses of the legislature. Still, Rangel had sent a strong message. Higher education in South Texas, and the state for that matter, would be one of her priorities during her tenure as a state legislator. From the San Antonio meeting came a plan, a program, to follow and Rangel would be its leader. The plan included higher-education initiatives for several universities. They were:

1. Allied health for A&M-Corpus Christi,
2. a medical school in the Rio Grande Valley at Texas-Pan American,
3. a pharmacy school for A&M-Kingsville and
4. other professional schools for Texas-El Paso and Sul Ross in Alpine.[77]

The plan was known as The South Texas Border Initiative and had its roots in a lawsuit filed by the Mexican American Legal Defense Fund in 1987. The plan was approved by the Texas Legislature in 1989. The momentum had started to change the scope of border universities, as reported by Susan Combs, Texas Comptroller of Public Accounts, on a report to the governor and state legislature titled "Window on State Government – Bordering the Future," in July 1998.[78]

Combs said in the report:

> "Since the creation of the El Paso College of Mining and Metallurgy (in 1914), Border leaders have sought additional funding for local colleges and universities. Also at play has been a desire to

offer programs as good or better than the academic offerings of other public colleges and universities across Texas. But it took a lawsuit to draw the attention of state leaders outside the Border. In 1987, the Mexican American Legal Defense and Educational Fund (MALDEF) sued in state district court alleging that Border universities were not getting their fair share of state funding. A major contention of the suit was that other Texas colleges and universities were offering more and better undergraduate and graduate degree programs in better facilities than what were available in the Border institutions. And while the Texas Supreme Court overturned a lower court's finding in favor of MALDEF, the resulting public debate over the needs of Border institutions drew the attention of lawmakers, who in 1989 approved the wide-ranging South Texas/Border Initiative."[79]

With the passage of the South Texas Border Initiative secured, the border legislators from Brownsville to El Paso and all who represented South Texas now had more influence in future legislation. In 1993, Rangel secured $450 million for institutions of higher education in her region of the state.[80] Rangel had been appointed chair of the Texas Higher Education Committee in 1993 by newly elected speaker Pete Laney, due in part to some crafty political maneuverings when the Mexican American Legislative Caucus was split on whom they were support for the top position on the Texas House. Rangel had supported Laney and was not embarrassed to ask for the chairmanship of the Higher Education Committee. "I am going to do a good job. I don't know what we are going to do, but I am going to do a good job. I won't embarrass you," she told Laney.[81]

But she didn't get marching orders from Laney, who was aware that Rangel was a maverick and would do only what she felt was right for her conscience and her constituents. "I didn't tell him I am going to do what you want me to do, *tampoco,* (either), you know . . . . I was never a team member, never. But Pete Laney was a different kind; he was a respectable man, and I liked the guy." As she lobbied for the position with other state legislators, she assured them she would do a good job and explained there was still much to do in the area of higher education. She felt that it was the state legislature's duty to "really make education accessible to everyone . . . I mean some universities had too much and other universities didn't have enough."[82]

From 1993 to 2003 Rangel served as chair of the powerful House Higher Education Committee. She would make a big impact and would be the author of one of the most controversial pieces of legislation in the latter part of the 20th century – the "Top Ten Percent Rule" – guaranteeing admission to Texas public universities and colleges for all Texas high school students graduating in the top 10 percent of their class.[83] It was in response of the U.S. Circuit of Appeals decision on *Hopwood v. Texas* that essentially killed affirmative action measures in Texas. In 1997, Laney appointed her committee the responsibility of studying the impact of the *Hopwood* decision, which in effect banned consideration of race in university admissions. The case stemmed from admission controversy for the University of Texas Law School. Affirmative Action, to that point, allowed university to use some race-based criteria for admission. The battle lines were drawn; it was time for Rangel to go to work. Working with both Republicans and Democrats and meeting with members on both chambers – the House and Senate – Rangel was able to get a coalition together that wanted an alternative to *Hopwood*. She even met with the Hopwood's lawyer Terrell Smith (a Republican), later appointed as Gov. George W. Bush's legislative counsel. She left no stone unturned, maneuvering politically, all meetings of the Higher Education Committee and search for votes to pass new legislation that would negate the Hopwood decision in Texas. She even got Republican Sen. Ted Bivins, chair or the Senate Higher Education Committee, to eventually support the legislation. Laney was hesitant to allow House Bill 588 to make it to the floor and move up to the Senate where support seemed solid. He met privately with Rangel and many thought that was the end of the legislation. But, always the political strategist, Rangel brought a cadre of nine Mexican American professional experts to support her case for the legislation.[84] Still, Laney felt more study was needed. On the House floor, when the bill came up for discussion, he called for more "study" before a decision was made. Rangel got up from here desk and shouted, "We've studied it."[85] Laney went quiet and HB 588 was approved on a non-recorded voice vote, barely with most votes along party line, in the House and went to the Senate where it passed by a wide margin. It was now up to Gov. Bush to make it law. Three days later he signed the bill.[86]

Ironically, after all the hard work Irma Rangel and her supporters went through to assure passage of the Ten Percent Rule, Gov. Bush started to claim responsibility for its passage. Of course, he could have vetoed the bill and it would not have become law. After the Ten Percent rule passed, Bush took credit for the legislation. Rangel was livid, but understood politics; the bill passed and that was what was important. *"Ni modo* (whatever), Irma would say. It doesn't matter. He could claim credit if he liked."[87]

Leo, in the article for *The Texas Observer* after Rangel's death in 2003, also wrote: "The top 10 percent of students from the high school in Roma (in the Rio Grande Valley) were likely to be 100 percent Hispanic. The top 10 percent of students from Jack Yates High School in Houston were likely to be all black. And every one was automatically admitted to the state's best universities. That was Irma's legacy."[88] Rangel, however, wanted to make sure credit was given where credit was due and Leo, who used to work for the South Texas legislator before she headed for a career in journalism and politics herself, recalled Rangel's efforts to set the record straight. Leo wrote, "Irma felt strongly enough about setting the record straight that she took it upon herself to meet with reporters and editorial page writers to tell them that (Bush) had little to do with passing the bill. Irma was fearless when it came to proper protocol."[89]

Irma's biggest battle was yet to come. The South Texas Border Initiative always was "the plan." Soon, the opportunity would arrive for her to make a difference in the higher education fortunes of her alma mater – Texas A&I, now Texas A&M University-Kingsville. In 2001 she introduced House Bill 1601, urging its passage to fund the first professional school in South Texas – college of pharmacy on the Kingsville campus.[90]

The battle for the college of pharmacy in South Texas was to be one of the most contentious battles for the state legislature in the early part of the 21ˢᵗ century. It was a battle that Rangel would see come to an end, but not enjoy the fruits of her victory. She would get a professional school – a college of pharmacy for her alma mater – but she would not live to see the building go up. Her battle with cancer claimed her in 2003 before the college of pharmacy was built and was occupied by students. Cancer slowed her down, but did not defeat her. She underwent successful treatment in 2002 at the Center Therapy and Research Center in San Antonio for inflammatory breast cancer and ovarian cancer. But, the cancer did not go away. She had gone public about having breast cancer in February 15, 2000, and the *Corpus Christi Caller-Times* reported the then 68-year-old Rangel was undergoing chemotherapy treatments at the Cancer Therapy and Research Center in San Antonio. "Chemotherapy usually results in hair loss, so Rangel cut her hair," the newspaper reported.[90] "I'm not 'out of it.' I'm very much 'in it,'" said Rangel, who now represented District 35 and was chairwoman of the House Committee on Higher Education. "I intend to continue participating and exercising my responsibility to my district."[91]

As promised, she kept at her job. As the signs of therapy began to show, she seemed to generate even greater support and respect from her fellow legislators. Soon, her hair short now and not growing, she resorted to wearing hats so that the impact of the cancer would not show as much. She would wear brightly colored hats that stood out on in the House Chamber like wildflower on a sun-drenched Texas landscape. "One day, fellow female legislators walked into the House sporting hats in a show of support. With them were two male mascots – Rep. Tony Goolsby, R-Dallas, and Tom Uher, D-Bay City, also wearing woman's hats." They came into a roaring applause from the House membership.[92] They would have been even louder if they had become aware of the struggle it would take to make Rangel's last piece of legislation. Construction and occupation of a pharmacy school at now Texas A&M University-Kingsville almost didn't happen. Finding funding became the chief battle until the Texas A&M University System announced March 1, 2006, that it would transfer the management of the Rangel College of Pharmacy from Texas A&M University-Kingsville to The Texas A&M University System Health Science Center. In a news release the TAMU System noted: "The decision to transfer management of the college, which is located on the campus of Texas A&M University-Kingsville and slated to open in fall 2006, was made for a variety of reasons, including funding support and critical academic resources that the health science center can offer to support opening the school as scheduled in fall 2006."[93]

Prior to that day, funding was uncertain, occupation of the building questionable and the reality of the college of pharmacy not open at all began to take hold. Texas A&M University-Kingsville president Rumaldo Juarez, who had fought alongside Rangel to help make the pharmacy school a reality, was desperate. As the Texas legislature failed to provide the necessary funding, he said he would go out and borrow the money. "There is no change in the funding status of the college. We have done all the preparations we can do to open the program. However, without assured funding, we can't go any further. At this time we are exploring possible avenues of borrowing money. This is a most unfortunate situation that we must entertain."[94]

A bill creating the pharmacy college was passed in 2001 and lawmakers approved more than $300,000 in startup money for construction of the college, which was less than what was needed at the time. A&M-

Kingsville borrowed $3.1 million from the A&M System to proceed with the plans to build the school. Juarez reported to the A&M System and the legislature that an additional $13 million would be needed to make the pharmacy college a reality. In May 2006, the legislature allocated $275,000 for 2006 and not a dime for 2007. Juarez lobbied the Legislative Budget Board, which recommended $10 million for the project.[95] "(A)lthough $10 million was included at one point in the supplemental appropriations bill, at final passage the funding was denied."[96]

Meanwhile, the building was going-up and plans for pre-accreditation were proceeding with Dr. Mauro Castro, Regents Professor of Chemistry at A&M-Kingsville, serving as interim dean. "We were going to make this happen. We couldn't wait," Castro said in a 2013 interview.[97] In essence, what the A&M-Kingsville campus got was a "big empty buiding."[98] In a column scathing the legislature for non-action on the mater, Nick Jimenez, editorial page editor of the *Corpus Christi Caller-Times* said:

> "There is a big empty building in Kingsville on the campus of Texas A&M University-Kingsville. That building was supposed to fulfill the dream of the late Irma Rangel, one of the great guiding forces of higher education in Texas. Her dream was that a professional school would be located in South Texas. . . . Yet, when the 79th Texas legislature was gaveled to a close this week, the $13million to allow the Irma Rangel School of Pharmacy to open on schedule in 2006 wasn't there."[99]

Jimenez quoted Juarez who said, that other than borrowing money, there was no Plan B. "The struggle to fund the pharmacy school is a perfect example of hot tough that battle can be. It is a chronicle of political firefights and legislative hand-to-hand combat. But lost in all that are the students."[100]

Lost in the column was the fact that Rangel was not present to fight her best fight. Her death had robbed her of that moment. Is there any doubt that with Rangel's legislative strategy, funding for the pharmacy college at her beloved Kingsville campus would not have become reality? However, poignant in Jimenez's comments was his attention to the fact that students would suffer because of the legislature's inaction. It was Leo who said in 2003 in a reflection of Rangel's life after her death that "it was all about the students" for the South Texas legislator.[101] Ironically, or perhaps with all intention in mind, Jimenez that night (the column was posted on the *Corpus Christi Caller-Times* website at midnight June 5, 2005) ended his column with the phrase. "Never forget, it's always about the students."[102.] Rangel would have agreed.

Rangel died March 18, 2003, at the age of 71, of brain cancer after a lengthy battle with breast and ovarian cancer.[103] The day after her death, the members of the Texas House attempted to honor her in any way they could. A glass vase with 27 long-stemmed yellow roses, one for each year Rangel served, sat atop her desk as colleagues wept openly. "She lived and died full of passion, for higher education, for the poor," said Rep. Pete Gallegos, D-Alpine. "Those like me, who worked with her, are proud and touched by her. She always had a smile." Rangel's seatmate in the House, Moreno of El Paso, choked up as he recalled how they sat side-by-side for years. State Sen. Leticia Van de Putte, D-San Antonio, said: "Today a hero has fallen but an angel has risen. I really cannot imagine a Texas Legislature without Irma." Texas Gov. Rick Perry ordered flags flown at half-staff at state buildings in Rangel's memory.[104]

At her funeral at Our Lady of Guadalupe Catholic Church in Austin and burial service at the Texas State Cemetery on March 21, 2003, Rangel was memorialized as a hero for Texas and much more. Rangel's life's work was described by Father J.C. Cain as a vocation dedicated to helping the poor and marginalized, bettering the Hispanic community, and fighting for justice and equality. The priest said her passion and compassion were such that, "I think she would have been a wonderful priest. She would have made it to being the pope," he said, drawing laughter. "She could have been the first female pope -- the first female Hispanic pope."[105] The music at the burial service at the Texas State Cemetery helped tell Rangel's life story - proud to be Mexican American and happy to be with family. "It ranged from the civil rights hymn <u>"We Shall Overcome"</u>" to mariachi music to <u>"Jesus Loves Me"</u> played on two French horns and a trombone by a nephew and two great-nephews.[106]

Irma was gone, but the battle for funding continued for three more years.

Finally, on March 22, 2006, it was reported that funding for the pharmacy school had been secured. It would come from the Texas A&M University Health Science Center and would ensure opening of the Irma Rangel College of Pharmacy, as it was now officially referred to in all venues, that fall. "The first professional school in South Texas will open under the umbrella of the Health Science Center."[107] The article detailed the agreement between A&M-Kingsville, the A&M System and the A&M Health Science Center. It was a bittersweet pill to swallow, especially for

Juarez and Castro who, along with Irma Rangel, had wanted the College to be part of A&M-Kingsville. Still, the building would be there on the campus for all to see and realize the struggle it took to get in South Texas. Among those taking the news lukewarm was Irma's sister, Minnie Rangel. "As long as (Irma) knows it's getting funded, I know she is right there. It's going to be a success because we have young men and women who want a professional degree and want to use it to help the people of South Texas."[108]

The struggle over funding and staffing started to move briskly on the campus of Kingsville. There was money now for equipment and, more important, professors. Letters were sent out to prospective students and the first class was formulating just as Cast and Rangel had envisioned. "We wanted them to be Javelinas, like us," Castro said. "But, at least they were on our campus."[109] Plans to honor those responsible for getting the College of Pharmacy to the Kingsville campus proceeded briskly as well. There was even talk for a statue of Irma Rangel to be located in front of the building.[110] The celebration had actually started in 2001 when Castro and the A&M-Kingsville hosted an "Appreciation Banquet" to honor Irma Rangel and State Senator Carlos Truan for their role in making the pharmacy school a reality for the campus. Ironically, that invitation, which appeared in the Tamuk Chemistry Department's newsletter – *Javelinium* – had the Coastal Bend Pharmacy Association and the Texas A&M University-Kingsville School of Pharmacy hosting the banquet July 27 on Ballroom A of the Memorial Student Union Building in the A&M-Kingsville campus. It was said to listed as the "First Annual Appreciation Banquet." It was also the last. An article, in the newsletter, also bragged in its headline: "Chemistry Department Instrumental in Getting Pharmacy School Bill Passed."[111]

However, it wasn't until 2006 that letters to prospective students were sent out. In an article in the *Corpus Christi Caller Times* in March 22, 2006, Juarez confirmed that letters to more than 140 candidates for the school would be sent out soon and the interview process would begin within a few weeks.[112]

The official opening of the College of Pharmacy was on August 10, 2006. Indra Reddy, appointed as dean of the Irma Lerma Rangel College of Pharmacy, earlier that year, welcomed 300 students, state and university officials and parents at a ribbon-cutting ceremony. It was made very clear that The College of Pharmacy on the campus of Texas A&M-Kingsville would be under the guidance of the A&M Health System. In the near 100-degree heat, the $14.5 million, 63,000 square-foot building stood as an example of what can be accomplished when people with a common purpose get together, Reddy said. "Many people have worked to open these doors," Reddy said as she spoke to a freshman class of 70 pharmacy students. "We hope that you give back, not only to the profession, but to South Texas."[113] More than 60 percent of the inaugural class was from South Texas and almost 40 percent were Hispanic.[114] That would have pleas Rangel. Again, the ribbon-cutting ceremony was bittersweet.

Now all that was left was to honor Rangel with a commemorative statue. On January 18, 2007, the statue went up. During her tenure as a state representative for Texas, her friends and family remembered Irma Rangel as "bigger than life," an article announcing the statue's unveiling proclaimed. "Now students who enter the pharmacy school building will see her (Rangel's) name at Texas A&M University-Kingsville will know her that way, too."[115]

The 6-foot tall statue cost $55 thousand. The statue was designed and created by Laredo artist Roberto Garcia.[116] Castro and Coastal Bend area pharmacists raised the money for it and physicians like Ron Garza and Dr. Jose Ugarte and an organization known as Los Sembradores de Amistad (Planters of Friendship) Chapter in Kingsville. "The statue was funded through private community donations," Castro affirmed. "This is from the community who knew her, her friends in South Texas."[117]

Her friends and family showed up for one last sample of gratitude that day on the northern edge of the A&M-Kingsville campus. Grateful for her leadership, vision and dedication to her principles, those present honored Rangel by one speaker after another.

"This statue will help people remember Irma Rangel's contribution to Kingsville and South Texas," Ugarte said. "Her neighbors, her constituents and others from South Texas made this project a reality." Castro was near tears as he said, "I worked 15 years with Mrs. Rangel. During that time she was a champion of education. She didn't want students to leave from this area (to get a good education). She felt that if more educational and professional programs were brought to South Texas, it would give the opportunity for students to stay (and study) in this area. The pharmacy school was the last part of her legacy."[118]

Castro, in a column he was asked to write for a special edition on Rangel for *The South Texan,* wrote, "I can still see the smile on her face and hear the pride in her voice when she spoke about creating the first-ever professional school for South Texas, for all Texans, to educate trusted professionals in the field of pharmacy . . . Even now, four years after her passing, her friends are still coming together to honor her one more time by erecting a statue of her to remind all of us of her contributions."[119]

Kleberg County Judge Juan M. Escobar, who represented Rangel's district and fought for the establishment of the school after her death was equally moved by the statue's dedication. "It's a unique opportunity to show the people in South Texas how one person can make a difference. Irma got her education and never forgot where she came from."[120]

The statue was the last of several fitting tributes for Irma Lerma Rangel. Her awards and tributes include:

1. First Mexican American woman elected to the Texas legislature

2. First Mexican America woman to serve as chair of the Kleberg County Democratic Party.

3. First Mexican American woman clerk for a Federal District Judge.

4. First Mexican American Assistant District Attorney, Nueces County.

5. The Irma Rangel Science and Technology Building at Texas State Technical College in Harlingen.

6. Establishment of the The Irma Rangel Public Policy Institute, a research unit of the University of Texas at Austin in the Department of Government and the College of Liberal Arts, focuses on public policy issues salient to the State of Texas.

7. The Irma Rangel Young Women's (Grades 6 to 12) Leadership School in Dallas. It was the first public all-girls' school in the nation.

8. Selected as a Fellow of the State Bar of Texas in 1984.

9. Inducted into the Texas Women's Hall of Fame in 1994.

10. GEMS Television Woman of the Year, 1997.

11. Recipient of the G.J. Sutton Award from the Legislative Black Caucus, 1997.

12. Legislator of the Year by the Mexican American Bar Association in 1997.

13. Recipient of the Mirabeau B. Lamar Award from the Association of Texas Colleges and Universities, 1998.

14. Voted Woman of the Year in 1998 by the Texas Young Democrats.

15. Bestowed the "Margaret Brent Women Lawyers Achievement Award" in 1998.

16. Honored by the Hispanic Caucus of the American Association for Higher Education with the "Outstanding Support for Hispanic Issues in Higher Education" Award, 1998.

17. First woman to chair the Mexican American Legislative Caucus.

18. First woman and Mexican American to chair the Higher Education Committee of the Texas House of Legislators.

19. Establishment of the Moreno/Rangel Legislative Leadership Program by the Mexican American Legislative Foundation to encourage the involvement of young Hispanics in the political process.

20. The naming of the Texas A&M University Health Science Center College of Pharmacy being named in her honor.

21. First person to have a statue of her erected on the campus of Texas A&M-Kingsville.

22. Storage of her legislative collection is stored at the South Texas Archives and Special Collections at Texas A&M University-Kingsville.121 122

And so Irma Lerma Rangel was home. Her old home is just a few blocks away from the building that bears her name and that is adorned by her statue. On crisp fall nights the roar of the fans during a football game at Javelina Stadium echo past her statute and the College of Pharmacy building and can be heard all the way to Santa Gertrudis Avenue near the house where she and her family owned so many years ago where some did not want Mexican Americans in that neighborhood. Across from the College of Pharmacy Building where Rangel's well-lit statue stands, hundreds of students are seen coming to and from the Student Recreation Center. And, inside the building, there are now hundreds of students studying pharmacy in the first professional school in South Texas.

Rangel would be happy. Look at her statue. She's facing north toward Austin, but her feet are firmly on the ground of her beloved campus and alma mater – Texas A&M-Kingsville. And, if you look closely at the statue, it's almost as if she is smiling.

She won a big victory for her beloved Kingsville campus and for students everwhere.

Note: Sources available upon request – **manuelf78407@yahoo.com**

Cuentos Tejanos

Episode 2

Ben Garza - Corpus Christi Leader and First LULAC President

-By Cynthia Orozco

While not the true founder of the League of United Latin American Citizens (LULAC), Corpus Christi's Ben Garza was it first national president and widely respected in his time from the organization's start in 1929 to his death.

Bernardo F. Garza was born in 1892 to Mexican immigrants in Brownsville, but grew up in Rockport where he finished the sixth grade. A high school education was not common for Mexican Americans in the 1910s, but he helped his brothber Joe become the first to graduate from high school in Rockport. Garza waited tables in a restaurant and worked on a construction crew during World War I.

After he moved to Corpus Christi, he and several other men opened the Metropolitan Café on North Chaparral downtown. Popular with businessmen, the middle class, and city leaders, Garza found his business niche. He finished paying for the restaurant in 1937. He also entered the real estate business. He was one of the most successful Mexican American businessmen in the Corpus Christi area at the time. More typical were small family businesses.

Despite limited education, Garza crossed numerous racial boundaries.

Racial segregation against people of Mexican descent and African Americans in schools, restaurants, and public accommodations was the order of the day. Banks would not often offer loans to Hispanics. Garza was active in both Hispanic and traditionally Anglo organizations. He was active with the Chamber of Commerce and the Salvation Army Advisory Board. He was also president of the Woodmen of the World and even worked with the Mexican philosopher and politician and philosopher Jose Vasconcelos for President of Mexico.

However, the most important civic organization Garza was involved with the Sons of America, one of numerous mutual civic rights organizations in Texas at the time.

The Sons started in San Antonio in 1921 but spread to Corpus Christi by 1924. In Corpus Christi, the Sons fought for a new Mexican school, the Cheston Heath School; desegregated the Palace Bath House; helped take down a "No Mexicans Allowed" signs from North Beach; and got the first Mexican American on a jury in Nueces County.

Garza became president of the Sons of America in late 1926 and steered this group toward a merger with two other San Antonio Mexican American civil rights groups. His chapter called for unification, which led to the founding of the League of United Latin American Citizens (LULAC) on Feb. 17, 1929. He became the first president of LULAC, which grew to become the largest Mexican American civil rights organization in the nation.

Mexican Americans in San Antonio had initiated civil rights activism in 1921 with the Order Sons of America. Key leaders in the 1920s of this movement included M.C. Gonzales and Alonso S. Perales and James Tafolla Sr., all of San Antonio. Perales, an attorney, believed the best person to first preside over LULAC was Garza. Perales called Garza "intelligent, energetic, honest, and sincere." Garza wrote Perales, "My intentions are good, but I know that I lack the education to be at the front of such an organization. Nevertheless, I am willing to put the shoulder to the wheel and see it through."

Because Perales believed in Garza, he orchestrated his election as the first LULAC president despite the fact that it was Perales who was the key South Texas leader from 1924 to 1929 and despite his attorney status and George Washington University education in Washington D.C.

Almost as soon as Garza became president, the Depression began. Despite this economic challenge, LULAC survived. By January 1930, there were 19 LULAC chapters and 2,000 members. Members were committed because school segregation and the lack of access to high schools was still common. Inferior Mexican schools, lacking appropriate facilities, were common. In 1931, LULAC lawyers filed the *Salvatierra vs. Del Rio ISD* over the issue. The Depression hurt Garza's restaurant and in 1933 he took a job with the Southern Alkali Company's employment office.

Garza testified at a Congressional hearing on immigration in Washington. He proved a competent and able LULAC leader.

Unfortunately, Garza had tuberculosis and spent some time in Kerrville and Arizona to address his illness but he passed in 1937.

It was the community and city officials' tribute to Garza after his death that exemplifies what kind of man he was. The White House sent a representative. City Hall and the county courthouse closed. The city council passed a resolution of respect. One hundred men served as his pallbearers.

Ben Garza Park was dedicated on March 5, 1939. Garza left his wife Adelaida Carrilles Garza and five children behind. In 1939 and as late as 1969 in New Braunfels, Texas parks were often closed to Mexicans. So Ben Garza was a much respected man in the Hispanic and Anglo community in the city of Corpus.

Note: Dr. Cynthia E. Orozco is Professor of History at Eastern New Mexico University, Ruidoso, N.M. She is the author of _"No Mexicans, Women or Dogs Allowed,"_ a history of the origins of LULAC. She has a bachelor's from the University of Texas and master's and doctorate degrees from UCLA.

Cuentos Tejanos

Episode 3

Placido Benavides, "The Paul Revere of Texas"

-By Dr. Manuel Flores

Tejano Plácido Benavides was a most unlikely hero during Texas' quest for independence from Mexico in 1836.

Benavides so hated the Mexican federal government and Gen. Santa Anna that he stepped into the chapters of Texas history and became known as the "Paul Revere of Texas."

However, he did not join in Texas' revolution against Mexico. He just "warned" Texas troops of impending danger as a second Mexican Army marched from South Texas toward San Jacinto to reinforce Santa Anna's Army. Santa Anna's army would almost double, forcing Sam Houston's hand to move soon and embark on the historic Battle of San Jacinto where the Texans army prevailed and thus forged the Republic of Texas.

Benavides' saga all started at the Battle of Agua Dulce Creek where Mexican troops en route to San Jacinto surprised a regiment of Texas rebels. Their troop movement from Mexico City into what is now South Texas was part of Mexico's "Goliad Campaign" to retake the Texas Gulf Coast and help Santa Anna secure Texas for Mexico.

The battle occurred about 26 miles south of what is now San Patricio in what was then the Mexican State of Tamaulipas.

Benavides and 24 other men were in a Texas detachment searching for wild mustangs for Sam Houston's Army. They were under the command of Texas Col. James Grant. The Mexican army had already captured San Patricio, killing several Texan and Tejano volunteers. Grant's troops stumbled into a trap set by the Mexican army at Agua Dulce Creek. Benavides tried to rejoin the Texas rebels but was ordered by Grant, who was killed in the skirmish, to save himself and warn Fannin and other Texans of Mexican Army Gen. Jose Urrea's approach with more troops.

Upon reaching Fannin, Benavides learned that the Texas Declaration of Independence had just been signed at Washington-on-the-Brazos.

Benavides informed Fannin he did not wish to help Texas to be torn from Mexico, but wanted the Mexican Constitution of 1824 to be the law of the land and for Santa Anna to be defeated. Fannin discharged Benavides from the army and sent him home to Victoria.

From San Patricio to his final destination of Victoria, Benavides warned every person and town along the way of the Mexican army's approach.

In the process he saved hundreds of lives.

Benavides' ride and heroics after the Battle of Agua Dulce Creek have been compared to Paul Revere's famous ride in the American Revolution, as both men spread the news of oncoming enemy assault.

Born in 1810 in Mexico, Benavides moved to Texas in 1828. He found work in Victoria with the family of *empresario* Martín De León. Benavides married De León's daughter Agustina and became the city's *alcalde* (mayor).

By 1835, Benavides had joined the Texans in opposing Mexican dictator Santa Anna. As head of Victoria's militia, Benavides stood up to Mexican soldiers trying to arrest suspected rebels. This defiance made him a rebel, too.

Benavides helped take Goliad and San Antonio for the Texans. Soon after, he was among the men ambushed by the Mexican army near San Patricio.

Benavides did oppose Santa Anna, but he was fighting for Texas as part of a federalist Mexico, not for Texas independence. His relations with the Texas rebels soon soured. After the Texan victory in 1836, Benavides and the De León family left Victoria for exile in New Orleans.

Benavides never returned to Texas. He died in 1837.

In 2011, the city of Victoria dedicated a plaque at city hall honoring Benavides. He was elected "alcalde" of Victoria twice, an office whose duties included those of present-day mayor, sheriff, and local judge.

He led a unit of Tejano fighters at the Battle of Goliad ,and then he proceeded with his company to San Antonio, where they fought against Mexican Gen. Martín Perfecto de Cos in the Siege of Bexar. On Feb. 11, 1836, Benavides sent a warning to James Bowie inside the Alamo that Santa Anna was approaching.

Texas Historical Marker number 6563 placed in 1936 at the SW Corner of S. Main and Juan Linn streets in Victoria, marks the site of the Benavides Round Top house.

Benavides, Texas, located in Duval County deep in the South Texas brush country on U.S. 359 bears his family's name. It is named for his nephew Plácido Benavides who was a confederate army veteran and who in the 1870s built Rancho Palo Alto. When the railroad spread throughout South Texas, the younger Benavides donated 80 acres to help form the community of Benavides. In 1881, a post office was established with name Benavides Post Office.

A town in the Victoria area – Placedo, Texas - bears Plácido Benavides' name, albeit with a different spelling. The San Antonio and Mexican Gulf Railroad established a station at Placedo in 1860, where Benavides' ranch was located. In 1906, the St. Louis, Brownsville and Mexico Railway crossed the old line and renamed the station Placedo Junction. Today it remains an unincorporated community of approximately 800 residents. Placedo is on U.S. Highway 87 fourteen miles southeast of Victoria in Victoria County.

Plácido Benavides was a most unlikely hero, but he will forever be remembered as the "Paul Revere of Texas" for his role in the Texas Revolution.

Cuentos Tejanos

Episode 4

Don Martín de León – "Founder of Victoria, Texas"

-By Juan M. Escobar

Alonzo de León y Pérez, "El Mozo," is an iconic Spanish legend that often does not get the credit he deserves. He was a soldier, colonial administrator and explorer from New Spain, remembered for having led several expeditions in northeastern Mexico and into South Texas in the 17th century. He founded the Villa de Santiago de la Monclova (Coahuila). He was captain, mayor of Cadereyta and governor of Nuevo León and Coahuila.

From this lineage comes the founder of Victoria, Texas, Don Martín de León y Galván, one of Alonzo de León y Pérez's great-grandsons. Martín de León y Galván was known "El Empresario."

He was a man of great vision and, at the time of the Texas Revolution, his family was one of the wealthiest in South Texas. The De León family also became one of the most influential backers of the Texas Revolution for Independence from Mexico.

Martín de León y Galván was born in Burgos, Nuevo Santander, Nueva España (now Mexico, but also part of today's Texas) in 1765. His parents were Joseph Bernardo de León y García and María Antonia Galván y de Las Rivas. Martin carne from a wealthy family and at an early age was presented with the opportunity to obtain an education at the finest universities of México and Europe. Instead, at age 18, he chose to become a rancher and a businessman. He would earn the reputation of being Texas' first cattle baron.

He also joined the Spanish military and rose to the rank of captain, the highest rank a New World born was allowed to attain.

In 1795 Martín married Patricia de la Garza in Soto La Marina, Nuevo Santander, Nueva España. They had the following children: Fernando, Candelaria, Silvestre, Guadalupe, Félix, Agapito, María de Jesús, María de Refugio, Agustina, and Francisca.

By 1801, Don Martín and his family arrived in Texas. By the year 1806, the De León family had settled on the banks of the Aransas River. Don Martín immediately got involved in ranching. He raised cattle, goats, mules and horses. Seeing the great profits of the business, he wanted his own ranch and therefore petitioned to the Spanish Governor in San Antonio for land. Governor Manuel María Salcedo in San Antonio rejected his petitions several times. Don Martín de León consequently decided to move his family east of the Nueces River. They settled close to present-day San Patricio, Texas.

The year was 1809 and Indians were constantly attacking the settlers, making it dangerous for the De León family. Therefore, Don Martín moved again, this time to Presidio La Bahía for protection. However, matters worsened for him when Mexico revolted against Spain in 1810 and the Presidio of La Bahía withdrew its military forces back to Mexico City. Without protection for his family and at the mercy of the Indians, Don Martín decided to move his family back to Burgos, Nuevo Santander, Nueva España. Between the years 1810-1816, Don Martín spent his time between his family in Burgos and his ranching business in Texas. By 1816, he owned nearly six thousand head of cattle. Don Martín had a reputation for owning the best horses in Texas and his mules were in constant demand. He started making trips to New Orleans, Louisiana, where he made huge profits selling his stock.

On one of his ventures from the Nueces River to New Orleans, he discovered a location near the Guadalupe and Lavaca rivers. On April 8, 1824, Don Martín de León petitioned to the government at San Antonio to establish 41 families from Tamaulipas at a place he named Nuestra Señora de Guadalupe de Jesús. By April 13, 1824, a charter was approved and "The Great Empresario" Don Martín de León was authorized to settle and occupy any vacant land between the Guadalupe and Lavaca rivers. That location had the following boundaries: Matagorda Bay on the South, Lavaca River on the East, Mission Valley on the North and Coleto Creek on the West.

On his return trips from New Orleans, Martín would return with supplies for his family, friends and hired help. It was on one of those trips that he met a French pirate named Ramon La Fou. A wanted man in Mexico, La Fou and Don Martín worked out a deal. La Fou promised to bring supplies to the mouth of the Rio Grande at Brazos de Santiago (near present day Brownsville) and Don Martín in, return would assist in getting the Mexican government to grant him a pardon. This friendship gave Don

Martín his greatest economical edge. Through this deal he obtained and transferred vast numbers of supplies quickly in and out of Texas.

The De León Colony settled in present-day Victoria, Texas. The town was named in honor of Jesús Guadalupe de Victoria, first President of Mexico and a close personal friend of Don Martín. They developed their town around the main street, known as *"La Calle de Los Diez Amigos"* named after the 10 most trusted citizens of Don Martín's colony, which included family members.

The settlers went through much trouble with Indians and bandits. Don Martín de León died in 1833. He had become the first victim of the 1833 Cholera Epidemic, which had hit the colony.

In 1836 Victoria was involved in war against Mexico. The leaders of the revolt against Mexico advocated the Constitution 1824. The De León family, now led by Martín de León's son, Fernando, bought $35,000 worth of supplies and ammunitions to fight the war. They also supplied many of the men to fight in the war, including all the De León men and all the husbands of the De León women.

After the war for Texas Independence, the De León family was subjected to horrible injustices. As one historian put it, "They became the victims of the most unjust discrimination ever known in Texas."

The family was robbed of their dignity and all of their lands. They did not even have monies to pay for tombstones for their dead.

The De León family suffered one tragedy after another at the hands of the Texans, even though they had fought alongside the Texans against Santa Anna and his cruel form of government.

The De Leon's were one of the most influential families in the making of Texas history, whose historical actions are improperly recorded in Texas history. Maybe one day historians who rewrite the true Texas history books will have the heart to remember that it was families such as the De Leóns who were instrumental in giving us the freedom we have today. Today, Victoria, Texas, named for the first president of Mexico, has mainly forgiven the De Leon family and recognized their ancestors for their valor in helping fight and secure Texas' independence from Mexico.

Juan M. Escobar is a historian, genealogist, past president of the Kingsville and Brooks County school boards, a retired federal law enforcement officer, as well as a former Texas state representative and Kleberg County Judge. "Tejano Talks" is prepared by the Tejano Civil Rights Museum and Resource Center with Texas A&M University-Kingsville.

Cuentos Tejanos

Episode 5

Lorenzo de Zavala – "The True and Real Father of Texas"

-By Dr. Manuel Flores

Lorenzo de Zavala is a Tejano and Texas patriot who often does not get the credit he deserves in the history of the Lone Star State. Truth is, he deserves to be referred to as "The True and Real Father of Texas." Today, Stephen F. Austin usually holds that designation.

De Zavala was born Manuel Lorenzo Justiniano de Zavala Y Sàenz in Yucatan, New Spain, in 1788 and went on to become a political leader in the governments of New Spain and Mexico and later the Republic of Texas.

He studied at Tridentine Seminary of San Idelfonso in Merida, Spain. His studies earned him a membership in the prestigious Geographical and Scientific Society of France. It is with these tools he served the Spanish and Mexican governments loyally for nearly 25 years.

After Mexico earned its independence from Spain in 1821, de Zavala had a hard time adjusting to the new centralist government. In Mexico, he had fought to improve the conditions of the middle and lower classes. He served as governor of the State of Mexico and also was Mexico's first minister to France. But, when the despotic Santa Anna rose to power, he resigned.

Fearful for his life, he moved to Texas where he owned land, having been an "empresario" and helping colonize the Texas frontier. During this time, Texas was part of the Mexican state of Coahuila y Tejas with the capitol being in Saltillo, too far Texans felt for effective leadership and governance. From the start, de Zavala favored separate Mexican statehood for Texas and encouraged Tejanos to fight for that right.

Once in Texas, de Zavala realized he was needed to help ferment an uprising. In Texas, the scent of revolution and independence from Santa Anna and Mexico filled the air. While Tejanos and the newly arrived Texans were fighting for the institution of the Mexican Constitution of

1824, de Zavala was the first to openly advocate separation of Texas from Mexico. Later he would advocate for Texas to join the United States. He helped the native Tejanos and the newly arrived Texans to organize and his efforts led to the revolution that resulted in Sam Houston's Texas troops iconic victory in the Battle of San Jacinto.

De Zavala was among those who signed the Texas Declaration of Independence, helped write the Texas constitution, and served as the Republic's first vice president.

He also was on a commission assigned by Texas President Sam Houston to design a flag for the Republic of Texas. Today, "The Zavala Flag" is traditionally referred to as "The First Flag of Texas." In the TV mini-series "Texas Rising" the Zavala Flag is shown waving across the Texas plains after the signing of the Texas Declaration of Independence.

In Texas, de Zavala settled his family on Buffalo Bayou across from what would become the site of the Battle of San Jacinto. The Texas Army used his home and ranch as a shelter and hospital before and after the historic battle.

Politically, he represented Harrisburg Municipality at both the Consultation of 1835 and the Convention of 1836, where he signed the Texas Declaration of Independence from Mexico. At the Convention of 1836, de Zavala was elected vice-president of the ad interim government of the Republic of Texas.

Unfortunately, de Zavala did not live to see his vision of an independent and vibrant Texas that would become part of the United States. Zavala died at the age of 48 on Nov. 15, 1836, and is buried in the family plot near the San Jacinto Battlefield.

In death, he has been given numerous honors. De Zavala was an early advocate for an expanded system of public education in Texas. As a result, several schools, including and elementary school in Corpus Christi ISD, have been named in his honor. Several cities have streets named Zavala and a town named Zavala once existed in what is now Jasper County. Zavala County was formed in 1858 and named in his honor. In 1931, the state of Texas erected a monument at his gravesite.

The Lorenzo de Zavala State Archives and Library, located on Brazos St. in Austin, is named for him because of his scholarly reputation. De Zavala wrote two books: "A Historical Essay of the Revolutions in Mexico: 1808-1830" and "Journey to the United States of North America." In the latter, he predicted emergence of Tejanos (Texas) as a social, political and economic force as part of the United States. Both were written in 1834.

Zavala's leadership, patriotism to his beloved Texas and statesmanship is enough for him to be embedded in the pages of the history of Texas. From helping forge the revolution against Mexico in Texas, to designing the first Texas flag and serving as vice president of the First Republic of Texas, Lorenzo de Zavala is a true Texas hero.

And, because of his statesmanship and courage, there are some scholars who believe he deserves the title of "The True and Real Father of Texas."

Cuentos Tejanos

Episode 6

Tejano 20th Century Generals

-By Manuel Flores

A row of palm trees points the way toward the replica of the famous Iwo Jima Memorial depicting American victory during World War II. But this road does not lead to Arlington Va. in the shadows of our nation's capital.

It leads to the on campus of Marine Military Academy in Harlingen where a replica of the famed monument rests among the palmettos and yuccas and reminds us all of America's sacrifice for liberty.

The monument area was forged from the original cast of the monument in the Washington, D.C. The tribute to the heroism of the American soldier during World War II has found a suitable home in South Texas. For, South Texas is the home of *"El Soldado Razo,"* the Mexican-American, Tejano soldier who fought bravely to ensure our country's freedom in WWII and to assure his posterity to American citizenship.

It is well documented that the Mexican-American solider is known for his bravery.

Sixty men of Hispanic heritage have been awarded the Medal of Honor, our country's highest and most prestigious honor for military valor.

Of the sixty Medals of Honor presented to Hispanics, two were presented to members of the Navy, 13 to members of the Marine Corps and 46 to members of the Army. Forty-two were presented posthumously.

Thousands more have also been awarded the Purple Heart for being wounded or killed while serving with the U.S. military.

But Hispanics do more than just serve. Hispanics also lead. South Texas — an area bordered by Houston, San Antonio and Del Rio on the north and the Rio Grande on the south — has produced its fair share of top leaders for the U.S. military. In the 20th century, this area, smaller than most states, produced at least 10 top leaders.

They are:

1. ***Gen. Richard Cavazos*** – He was the Army's first Hispanic four-star general, who was instrumental in developing the Army's Battle Command Training Program. Born in Kingsville, he graduated from Texas Tech University in Lubbock and has elementary schools named in his honor in Killeen and Nolanville.

2. ***Lt. Gen. Marc Cisneros*** – He was a three-star Army general whose forces captured Panamanian dictator Manuel Noriega. A direct descendant of a Spanish officer who helped colonize South Texas, Cisneros also served as president of Texas A&M University-Kingsville. He was born in Brownsville and raised in Premont.

3. ***Lt. Gen. Ricardo Sanchez*** - Sanchez was the Army's longest serving commanding general of V Corps. He also commanded the multi-national forces in Iraq during Operation Iraqui Freedom. He was born in Rio Grande City and is a graduate of Texas A&I University.

4. ***Maj. Gen. Alfred Valenzuela*** - He commanded Army South and served in three combat corps and six infantry divisions. He was born in San Antonio and graduated from St. Mary's University.

5. ***Major Gen. Angela Salinas*** Salinas is the longest-serving and most senior-ranking female Marine in the corps' history as well as the most senior-ranking Hispanic Marine. She was born in Alice and graduated from Dominican College of San Rafael in California. She was the first Hispanic woman promoted to general in the Marine Corps.

6. ***Bvt. Maj. Gen. Belisario Flores*** -He served the U.S. Air Force in many capacities, including his appointment as Asst. Adjutant General of the Texas Air National Guard. In 1974, he was the first Hispanic promoted to Brigadier General in Texas to the U.S. Air Force Reserves. He was born in Eagle Pass and graduated from St. Mary's University.

7. ***Brig. Gen. Manuel R. Flores*** He was born in Laredo and graduated from St. Mary's University. He is the former director of enlisted training program for the US Army Reserve School.

8. ***Brig. Gen. Victor M. Ortiz Jr.*** – He was born in Galveston and served as director of the enlisted training program for the U.S.

Army Reserve School. He also served as commander of the 49th Armored Division. He is a graduate of St. Mary's University.

9. ***Brig. Gen. Joe E. Ramirez Jr.*** -He was the Army's deputy Chief of Staff for the US Central Command during Operation Iraqui Freedom. He also served as commandant of the Texas A&M University Corps of Cadets. He was born in Houston and graduated from Texas A&M.

10. ***Brig. Gen. Manuel Ortiz*** – He served as Adjutant General of the Texas Army National Guard. He was born in Crystal City and is a graduate of Texas Tech University.

Of course, each of them have outstanding military records and many commendations during their service to our country. It is appropriate that we look to their courage and leadership as an example of what it is to serve our country.

We salute them.

Generals from South Texas

Lt. Gen. Marc Cisneros
U.S. Army (Retired)
Premont, Texas

Lt. Gen. Ricardo Sanchez
U.S. Army (Retired)
Rio Grande City, Texas

Gen. Richard E. Cavazos
U.S. Army (Retired)
Kingsville, Texas

Maj. Gen. Alfred Valenzuela
U.S. Army (Retired)
San Antonio, Texas

Maj. Gen. Angela Salinas
U.S. Marines (Retired)
Alice, Texas

Maj. Gen. Belisario Flores
U.S. Air Force (Retired)
Laredo, Texas

Brig. Gen. Manuel Flores
U.S. Army (Retired)
Eagle Pass, Texas

Brig. Gen. Victor Ortiz
U.S. Army (Retired)
Galveston, Texas

Brig. Gen. Joe Ramirez, Jr.
U.S. Army (Retired)
Houston, Texas

Brig. Gen. Manuel Ortiz
U.S. Army (Retired)
Crystal City, Texas

"Note: Fort Hood was renamed to Fort Cavazos in recognition of Cavazos' military service.[3] The re-designation as Fort Cavazos occurred on May 9, 2023.[5] Cavazos' Korean War Distinguished Service Cross was upgraded to the Medal of Honor   and posthumously awarded to him on January 3, 2025 Gen. Richard E. Cavazos, is a native South Texan (Kingsville, King Ranch) and the US Army's first Hispanic four-star general. (Richard E. Cavasos, Medal of Honor, www.army.mil › medalofhonor › Cavazos).

Cuentos Tejanos

Episode 7

A Monument to the Tejano in Austin, Texas

-By Manuel Flores

Seen between the busy metropolis and the high-rise buildings of Austin, Texas, the monument seems slightly out of place.

Dedicated it on Sept. 19, 2012, it is nestled between the majestic Capitol Building of Texas with its granite tower reaching for the Texas sky as the reflection of glass windows shed their light on both the Capitol and the monument.

Standing there on the south lawn of the Capitol is the Tejano Monument. The closer you get to the Capitol, the more you realize it belongs there and was long overdue. The monument is majestic and marvelous tribute to the first Euopean settlers of Texas – the Tejanos.

Located on the south lawn of the Capitol Building, the Tejano Monument cost $1.8 million to build. It is regal in scope and sends a powerful message that the Tejano contributed to the development of Texas and continues to influence its present and future

The Tejanos were the Europeans who first forged the development of modern Texas. Exploring and settling the land, developing a thriving ranching and agricultural industry, and ushering in politics and government while developing a unique culture that has survived centuries.

Numerous figures and statuettes depicting the lifestyle of the first settlers accent the monuent. They seem to reach out for the passersby. encouraging them to hear their story. This what artist and sculptor Armando Hinojosa felt when he carved each figure and figurine meticulously in his art studio in Laredo, Texas.

A three-year project to construct and a more than 10-year dream to become reality, the Tejano Monument is the most visited in the Capitol Grounds where a myriad of statues depicting Texas history – including several monuments to the Confederates – glare into the crowded streets of downtown Austin.

A Spanish explorer seems to gaze at this strange new world he sees. He must wonder what he has wrought. With one hand over his eyes, he studies his surroundings. Texas must have been beautiful and scary land when he first struck this pose. Next to him is a well-dressed Spanish don, perhaps a hacienda owner, riding a fine Spanish mustang. The days of cattle and horses as a means of transportation have disappeared, but here he is on horseback exploring the landscape and seemingly feeling right at home in this brave new world. This is where the Tejanos belong, in a place of honor, for this land was wild and treacherous and has been tamed.

The conquistador's sword and Spanish armor depict him in the 16th or 17th century, but he is at home here where he will help tell the story of the Tejano's impact on the Lone Star State. The Spaniards, Tejanos, would settle the land. Some, like the hacienda owner depicted as one of the figures in the monument, would do very well. Families would thrive.

Goats and cattle would become lifelines to the ranching and agricultural land. Thousands of mustangs would roam Texas' grassy lands as the evolution of Texas progressed almost overnight. The statue also has two Longhorns who seem to be rumbling toward the east side of the city with a destination to reach yet another site. Longhorns are native to Texas. They were Spanish cattle who developed long horns as they maneuvered through the tall grass of 17th and 18th century Texas. Meanwhile a Tejano family tends to other livestock. The children pull on a goat's tail as if saying this is going to be a fun trip.

But it wasn't. Somehow the Tejanos survived. Somehow they had a hand in building Texas and save the most sacre thing any Texan had to offer – pride in the land, pride in your heritage and proud of being Texan – Tejano.

Hinojosa, the sculptor for this magical monument, summarized the work. "The explorer shields his eyes as he looks toward the Capitol," Hinojosa says. "That was our future."

Finally, the contribution of the Spanish and Mexican settlers who tamed the vast frontier that is now Texas is being properly recognized.

The Tejano Monument was an idea whose time had come, and there was no holding it back. The Legislature first approved creating a Tejano monument in 2001. Lawmakers dedicated $1 million in 2007, and about $800,000 more came from private donations, including $200,000 from Walmart.

The massive granite and bronze memorial that took 12 years to complete is 525 square feet. The monument is among the largest on the Capitol grounds. Mounted on a 250-ton slab of pink granite, bronze statues depict a Spanish explorer, a vaquero on his Spanish mustang, a longhorn bull and cow and a family of settlers.

The artist, Armando Hinojosa, a graduate of Texas A&I University (now Texas A&M-Kingsville) calls it the most important work he has done in his impressive career. "This piece was dedicated in the honor and the glory of the strong men, women and children who many times, with bleeding feet and broken hearts moved forward so that we could stand on this hallowed ground today. Remember that we are the products of great people," Hinojosa said during the dedication ceremony featuring Texas. Gov. Rick Perry and many other state dignitaries as well as family members and representatives from the original settlers of Texas.

Among them was Joel de Léon, a descendant of Martin de Léon, recognized as the founder of Victoria, Texas. The 80-year-old was part of the ceremonies involving descendants of many of the original family who helped settle Texas and whose ancestors fought in the Texas Revolution for independence from Mexico. He and others helped pull the veil off the part of the statue that showed a Tejano couple holding their infant and depicting the coming colonization of Texas.

With a mariachi group greeting an enthusiastic crowd that appeared to number well over a thousand, the monument, a grand 250-ton tribute to Texas' early Spanish and Mexican explorers and settlers, was dedicated Thursday on the Capitol's south lawn. The unveiling culminated a grass-roots campaign begun in 2000 to make the monument a reality.

The unveiling ceremony could easily be called a "pachanga" – A Tejano celebration – adjacent to the state's Capitol Building in under the brilliant Texas sun and blue sky. There was music, abrazos (hugs) and tears. Si señor (yes sir) we were in Texas, Tejano Texas.

"This important monument reflects a larger truth about the origins of Texas, about the contributions of so many Hispanic citizens to the creation of the state we love and the lives we share," Gov. Perry said to cheers at the ceremony.

Texas State Capitol in Austin, Texas. (*Texas State Capitol Images, www. austintexas.org › listings › texas-state-capitol, Austin, TX*).

Cuentos Tejanos

Episode 8

Servando Hinojosa - Tejano Artist

As you approach downtown Alice, a strange silhouette pops up on the horizon.

Next to the railroad track and close to the busy business district of this South Texas oil boom town you can see a metal sculpture of *"Alicia and Juan"* dancing the day and night away, their motion frozen in time for all to join in their joy.

The 7X12-foot metal sculpture, completed in 2008 by Tejano artist Servando Hinojosa, with the help of metal artist John Farias, has become one of the city's and South Texas' iconic sites. It also the city's connection with Tejano music. Alice is also the home of the Tejano Roots Hall of Fame Museum, honoring Tejano music artists, and the famed La Villita Dance Hall, often referred to as "Grand Ol' Opry" of South Texas.

But the figure of *"Alicia y Juan"* is singular in its visibility. It portrays a Tejano couple enjoying a dance at a fandango in the 19th century. Hinjosa chose the names simply because they were "Spanish" and he felt it would make people recall a bygone era when ranching and agriculture kept the South Texas economy vibrant.

"It was hard work, still is, but the people had fun, too," Hinojosa said.

A 1965 graduate of Texas A&I (now Texas A&M University-Kingsville), his art work reflects the revolutionary spirit of the times. It is varied and can range from sketches to murals to metal work and plastic sculptures.

"Being a Tejano is something to be proud of and something to fight for," he said. "Our way of life must be remembered and should survive in some form. Public art will help."

One of Hinojosa's premier pieces is a sketch of 19th century civil rights advocate Catarino Garza talking to a group of men in a South Texas *"mezquital* (mesquite grove)" laden with *"nopales* (prickly pear)" and fallen tree trunks used as seats for those who gathered to hear the respected freedom fighter and orator. So well-known were Catarino Garza's rides throughout South Texas that *Harper's Magazine* published a cover story on him and his ambitions to protect Tejanos from atrocities of the Texas Rangers and others. Garza's legacy was inspirational to Hinojosa. He wanted to preserve Garza's legacy for generations of Tejanos in the 20th and 21st centuries. He did not want people to forget the freedom fighter's urgency to unite or perish and lose their culture, he said.

"I remember my "*abuelo* (grandfather) and older "*tios* (uncles)" and other family members talking about Catarino Garza. He was a man of courage and discipline, well-educated, a journalist and an orator but he would speak with his gun as well. He helped many vaqueros and South Texas rancheros survive those days." Garza was one of Texas' premier newspaper publishers and owned a chain of four newspaper he used to promote his message.

Hinojosa displays his heritage through art.

"*Soy* (I am) Tejano," Hinojosa says proudly. "I live in Alice, a city resident I guess, but my heart and passion is Tejano and the vaquero and rancho culture they blessed this area with."

He has done numerous exhibits and designed artwork for books and scholarly publications. His public art is on display in buildings and sites throughout South Texas. His art work has been on the books such as *"Llanos Mestenos (Mustang Plains)"* by Agnes Grimm, in *"Stories That Must Not Die"* in 1977 and *"Across the River"* in 1978 by former Texas A&I professor Juan Sauvegeau. His artwork is also in the Tejano classic *"Tejano Empire"* by Andres Tijerina.

"All those depict South Texas legends or a way of life," he said. "But I also want to show that the Tejano has impacted not only South Texas, but the state and nation," Hinojosa said.

"Servando Hinojosa's drawing of Tejano journalist and revolutionary Catarino Garza rallying his troops in the Brush Country near Alice, Texas, in the 19th century."

Among his favorite art pieces is *"Ameramorfosis"* - a mural diagram that explains the transition of the Americas from the discovery of the New World by the Spanish to modern times. At the center of the mural are Abraham Lincoln, the Liberty Bell and George Washington. Below them are scientists and scholars and toward the bottom is Mexican icon *"La Virgen de Guadalupe"* and Mexican President Benito Juarez. Cattle, missions, horses, vaqueros are all included in *"Ameramorfosis"* through which he claims that the United States is morphed from many segments of our history.

"You see, Hispanics – in particular Mexicanos and Tejanos – have been and continue to be an integral part of the United States. Perhaps my art will help depict that contribution and impact and realize that the battle for acceptance as an American continues.", he said

Silhouette of metal sculpture titled "Alicia y Juan" by South Texas artist Servando Hinojosa. It is located new downtown Alice, Texas.

(Printed with permission from the artist)

Cuentos Tejanos

Episode 9

The Hanging of Chipita Rodriguez - "No Soy Culpable"

-By Manuel Flores

"No soy culpable (I am not guilty)."

Those were reportedly the last words of legendary Tejana Josefa "Chipita" Rodríguez, who at one time was thought to be the first woman hanged in Texas.

After her death, several sightings of her ghost were reported. She was seen roaming the banks of the Nueces River and sometimes the Aransas River voicing a plaintive wail of sorrow.

"No soy culpable."

This went on for more than 120 years until she was declared "not guilty" by the Governor of Texas.

Her death and legend are as pertinent to the state of Texas as any other intriguing tale of the Lone Star State. It was in death that Chipita Rodríguez became part of Texas lore.

Her story, mostly based in fact, is as captivating as any ghost story ever told in the state. The nature of her death was the stuff of legend and it was often repeated at cowboys' campfires and family gatherings. Always, she would roam the river banks asking for clemency, forgiveness, a fair hearing, the story tellers claimed.

Chipita was hanged in 1863 for murdering cotton merchant and horse trader John Savage with an ax and stealing $600 in gold from him. Savage's body was found wrapped in a burlap sack in the Nueces River north of San Patricio.

Some records indicate she was born in what is now Texas in 1773, others that she was born in Mexico in 1799. Some believe her name was Josefa, but it cannot be verified. It is known her father was Pedro Rodríguez. There is no record of her mother's name. Her father was believed to have abandoned the Mexican army during Santa Anna's march to San Antonio in 1836, and that is when the family moved to the banks of the Nueces River near San Patricio.

Legend holds she married when she was 20 and had a baby, but her husband abandoned her and left with the baby.

After that, she lived on the banks of the Nueces River and had a modest *jacal* (hut) that became a resting place for travelers who wandered the South Texas plains after the Texas Revolution and into the Civil War era. There, the travelers could find a cot or lay down their bed roll as Chipita would provide cooked meals, trying to make a living in the harsh sun-bitten, mosquito-infested and mesquite-laden terrain.

Savage, the man she allegedly killed, was among those "guests" one fall night in 1863. He had been at the saloon in San Patricio bragging about his sale of horses to the Union Army. The Civil War was still raging, especially in South Texas and the Rio Grande Valley, and this news was not welcomed in Confederate Texas. After a night of drinking, Savage drove over to Chipita's hut and asked for a place to spend the night. He was prepared a hot meal for a "*peseta* (quarter)" and told he could sleep in his bedroll in front of the hut.

The next morning, he could not be found. Two days later, two slaves found Savage's dismembered body in a burlap sack by the river.

Sherriff William Means' investigation led him to Chipita's place and he arrested her, claiming the motive was greed, even though legend holds the saddlebags with the gold were found nearby.

Chipita refused to speak or could not defend herself in English.

She kept insisting, "*No soy culpable ...*"

Some felt she was protecting someone, perhaps Juan Silvera, who some sources claim was her illegitimate son and had recently arrived back at San Patricio. Both were indicted and tried in the 14th District Court under Judge Benjamin F. Neal, but only Chipita was found guilty, according to records.

The jury pleaded for mercy because of her age, but Neal sentenced her to death by hanging on Nov. 13, 1863. Depending on what birthdate is accurate, she was either 90 years old or more like 45. Stories make her sound like she was strong and could take care of herself, a point that was brought up in the trial. One theory holds that the jury pleaded for justice because she was a woman and hanging of a woman should not be tolerated. The jury members were led to believe that no woman had ever been hanged in Texas, thus they pled for mercy.

She was first held at Sheriff William Means' home in Meansville, about three miles east of present-day Odem, Texas. According to legend, Chipita was kept in leg irons and chained to a wall in the courthouse where she was later moved "for her safety."

But, some wanted her dead and would stop at nothing to have frontier justice. There were two attempts by a lynch mob that were thwarted by Sheriff Means and his deputies.

Soon, Chipita was taken to a grove of trees along the river and hanged from the tallest oak. She was buried in a coffin along the banks of the river under the tree from which she was hanged.

Shortly after her impromptu burial, the rumors started. One of the onlookers said he heard a moan coming from the coffin. For decades, witnesses have claimed they have seen the shadow of a mournful woman gliding near where her jacal once stood, her cries echoing off the river banks and into the near mesquital.

"No soy culpable!", the cry echoes down the river banks.

The tale of this woman who was unjustly hanged has inspired countless books, articles, poetry and even a southwestern opera. In 1993, the University of Texas music department performed the opera Chipita Rodríguez, composed by Texas A&M University-Corpus Christi professor Lawrence Weiner. In 2010 a screenplay was written by Del Mar College and Texas A&M University-Corpus Christi student screenwriter Cary Cadena. All acknowledged her cries of *"No soy culpable!"*

However, someone did hear Chipita's cry. A historical marker in Old San Patricio details her tragic tale. It is more of a tourist attraction than a historical market detailing Chipita's life and struggle.

But, in 1985, Texas state senator Carlos Truan of Corpus Christi asked the Texas Legislature to absolve Chipita Rodríguez of murder. The Sixty-ninth Legislature passed the resolution, and it was signed by Gov. Mark White on June 13, 1985.

At last, Chipita was declared innocent and her spirit could rest.

At last, her words *"No soy culpable,"* were heard.

No recent apparitions of Chipita's ghost have been reported.

Cuentos Tejanos

Episode 10

Cinco de Mayo and the Texas Connection – Gen. Zaragoza saves Mexico and the U.S.

-By Judge Juan
Escobar and Manuel Flores

Cinco de Mayo should be a Texas and American holiday.

Surprised? Don't be. With the help of several valiant Texans, Tejanos to be exact, the celebrated victory of the Mexican Army over the French in 1862 in Puebla may never would have happened. And, that changed the course of history.

Had the French succeeded in defeating Mexico, the Union victory in the U.S. Civil War was at stake, not to mention international trade and stability of the hemisphere. The Monroe Doctrine would have been violated.

Neither is Cinco de Mayo Mexican Independence Day. That is on Sept. 16. Cinco de Mayo, however, is a holiday in Mexico but it seems to be observed more fervently in Texas and the American Southwest.

There is a reason.

The fight for victory on this significantly historic battle began with Gen. Ignacio Zaragoza, born in Goliad, Texas, and educated in the best Spanish and Mexican universities. When the French invaded Mexico, Zaragoza sounded a call to arms from his compatriots in the Brush Country and Rio Grande Valley of South Texas. He rounded up vaqueros by the hundreds and marched to Mexico to confront the French. There he and his Tejanos helped train and prepare the Mexicans of the area to fight the French. Badly outnumbered and not properly equipped for warfare, Zaragoza and his men prevailed. This victory allowed time for Mexico to prepare for war against France and eventually run them out of Mexico.

Here's how it all unfolded:

Benito Juarez was elected President of Mexico in 1861 and took over a government that was in financial crisis. On July 17, 1861, Juarez decided to freeze all foreign debt, for two years. Mexico's decision to default on their debt was met with resistance from France, Spain and Britain. As a consequence, these countries sent their naval forces to block the Port of Veracruz and force Mexico to pay its debt.

Spain and Britain came to a settlement with Mexico and withdrew. France, under the leadership of Napoleon III, however, saw this as an opportunity to conquer Mexico and expand its empire.

On the eve of 1861, France landed a well-armed Army at Veracruz and forced the Mexican Army into a full retreat. Some historians estimate that there were 8,000 soldiers and others that there were 6,000 soldiers under General Charles Latrille de Lorencez. This well-trained force set forth to a small village, Puebla de Los Angles, setting the stage for what became known as the "La Batalla del Cinco de Mayo."

The date for this battle was May 5, 1862. More than 2,000 Mexican peasants, led by Goliad, Texas-born General Ignacio Zaragoza awaited their fate as they defended the forts at Guadalupe and Loreto in Puebla, with the assistance of many South Texas and Rio Grande Valley vaqueros. The Mexicans were poorly trained and armed with short supplies of ammunition, weapons and practically no artillery. Zaragoza and the South Texans did their best to prepare for battle.

In the early morning of May 5th the French attacked the small forts and were met with fierce resistance by the Mexicans under Zaragoza's command. The battle lasted until the late evening hours. The French were defeated and lost more than 600 men. The Mexicans lost 100.

Several of the illustrious leaders of the Battle of Puebla had direct roots to South Texas. According to some leading historians, more than 500 Tejanos were recruited to fight at Puebla. A list of some of these men has been compiled at the University of Puebla.

Captain Porfirio Zamora y Galvan, another leader of the battle, was born in Matamoros and later lived in a ranch near Palito Blanco, Texas, south of Alice. He was under the command of Gen. Porfirio Diaz, who would become president of Mexico.

Zamora's bravery and actions during the battle of Puebla did not go unrecognized. He was awarded *"La Condecoración de Segunda Clase,"* Mexico's second-highest award for bravery. He also was honored by the

Mexican President and today Mexicos 500 Peso bill bears his image. Many of Zamora's descendants live in Jim Wells and Nueces County.

After the battle, the name of the city of Puebla de Los Angeles was changed to Puebla de Ignacio Zaragoza in honor of Zaragoza's victory. Sadly, only months after his historic victory, Zaragoza died at age 33 from typhoid fever. He was honored in a state funeral and only days later President Juárez issued a decree making Cinco de Mayo a national holiday.

This victory gave Mexico a much-needed morale boost and a reason to unite as a country. The victory was celebrated all over Mexico and President Juarez declared that this would be a holiday named "El Cinco de Mayo."

The victory at Puebla was short-lived. The French Army eventually attacked Mexico City, with a force of more than 30,000 troops, setting Emperor Maximilian I as emperor of Mexico.

French forces continued fighting all over Mexico. Napoleon III and his Emperor Maximilian I were determined to gain control of Mexico and eventually the United States, in clear violation of the Monroe Doctrine. At the time of the battle of Puebla the United States was involved in the Civil War. Historical records indicate France intended to help the Confederacy.

The French continued to march toward the United States-Mexican border. They saw a weakness in the United States with the cost incurred by the Civil War and were determined to invade the United States. On June 16, 1866, Mexican Forces under the command of Gen. Servando Canales confronted the French at La Mesa del Ebanito, about three miles east of Rio Grande City, Texas, on the Mexican side of the river. The Mesa is on hills known as Lomas de Santa Gertrudis. According to Ernesto Garza-Saenz historian from Camargo, Tamaulipas, Mexico (This community is located across the Rio Grande River from Rio Grande City, Texas), Saenz states that after a one-hour battle, forces from Camargo defeated the French. This battle became known as the Battle of Santa Gertrudis. Nine days later, French forces surrendered at Matamoros. This was the beginning of the end of the French intervention in Mexico. With the assistance of the United States, the French surrendered to Mexico five days after the Battle of Santa Gertrudis on June 21, 1867.

Mexican historian Justo Sierra (1848-1912), in his writings "Political Evolution of the Mexican People," states, that had the French won the Battle of Puebla the Mexicans would have lost their fighting spirit. This would have expedited the war in Mexico and the French would have joined forces with Confederate Army with a higher probability of defeating the Union. The Battle of Santa Gertrudis was also significant, because it this was the beginning of the end of French occupation of Mexico. Five days after the battle the French finally surrendered.

So, next time you celebrate Cinco de Mayo and get ready to drink some *cerveza* and perhaps imbibe some tequila and munch on some tacos, remember there are several reasons to celebrate the holiday. The hero of the battle was born in Texas and his family had deep Texas roots noted in the Texas Land Office. In addition and more importantly, many of those soldiers who led the charge against the French came from South Texas.

Salud!

Juan M. Escobar is a former county judge of Kleberg County and a former Texas State representative and is a seventh-generation Tejano.

Statue of Gen. Ignacio Zaragoza, hero of Cinco de Mayo, at La Bahia in Goliad, Texas. *(Goliad State Park tpwd.texas.gov).*

Cuentos Tejanos

Episode 11

La Matanza (The Massacre) – A Dark Time in the history of South Texas

-By Ramiro Molina and Manuel Flores

When a historical marker is dedicated in Texas, there is usually a sense of pride among survivors or relatives of those associated with the history-making site and event that led to the plaque being dedicated. The mood is often celebratory as the marker is unveiled, validating an event so significant that the Texas Historical Commission has decided it merits to be recognized. That was not the case on Oct. 14, 2018, near San Benito, Texas, in the Rio Grande Valley when the marker dedicated brought a spotlight — and admission — to a dark time in the history of South Texas.

The plaque is off southbound Exit 16 along Interstate 69E near San Benito. It commemorates the killing of thousands of Mexicans and Tejanos in the early 20th century.

The plaque is titled "*La Matanza* (The Massacre or Mass Slaughter)." The ceremony was somber, angry and cathartic, for many Tejanos. Here or nearby, more than 1,000 Tejanos were buried in a mass grave by the Texas Rangers and other vigilante groups after indiscrimate murder of Tejano men, women and children who lived in the Rio Grande Valley.

The plaque serves as a stark reminder of the sorrow and anger many Tejanos in South Texas felt during a scourge of killings that permeated in the Rio Grande Valley and South Texas between 1915 and 1917. Racial and ethnic tensions erupted into violence as Texas Rangers dispensed a form of frontier justice that led to the murder of thousands of Tejanos, who lost their lands and possessions as Anglos settled the area.

Author Benjamin Heber Johnson, who wrote "*Revolution in Texas,*" equated the killings to a form of genocide. He called the armed rebellion opposition by the Tejanos the determining factor in the claiming of American citizenship for the Mexican American residents of South Texas.

The book is subtitled *"How a Forgotten Rebellion and Its Bloody Suppression Turned Mexicans Into Americans."* He calls what took place in the Rio Grande Valley and in South Texas one of the nation's most intense and protracted episodes of racial violence.

Of course, the Tejanos and Mexican ranchers fought back. A militia called *"Ejercito Libertador de los Mexico-Tejanos* (Liberating Army of the Mexican Texans)"* was formed under the leadership of Luis de la Rosa and Aniceto Pizana. The Tejanos staged raids against the Rangers, the U.S. Army and vigilante groups hiding in ranches protected by the Rangers and Army.

Johnson notes that the rebellion by the Tejano army was really a cry to be accepted as full American citizens, as the Treaty of Guadalupe Hidalgo of 1848 called for after the U.S.-Mexico War. He called the atrocities by the Rangers and vigilante groups a form of genocide. Indeed, it was. The hangings and murders of Tejanos were taking place all over Texas. They were indiscriminate with the excuse of frontier justice being the only form reason for killing or stealing a person's property as the excuse for the action.

This violence also led to *"El Plan de San Diego,"* a revolutionary proclamation that was more of a desperate cry for freedom than an act of war. When it was made public, even more violence by the Rangers and others was perpetrated against the Tejanos. The plan urged residents to unite and stop the encroachment of the Anglo settlers.

The Plan de San Diego called for the execution of all Anglo males over the age of 16. Historical records show that 21 Americans were killed and numerous raids were conducted by the revolutionary army tired for seeing Tejanos treated like second-class citizens and denied their civil rights. The ragtag militia, which often crossed the border to escape being captured, was no match for the Texas Rangers and vigilantes. The Rangers and their associates stepped up their tactics in response to the *Plan de San Diego*. They roamed the Rio Grande Valley and the South Texas brush country with the authority to dispense frontier justice, which often came in the form of shootings, hangings and even dragging the dead through the prickly pear and thorny landscape.

Indeed, the Tejanos did not go down quietly. Ever since the Texas Revolution (1836) and the U.S-Mexico War (1846-1848) they were harassed, hanged, and killed by the Texas Rangers and vigilante groups who claimed the land we now call Texas for themselves. Allegiance to Mexico was natural for the Tejanos, but those in South Texas and Rio

Grande Valley wanted to claim their American citizenship which was guaranteed to them by the signing of the Treaty of Gudalupe Hidalgo. The mass slaughter celebrated that day was the turning point.

The killings stopped, for the most part, when President Woodrow Wilson, at the urging of Texas State Rep. J.T. Canales, sent 26,000 U.S. troops to patrol the border region. At first, many thought the Army troops were sent to discipline the unruly Tejanos (and they did do some of that policing work), but they were in South Texas to stop the violence and the indiscriminate shooting of American citizens perpetrated primarily by the Texas Rangers and vigilantes. The U.S. Army started arresting Texas Rangers who were plain ol' guilty of murder. Vigilante groups were calmed down. The mass shooting stopped.

The Texas Rangers — often referred to as *"Los Rinches"* — continue to be resented by many Tejanos. Canales was so upset by the actions of the Texas Rangers that he asked the Texas Legislature to dissolve the unit which he claimed was racist and at times acted without legal authority. Gov. James Hogg was the only one to react, disbanding one of the Ranger units in West Texas after the massacre at the hamlet of El Provenir. Texas. The Rangers and U.S. Army troops swept into the ranch community killing all of its male residents.

It was part of the ongoing violence and killings of Tejanos in Texas. Historians now estimate that 3,000 to 5,000 Tejanos died at the hands of the Texas Rangers and vigilantes during this period. Mass murders occurred.

Another mass murder site is near Edinburg. It lies just off the roadway on FM 1017 amid the tangled mesquite and cenizo. At least, there, graves commemorate the dead. The grave site and cemetery belongs to the Bazan and Longoria families.

Benjamin Heber Johnson wrote that the indiscriminate murders were reprehensible even at a time when frontier justice prevailed. Today, because of the Texas Historical Marker, we understand why he said those words.

For the longest time, the events associated with *"La Matanza"* remained forgotten, absent from the history books and not discussed. No one talked about it. People began to ask, "Did it even happen?" The answer now for all to see is as plain as the historical marker sticking out of the busy highway in the heart of the Rio Grande Valley brush country, in San Benito it did! It is but one of example of the killing of Tejanos by the Texas Rangers and vigilantes.

This dark time in South Texas history has finally been acknowledged. This event is also commemorated at the Bob Bullock State History Museum in Austin in its Texas history exhibit. But, with the dedication of the Texas Historical Commission marker, the bloodshed that marked that era is no longer relegated to the shadows of history. It serves as a sobering reminder of what can happen when hate envelops a region.

Somehow, Texas has survived and, so have the Tejanos.

Ramiro Molina is a Tejano historian and has one of the state's largest collections of historical maps, many of which are on display at the Tejano Civil Rights Museum and Resource Center in Heritage Park in Corpus Christi. He served as an adviser to the construction of the Tejano Monument in Austin, is an advisory board member of the Tejano Civil Rights Museum and has served as an officer of the Hebbronville Museum and Jim Hogg County Historical Commission.

Texas Historical Marker at site of "La Matanza" in South Texas. (La Matanza Historical Marker, photo by James Hulse, www.hmdb.org).

Cuentos Tejanos

Episode 12

The Chisholm Trail - Cattle Drives Part of Texas Lore

-By Manuel Flores

Cattle drives were as much a part of South Texas lore in the 19th century as the prickly pear patches of *nopal* (prickly pear cactus) and mesquite groves.

This was inevitable after the Spanish brought cattle to the New World in the 16th century and vaqueros settled what is now South Texas in the 1700s. Millions of cattle roamed the fertile grasslands north of the Rio Grande Valley and up to the Texas coast. These Spanish cattle evolved into the fabled Texas Longhorns, a sturdy beast designed to weather the harshness and drought of the area and survive and multiply.

They were good eating, too.

After the Civil War, a variety of cattle trails evolved as ranchers had their vaqueros take the hardy Longhorn cattle 1,000 miles north to faraway places like Kansas, Wyoming, and Missouri.

In the decades following the U.S. Civil War, more than 6 million — some accounts say 10 million — cows and bulls were led out of Texas to northern cattle markets.

There were many cattle trails. All started in Texas and all had cattle from South Texas where tens of thousands of head of cattle roamed the Wild Horse Desert as freely as a horned toad on a hot summer night in the Lone Star State.

The trails started in the lower Rio Grande Valley and the Brush Country of modern-day Jim Hogg, Books, Kleberg, Kenedy and Webb counties and meandered up what is now U.S. Highway 281, Interstate 35 and U.S. 77 toward San Antonio and points north.

The King Ranch and Kenedy Ranch in the heart of the South Texas Brush Country near the Texas coast by Baffin Bay on the Gulf of Mexico also got involved. Their vaqueros were called Kineños and Kenedeños, respectively. These massive migrations of Texas beeves would feed a nation. Some of those original drives from what is now the Kenedy County and Kleberg County meandered up what is now 6th Street in Kingsville. The City of Kingsville has renamed 6th Street to "6th and Kineños Trail" to commemorate those drives that brought economic vitality and fame to the area.

Among the cattle trails used by South Texas ranchers — small and big — were the Great Western Trail, the Matamoros Trail, the Shawnee Trail, and the Sedalia Trail. But it was the Chisholm Trail that was the major route out of Texas for livestock. In 2017, the Chisholm Trail celebrated its 150th anniversary and its impact on South Texas, the state and nation must be recognized.

From 1867 to 1884, the Longhorn cattle driven north along it provided a steady source of income that helped the impoverished state recover from the Civil War.

Ranchers and banking entrepreneurs realized there was a growing demand for beef in the United States. With the development of the railroad up north, markets in the Eastern and Western coasts could now be reached.

The Chisholm Trail started with simple banking negotiations by Joseph G. McCoy of Illinois. In the spring of 1867, he persuaded Kansas Pacific Railroad officials to lay a line in Abilene, Kansas. He began building pens and loading facilities and sent word to Texas ranchers that a cattle market was available. That year he shipped 35,000 head; the number doubled each year until 1871, when 600,000 head glutted the market.

Besides Abilene, other cattle drive destinations were Dodge City, Kansas; Sedalia and Kansas City, Missouri; Pueblo and Denver, Colorado; and Cheyenne, Wyoming.

The first herd to follow the future Chisholm Trail to Abilene belonged to O.W. Wheeler and his partners, who in 1867 bought 2,400 steers in San Antonio. The cattle came from the San Antonio River ranchos and the Goliad-Victoria area.

On average, a single herd of cattle on a long drive (for example, Texas to Kansas) numbered about 3,000 head. To herd the cattle, a crew of at least 10 cowboys and vaqueros was needed, with three horses per cowboy. The drive could take 14-18 weeks, depending on weather and even Indian raids.

Organizers of the original cattle drives planned to winter on the plains, then trail the cattle on to California, a treacherous journey through desert and mountain terrain. But the vaqueros who were leading the drive found tracks that would lead them to Kansas. The tracks were made by Scot-Cherokee Jesse Chisholm, who in 1864 began hauling trade goods to Indian camps about 220 miles south of his post near Wichita, Kansas. At first the route was merely referred to as the Trail, the Kansas Trail, the Abilene Trail, or McCoy's Trail, according to historical documents.

Texas cowmen soon gave Chisholm's name to the entire trail from the Rio Grande to central Kansas.

Today, a map of the Chisholm Trail clearly shows its start in the South Texas triangle starting at San Antonio with Del Rio to the west and the south Houston area to the east and meandering down to the Rio Grande Valley and Brownsville.

It was there where millions of cows fed on the leg-high grass that would grow in the spring and sustain the beeves through the harsh winters and blazing hot summers.

According to the Texas State Historical Association, the earliest known references to the Chisholm Trail in print were in the *Kansas Daily Commonwealth* of May 27 and October 11, 1870. On April 28, 1874, the Denison, Texas, *Daily News* mentioned cattle going up "the famous Chisholm Trail."

The trail drives started from various points and led up to San Antonio, Austin, and Waco, where the trails split. The Chisholm Trail continued north to Fort Worth, then passed east of Decatur to the crossing at Red River Station. From Fort Worth to Newton, Kansas, U.S. Highway 81 follows the Chisholm Trail. The trails from the Rio Grande Valley came up just east of what is now U.S. 281 and led to San Antonio. The Kingsville area trails started at the King Ranch and meandered on up what is now U.S. 77, crossing the Nueces River and wandering toward Lockhart, Temple and Waco before getting to Fort Worth.

A map of the Chisholm and other trails is like a series of tree limbs arching out through Central and North Texas and up to the Midwestern United States. But the trunk that kept it steady and sending cattle to feed America was from San Antonio on down.

Once in Kansas, Wyoming or Missouri, the cattle would be shipped by rail to other markets.

The Chisholm Trail led to the new profession of trailing contractor. A few large ranchers such as Capt. Richard King in Kingsville and Abel

"Shanghai" Pierce in Wharton delivered their own stock, but trailing contractors handled the vast majority of herds.

The Chisholm Trail was finally closed because of the proliferation of barbed wire that closed the vast grazing lands in Texas and became a barrier to following original trails. A tick outbreak also led to a quarantine of Texas cattle around that time.

Its legacy, however, lives on. South Texas, its large and small landowners and its vaqueros proved to be crucial to its success and to the color and heritage that is now associated with Texas.

Cuentos Tejanos

Episode 13

Mary Helen Berlanga – Education Advocate

-By Manuel F. Medrano

An advocate is a proponent or champion of a cause. Few policymakers in the history of South Texas have been more involved in the cause of educational equity than Mary Helen Berlanga, a Corpus Christi attorney whose mark on Texas education and politics earns her a place on the heroes mantle. For nearly three decades as a member of the Texas State Board of Education, she championed educational justice and fairness.

There is a Spanish proverb which says *"Camarón que se duerme se lo lleva la corriente* (The shrimp that falls asleep is swept away by the current)". One should never take things for granted or cease to make an effort.

Her life is an example of an educational leader whose ideas and passion were forged by growing up in a loving family who gained a foothold in the civil rights struggle for Mexican Americans by serving as leaders in the League of United Latin American Citizens (LULAC).

Mary Helen Bonillla Berlanga was born in Calvert, Texas about an hour from Waco. She was the youngest of eight children. Her father, Ruben Bonilla, was born in Mexico City on January 31, 1905 and knew no English when he immigrated to the United States at seventeen. Her mother, Maria Ramirez, was born on August 15, 1905. They married on September 16, 1927. They would become two of her best teachers and staunchest supporters. Her primary schooling was both academic and sobering. In first grade she remembers her best friend refusing to play with her because she was "Mexican." Bonilla Berlanga remembers, "I thought it was a disease, so I went to my first grade teacher."[1] Her teacher, regrettably, could not answer her question about the barriers in a segregated school. Her father later questioned the policy and persuaded the school board to allow his older children into the "Anglo school." They became the first Hispanics to attend that school in that town. Although Mary Helen Bonilla Berlanga was the beneficiary of that precedent, some prejudice persisted.

Even as a young girl Bonilla Berlanga loved learning and making speeches. On one occasion after she had learned about George Washington and Abraham Lincoln in class, she decided to speak about them at home. In her back yard on a downed mulberry tree, she gave a speech about these Presidents to her pets, the chickens. On another occasion, she decided to build her own office, so she gathered some bricks in her backyard and began "construction." After she told her mother about her plans, her parents built her a playhouse where she enjoyed "the freedom of pretending"[2] by acting and giving speeches. Neither of her parents had much formal education, but both recognized its value. They expected their children to excel in school. Bonilla Berlanga recalls, "Of course, Dad wanted straight A's and Lord have mercy if he ever saw a C on your report card… I don't think we ever had a C.[3]

Her mother also encouraged her. Once when Bonilla Berlanga was in second grade, her teacher suggested she enter a spelling bee. Her mother told her that she had nothing to lose, but could win a ribbon. Bonilla Berlanga not only entered but won the spelling bee and the ribbon. In 1958 Bonilla Berlanga's father suffered a heart attack and within a year the family moved from Calvert to Corpus Christi, Texas. She and her brother, Ruben, enrolled at Hamlin Middle School. The school counselor promptly informed them that although they had made A's at their former school, they were not in a "country school" any more. She also said there were few Hispanic children enrolled in Hamlin and that they were competing with outstanding Anglo students. They should expect a drop in their grades. As the children left the office, their father told them not to listen to what the counselor had said. They would continue to excel in school because that was the way they were reared. After middle school Bonilla Berlanga attended Ray High School and became very involved in public speaking. She enrolled for speech courses and participated in speech tournaments and debates. She remembers her Spanish teacher was outstanding, but "She expected me to know everything all the time; if I didn't raise my hand, she would call on me anyway. It was stressful, but I'm glad she did it because I really listened."[4]

Although her high school experience was at times challenging, it was generally positive. After graduation she enrolled at the University of Houston and continued the tradition that her older siblings had begun. All had graduated from college. In the Bonilla household attending college was not an option; it was a requirement. Her parents always told them education was their salvation and the key to their success in life. It was their destiny. In 1968, during her sophomore year, Bonilla Berlanga's resolve was severely tested when her father died. He had always told William, his second oldest son, that if anything happened to him it was his responsibility to take care of Mrs. Berlanga and the younger children, and he did. In May 1970 Mary Helen Bonilla Berlanga received a Bachelor's of Arts degree. It was then that her mother again challenged her to do more. Bonilla Berlanga remembers her mother saying, "Mary Helen, why don't you go to law school; you got brothers that are practicing attorneys, too… you'd be the first female in our family (to be an attorney)."[5]

For Bonilla Berlanga it was an interesting decision to ponder because there were virtually no female attorneys in Corpus Christi. Her mother, however, simply said that it did not matter, and it did not. Three of her older brothers - William, Tony and Ruben - were already practicing law and she could be just as successful, she felt. She soon enrolled at the South Texas College of Law in Houston. Although she originally preferred criminal law, she found her niche in immigration and social security law.

Bonilla Berlanga explains, "I think immigration law because I knew my parents were immigrants and I knew what they had suffered and I wanted to be able to unite families. I think social security law because it is administrative law and you are helping people who cannot work… because of a disabling condition, whether its mental or physical and I felt like I was giving to those people who needed help and did not have anyone to really help them, did not have anyone to defend them."[6] She knew that these individuals needed an advocate. At South Texas Law School there were approximately 400 students and only 10 were women. Bonilla Berlanga was one of those few and recalls seeing only one other female in all of her classes. The 15-hour course load was demanding and stressful enough, but because Bonilla Berlanga was usually the only female, she bore an additional responsibility. She recalls, "You didn't want the males to think you could not keep up with them… in a way that was good because it was more challenging… but it was difficult and it required a lot of dedication and a lot of time."[7]

In 1974 while still in college, she met her future husband, David Berlanga, on Labor Day weekend at a party her brother Tony Bonilla was hosting. They soon met again at a Fiesta Mexicana that the League of United Latin American Citizens was sponsoring. They dated for a brief time and, for Christmas that year, David gave Mary Helen a stocking with a doll inside. At the bottom of the stocking was a small box with an engagement ring. In May 1975 she passed the Texas State Bar Exam, and on June 6th they married. After their honeymoon in Puerto Vallarta, Mrs. Berlanga returned to practice law with the Bonilla Law Firm in Corpus Christi and Mr. Berlanga began his doctoral studies in bilingual education at Texas A&M University in Kingsville, graduating in 1976. Throughout thirty-four years of marriage, they were strongly committed to improvement education. Their first child, Christina Maria, was born on September 28, 1976. Less than one year later, the Berlanga twins, Monica Lisa and David were born on September 19, 1977. Mary Helen Bonilla Berlanga recalls, "Well, when she (Christina) was just a few months old, I started feeling sick and they told me I was pregnant… Well, at six months I said I'm just not feeling very well and the doctor said what we're gonna have to do is a scan on you.[8] From the scan the doctor confirmed that she was carrying twins. She readily admits that both her mother and mother-in- law were instrumental in helping care for their three young children. Cathy, her fourth child, was born on February 14, 1980. With her own children Bonilla Berlanga realized that "all children in this world have a gift, but I wanted to see if they could find their own gift, or sometimes we had to nourish to find out what that gift was."[9]

Having a family to care for did not slow down the whirlwind that was Bonilla Berlanga. There were immigration cases to tend to and social security issues for her clients to attend to as well. Now, with children of her own, the problem with educating South Texas children also came to the forefront. In January 1983 she was elected for her first term on the Texas State Board of Education, becoming the first Hispanic to ever be elected. She soon championed what would become her trademark cause for over a quarter of a century, a quality education for all the children of the state of Texas with no discrimination "from one student to another or from one campus to another with access to the same textbooks, computers and software, libraries and the best teachers."[10]

Initially, some State Board members believed that South Texas children did not need the same materials or to meet the same expectations as children from other regions of Texas, she said. One associate commissioner, Vicki Burgen, said that Hispanic children were born with less capacities. Bonilla Berlanga forcefully replied, "You're telling me that these children that I represent are not are not capable of reading the material that you're preparing for supposedly the kids in your district? I'm sorry; I totally reject that I will not be a part of this. I want the same material as I would for all of the children across the state."

That was the first line of battle.

Because of continued discriminatory comments, Bonilla Bevlanga started "walking out" of the Texas State Board meetings in protest of what was being discussed. "I did walk outs in the State Board (room). I had other Board members, sometimes Republicans, walking out with me," she said.[11] She demanded hiring only certified teachers and denounced the attempts by the State Board to adopt "watered down" books and curriculums. [12] Over the years Bonilla Berlanga worked tirelessly to empower the State Board and various Texas communities to understand the diverse needs of the student population. One venue for achieving this was through the textbook adoption process. She recalls, "I've faced a situation of the lady that comes up to me and says 'I want to make sure that you're going to include my great-great grandfather Stephen F. Austin,' and I say yes ma'am. I just want to make sure that the people who were here to greet him are also included in the book… We're not trying to steal anybody's history; were just trying to be accurate. This is a very important part of the work."[13]

Bonilla Berlanga remembers examining proposed textbooks that included only negative information about the Aztecs and other pre-Columbian civilizations and argued that they were also great scientists and mathematicians. In some books the slavery issue was virtually excluded because, according to one Board Member, "It's not nice for children to read about slavery, you know; maybe we can say a little bit less about it." [14] She responded by saying that if children don't know about the institution, how can they understand its later impact on issues such as discrimination? Additionally, photographs and illustrations about women and minorities were virtually excluded in those textbooks; however, females and Hispanics, for example, contributed to and participated in all of the U.S. wars since the American Revolution. Her point was, of course, that a more inclusive view of people and events in history was required to give students a better understanding of the past.

Her battles with the State Board of Education became legendary, garnering state and nationwide publicity as she fought to ensure Mexican American, Tejano, children received the same educational opportunities as other Texas students. She decorated her State Board of Education seat with a Mexican sarape and charro hat to emphasize that the Mexican American children of Texas could not and would not be forgotten as long as she had a voice in the situation.

Mary Helen Berlanga continues to champion the rights of immigrants and the rights of students throughout Texas, sometimes despite personal tragedy. Her husband, David, died on April 20, 2009 two weeks before their thirty-fifth wedding anniversary. The November before, he commented about her legacy to education and to him. He said, "She always put students first; she always put teachers first. She always has fought for their rights… To me her legacy is that she has been a wonderful mother; she has been a wonderful wife and she is the love of my life and my partner."[15]

What does she consider her legacy as an advocate? She replied, "I would like to think that I have somehow helped a child or children to take the challenge to either pursue a career or pursue their dream and know that they can be proud of who they are." [16]

She has done that and much more, and all the children of Texas are better for it.

Citations

1. Interview with Mary Helen Berlanga on November 14, 2008.
2. Berlanga interview Nov. 14, 2008.
3. Berlanga interview Nov. 14, 2008.
4. Berlanga interview Nov. 14, 2008.
5. Berlanga interview Nov. 14, 2008.
6. Berlanga interview Nov. 14, 2008.
7. Berlanga interview Nov. 14, 2008.
8. Berlanga interview Nov. 14, 2008.
9. Berlanga interview Nov. 14, 2008.
10. Berlanga interview Nov. 14, 2008.
11. Berlanga interview Nov. 14, 2008.
12. Berlanga interview Nov. 14, 2008.
13. Berlanga interview Nov. 14, 2008.
14. Berlanga interview Nov. 14, 2008.
15. Interview with David Berlanga interview Nov. 14, 2008.
16. Berlanga interview Nov. 14, 2008.

Cuentos Tejanos

Episode 14

Américo Paredes – A Texas-Mexican Cancionero

-By Rosa Canales Pérez

Along the Texas-Tamaulipas border, Américo Paredes sang and played guitar with old *"guitarreros"*, folk musicians who were the keepers of a musical tradition he would document in his book, *"A Texas-Mexican Cancionero – Folksongs of the Lower Border."*

Paredes was a folklorist and a scholar. A professor at the University of Texas at Austin, he introduced the musical folklore of the Border to the halls of academia. He taught from an extensive repertoire of ballads that the México-Tejano people called *"corridos* (ballads)". The *corridos* narrated oral histories of a native Tejano population whose historical perspective was non-existent as they faced the social challenges of Texas becoming part of the United States.

Paredes was born in Brownsville in 1915. As a boy he spent summers with his uncle on a ranch in the Tamaulipas countryside. At the ranch near Matamoros, Paredes was drawn to the tradition of oral lore. He sat around older men who smoked and told stories under mesquite trees after nightfall. Often the men brought out guitars to sing songs of the ranches, *"música ranchera"*. It was that rustic ranch sound that accompanied the narrative verses of the corrido ballads.

José Lopez Morín in his book *"The Legacy of Américo Paredes"* reveals that one of Don Américo's favorite corridos as a youth was *"El Hijo Desobediente"*, a ballad about a disobedient son. With roots in the *"romance"* tradition of 18th Century Spain, the corrido narrates a morality tale about a ruthless young man who disobeys his father and threatens to kill him. Before sunset that day, the disobedient son dies when he is gored by a black bull, *"el toro prieto"* from the corrido.

In his poem, "Guitarreros", Paredes describes a live performance of the corrido as two men at the ranch play guitars. Their fingers become "twenty nimble stallions" as the men throw their voices to one another, executing the verses of the song. "*Bajaron el toro prieto que nunca lo habían bajado* (They brought the old black bull that had never been brought down before)", reads the epigraph of the poem quoting a line from the ballad of "El Hijo Desobediente".

Over the years, Américo Paredes continued to gather with musicians who sang the corridos that circulated in the Lower Border region. The early 20th Century had seen Anglo-Texans and Native Tejanos clash in many areas of daily life. The anonymous verses of the corridos allowed the México-Tejanos to provide their own versions to the events that were being reported quite differently in newspaper accounts. Some scholars now refer to the verses of those corridos as literature of resistance.

In his book "*Texas-Mexican Cancionero*", Paredes includes the corridos of resistance in a section of the book titled "*Songs of Border Conflict*". Many of the conflicts involve clashes with law enforcement officials, among them the Texas Rangers.

The sentiment expressed in the corridos of border conflict was that a man had the right to defend himself against the abuses of law enforcement. Such was the case in the "*Corrido de Gregorio Cortez*", which Américo Paredes used as the subject for his doctoral dissertation at the University of Texas.

Gregorio Cortez defended himself with his pistol in his hand when a local sheriff unjustly shot Cortez's brother and tried to shoot Cortez as well. To the Tejano population, Cortez become a folk hero when he eluded the Texas Rangers for days as he made his way back to the Border from Central Texas.

Submitted in1956, the doctoral dissertation met with controversy as Paredes exposed injustices surfacing from the corrido with research to substantiate them. He had trouble finding work after graduate school. In 1958 he was teaching at the Texas School of Mines in El Paso (now the University of Texas-El Paso) when he received word that the University of Texas Press was publishing his dissertation as a book – "*With His Pistol in His Hand: A Border Ballad and Its Hero.*" That Fall, Paredes returned to Austin to accept a position as Assistant Professor of English at UT. His continued research and publications on South Texas folklore earned him considerable leverage in academic circles. In 1970 Paredes founded the Center for Mexican-American Studies at the University of Texas. The Center now carries his name.

Before he died in 1999, Paredes gave instructions for his funeral. He wanted to be cremated so that his ashes could be scattered at the mouth of the Rio Grande. Dr. Manuel Medrano, another Brownsville native, was present for the memorial. A professor at UT-Brownsville, Medrano had cultivated a strong friendship with Don Américo. Their conversations over the years had become material for Medrano's authorized biography of the Tejano icon. Medrano says that Américo Paredes was not only a folklorist and a scholar; he was also an "academic activist."

A photograph of a young Américo Paredes shows him holding a guitar in his classroom at UT. On the chalk board behind him he has written the rhyme scheme for a border ballad next to the words "corrido" and "*cancionero*". Years later a movie will appear, "*The Ballad of Gregorio Cortez*".

For the dedication page of his book: "**A Texas-Mexican Cancionero,**" Paredes writes, "To the memory of my mother who could sing a song or two; and to all the other singers of the Border, who left part of themselves in my keeping."

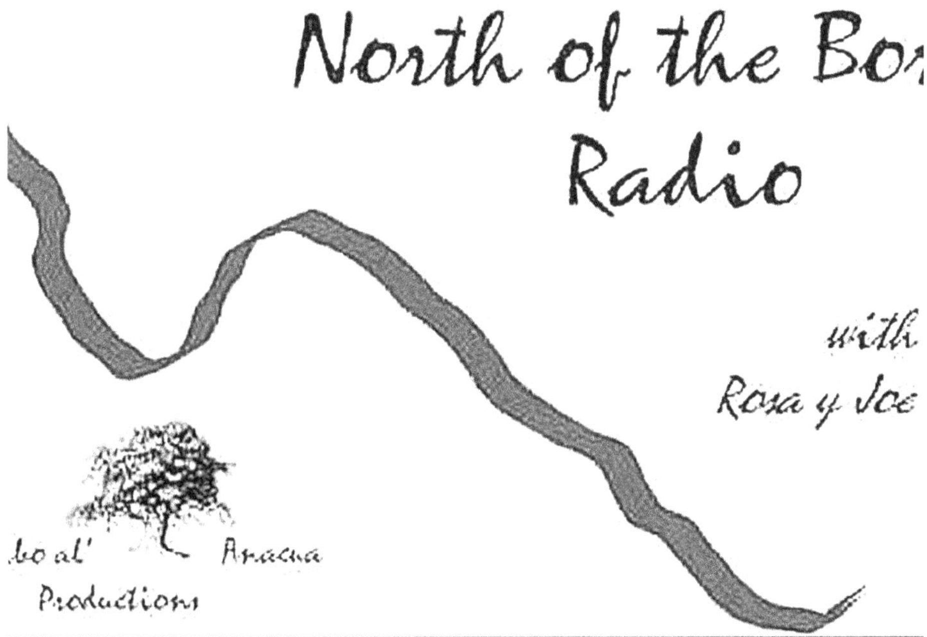

Note: Rosa Canales Perez is a graduate of Texas A&I University, now Texas A&M University-Kingsville. She was a long-time teacher in the Rio

Grande Valley and, after retirement, she and her husband started the musical group "Rumbo al Anacua (Toward the Anacua tree)." The duo has had a long-standing radio program and podcast on "North of the Border by Rosa y Jose".

They are musical scholars and are invited to community feasts and scholarsly events on a regular basis.

Rumbo al Anacua

Cuentos Tejanos

Episode 15

My Mestizo Family Crossed the Rio Grande in 1752

By Dr. Ricardo Romo

South Texas, a U.S.-Mexico borderland region extending for nearly 300 miles along the Rio Grande, has one of the most profound concentrations of Mexican Americans in America. In nearly every one of its communities extending from the Rio Grande River to the Nueces River 50 miles north, Mexican Americans represent more than 90% of the population. Many of these communities are over 200 years old, several, including Laredo, were founded 250 years ago.

In my historical research of this region, I recently discovered that the Sáenz branch of my family came with the original colonists that settled the region in 1750. I am not alone in claiming historical links to the early Spanish settlers, but in researching their history, I was unaware of the significance of these settlements to the future economy of Texas. Western historian Sandra L. Myres concluded that these settlers founded "a ranching frontier which was to become the 'cradle of the Western cattle business'."

The Spanish-Mexican communities of South Texas, extending today from Matamoros-Brownsville to Laredo-Nuevo Laredo along the Rio Grande, have their origins in the mid 1700s. The intrepid colonizer, José de Escandón, the Conde (Count) de Sierra Gorda, received a Spanish Crown commission in 1746 to settle the region. He recruited some 6,000 farmers and ranchers and their families from the northern provinces of Mexico, a region then referred to as the Seno Mexicano. The Seno Mexicano, a sparsely populated province of Mexico, extended from the Panuco River in Tampico to the headwaters of the San Antonio River.

Under Escandón the new colony was called Nuevo Santander and included the towns of Camargo, Reynosa, Revilla [Guerrero], and Mier on the south bank and Laredo and Rancho de Dolores on the north bank. In 1757, less than five years after the founding of new towns in Nuevo

Santander, official Spanish inspectors reported more than 80,000 heads of cattle, horses and mules and 300,000 sheep and goats in the region.

While teaching Texas history in Austin to 7th graders years ago, I encountered the chapter on Stephen F. Austin, "Father of Texas," who brought 300 colonists to Texas in the late 1820s and early 1830s. What was missing was the contribution of Mexican settlers.

Texas Historian Donald E. Chipman is exemplary in recognizing the achievements of Escandón n. Escandón, he wrote, "helped relocate more than six thousand Spaniards and congregate nearly three thousand Indians, and he helped lay the foundation of the cattle industry in the lower Rio Grande Valley." [Chipman, *Spanish Texas*]

By 1800, thousands of cattle roamed the plains of Texas and wild horses were plentiful. Most of us who taught history years ago, and even Texas school teachers today, had never heard of Escandón and few knew that he had been responsible for the first great migration to Texas and surrounding Mexican communities.

The Mexican province of Queretaro was Escandón's home base, and from there he recruited three thousand colonists. Among Escandón's colonization recruits from the Northern provinces of Cerralvo and Camargo were three Sáenz brothers, Juan Ángel, José Miguel, and José Gerónimo, descendants of my 10th generation great grandfather, Miguel Sánchez Sáenz.

I used numerous historical and genealogical sources to determine when and how the Sáenz family, my ancestors, arrived in South Texas. I was helped by the research done by Joel Rene Escobar y Sáenz in his book, *Family History of Capt. Miguel Sánchez Sáenz and His Descendants*, printed in 2002 by Munguia Printers of San Antonio. I grew up two blocks from Munguia Printers and visited often but only recently became aware of this book's existence. Mr. Escobar y Sáenz provided valuable information on research by Ramon Barrera regarding the founding of Roma-Los Sáenz (communities in the Rio Grande Valley east of Zapata on the Rio Grande).

Barrera, a native of Los Sáenz, has written an excellent history of the settlement of Roma-Los Sáenz, as the area was originally known. Barrera writes that the Sáenz colonists came from Mier, one of towns founded by Escandón on the Rio Grande. Mier was founded in 1752 and was adjacent to Roma. The Sáenz brothers established residence in the Roma area in the mid 1750s. In 1767 these three brothers were granted Porciones by the "General Vista of 1767." Their ranches, Porción 72, 73, and 74, were between the towns of Roma and Los Sáenz.

According to Barrera's research and the Roma Bicentennial Committee, the "Villa de Los Sáenz" was founded in 1763, prior to the land distribution. The founding of Roma-Los Sáenz is confirmed by Jerry Thompson's excellent narrative, *A Wild and Vivid Land: An Illustrated History of the South Texas Border.* Thompson discovered that "During the Colonial Era, what is today Roma was claimed as Porciónes seventy-one and seventy-two under the jurisdiction of Mier. In these Porciónes, two ranches, Rancho de Los Sáenz and Rancho de Buena Vista, were established with families from Mier around 1760."

On May 13, 2021, I was moderator for a presentation at the Witte Museum (in San Antonio) by historian Armando Alonso on the life and achievements of colonizer Jose de Escandón. This invitation reminded me that history has many deep secrets and rich details we know little about. We do not always have all the facts about crucial events and important individuals. Escandón's contribution to Texas history is significant and has long been overlooked. Escandón's exclusion from many Texas secondary textbooks is a slight that needs to remedied.

Ricardo Romo is an author, educator, and Latino Art connoisseur. He has degrees from the University of Texas at Austin (BA) and UCLA. He is the former president of the University of Texas-San Antonio May 1999-March 2017 and was a star track athlete for the University of Texas. A nationally respected urban historian, Romo is the author of "East Los Angeles: History of a Barrio," which is now in its ninth printing (one in Spanish). He graduated from Fox Tech High School in San Antonio. (Note: Dr. Manuel Flores and Dr. Romo are distant cousins through the Sáenz family tree).

Cuentos Tejanos

Episode 16

José de Escandón – Father of South Texas

-By Manuel Flores

Along State Highways 359 and 44, which cross through the center of the South Texas city of Alice, is a bigger-than-life statue of a man wearing a cape and hat dating back to colonial American days.

At first glance, he looks like a priest, perhaps a bishop to honor the Catholic tradition of South Texas. With the colonial style hat he dons, he may be an American colonist like George Washington or Thomas Jefferson.

But, one can't be sure.

Why is this statue there, just off the Tex-Mex Railroad track, across from the Alice Chamber of Commerce building and the thriving downtown of the oil and gas town who bills itself as "The Hub City of South Texas"?

The cars pass as if in a flurry to get through the congested traffic familiar to Alice residents. Some, however, slow down to get a better look at this statue in the heart of downtown Alice. Only upon closer inspection and stopping to view the statue can it be ascertained whom this statue represents.

The statue is of José de Escandón– a Spanish colonizer known in historical circles as "The Father of South Texas" and the "Father of the Rio Grande Valley" of Texas. Escandón was sent by the Spanish crown to settle what is now Northern Mexico and South Texas. His origin dates back to the 18th century when South Texas was a province of New Spain known as Nuevo Santander. He was known as The Count of Sierra Gorda.

He arrived in this area in 1746 with thousands of hand-chosen pioneers and soldiers to settle the arid land. He helped establish 23 settlements in South Texas, many which are still operating today as cities, town sites or ranches. He became the first governor of Nuevo Santander, which included parts of what is now Northern Mexico and territories in Texas up to the Guadalupe River and beyond.

His soldiers also settled Rancho Santa Petronila, southwest of modern-day Corpus Christi and just northeast of what is now the King Ranch. Santa Petronila became the largest cattle and horse ranch in the Americas and served as a way station for Spanish explorers headed north in search for riches and adventures.

The statue was established in 1999 as a donation from the family of Tomas and Eloísa Peña Martínez. The family was among the original Spanish settlers of South Texas.

Guadalupe Martínez, one of the descendants of the original Spanish settlers, said the family decided to donate the statue so that South Texans would never forget their Spanish heritage. In an article in the *Corpus Christi Caller-Times* in 2018, Martinez said, "Many people forget this was a Spanish colony. They forget that it was Spain who brought cattle and horses to the area, established the first towns and government, and set up a system of commerce which still operates today. At least, when people see the statue, they wonder, 'Who is that?' and perhaps they will stop and realize the proud history of our area."

Texas became part of Spain from in 1519 when Spanish explorer Alonzo de Pineda landed in in a bay now near modern-day Corpus Christi and claimed all the land for "Mother Spain." The land remained part of Spain until 1821 when it was defeated by Mexico.

Whatever happens, the statue has solidified the legacy of Escandón in South Texas. Many will continue to speed by, but some will stop and learn about the original settlers of the area and recognize Escandón as "The Father of South Texas" and the "Rio Grande Valley."

Cuentos Tejanos

Episode 17

Domingo Peña - Born to be an entertainer.

-By Manuel Flores

Domingo Peña was an entertainer.

There is no other way to describe the charismatic South Texas Spanish-language radio-TV legend whose antics and magnetic personality thrilled thousands of fans. He was the gracious host who helped *"la gente del pueblo* (the people of his community) while dominating radio and television programming in South Texas and mingling with music stars and politicians alike during his lifetime. Because of his work entertaining troops in Vietnam, hosting a Sunday morning community television show and sponsoring *"El Baile Grande* (The Great Dance)" in Memorial Coliseum on the Corpus Christi Bayfront, Peña became a legend and is still talked about today with a reverence reserved for community leaders.

Peña was born Dec. 16, 1917, in Kingsville, Texas, one of Placido and Rose Everett Peña's four sons. The family moved to Corpus Christi in 1935. There he would rise to fame despite some medical struggles and several bumps along the way.

As a teenager, he contracted tuberculosis and was hospitalized. But, even then, he was made for the world of entertainment. Even as a youth, he had a sparkling and energetic personality that seemed to draw people to him. A photo taken during his convalescence from tuberculosis shows him with a cigar in hand, wearing a polo coat and a dapper hat. Nothing was going to slow this young man down. Later in life, he often wore fresh flowers in his lapel and his boots were custom-made and embossed with his name.

His path to stardom began in radio. At age 28, he became a disc jockey on KCCT, a Corpus Christi Spanish-language radio station. His popularity soon spread due to his commanding voice and playful sense of humor. He became a dance promoter and would eventually sponsor *"El Baile Grande de Domingo Peña"* in Exposition Hall. The dance was so popular it was moved next door to Memorial Coliseum by the Corpus Christi Bayfront because of the large overflow crowds. Every Monday night for five years in the mid-1960s, Peña's dances showcased the best Tejano and Mexican musicians of the era.

The dances became immensely popular and were the beginning of a lifelong effort to use his growing fame and fortune to help the community in Corpus Christi and beyond. Peña initiated his philanthropic career while in radio and soon the dances became part of his charity work and fundraisers for those in need.

In 1964, as the Beatles begged to hold our hands on the Ed Sullivan Show, Peña launched what would become the nation's longest-running Hispanic community television show. "The Domingo Peña Show (Or as he liked to call it "El Show de Domingo Peña"). It aired Sunday mornings on KIII-TV Channel 3 in Corpus Christi. The show opened every episode with footage of Peña blaring in a gruff and commanding voice, "Are we ready to go?" There is a slight pause and then he barks "Put it on!," which became his trademark opening delivery. And, speaking of legendary American TV show host, Peña was a cut above but with a clear and distinct purpose to serve and entertain the people of South Texas, a demographic group that had been ignored by traditional and local media.

Peña had many accomplishments during his lifetime, including getting elected constable of Nueces County. His most notable accomplishment was when the U.S. State Department invited him to visit Hispanic troops in Vietnam with a cadre of Tejano musicians. He put together a twelve-person troupe of amazing performers that traveled on a seventeen-day tour of Vietnam, the only one of its kind offered during the war. It brought him much additional acclaim and placed him on the national map as a leader among the larger Hispanic-American community. His passion for the families who lost a soldier in the Vietnam conflict was legendary. He attended more than 100 funerals of soldiers from South Texas who died in Vietnam. Often, he was accompanied by Civil rights leader and founder of the American G.I. Forum Dr. Héctor P. García.

Events like this solidified his presence in South Texas and the popularity of his show. Sunday morning became Domingo Peña time.

Every Sunday as the viewers caught their first glimpse of the host, Peña's cigar was in his hand and his pants just high enough to catch a glimpse of his decorative boots.

One of Peña's favorite phrases was "*abuelita* (grandma)" as he went from sequence-to-sequence in his show asking all the grandmas to pay attention, because some exciting stuff was about to pop on the TV screen. Since his days in radio, Peña knew his audience. Always the marketing expert, he knew that in a Hispanic family, if Grandma watched, everyone would watch.

Between 1964 and 1983 his show was a "must-see" every Sunday morning for many Tejano families in South Texas. His show and his dances were memorialized in songs by famed Tejano musicians Paulino Bernal and Tony de la Rosa.

The show became a forum for activism that allowed for political commentary and discussion on community issues. Civil rights leader Dr. Héctor P. García and his sister Dr. Clotilde García, a community activist, were frequent guests, encouraging all viewers to get out the vote. García and his sister would appear on the screen and ask people to press the lever ("*La Palanca*") for all candidates in the Democratic Party running for whatever office was listed. However, all who wanted access to the show were welcomed, but they had to go through "*El Señor Peña*" first.

Spotlighting community barbecue fundraisers, church fiestas, educational opportunities and school functions and other events important to "*la gente* (the people)" became the staple of "El Show de Domingo Peña." He also presented opportunities for new Tejano musical groups to showcase their talent as they aspired to stardom. Peña was friends with President Lyndon Johnson and visited him in his Texas ranch. Then Texas Governor John Connally would visit Peña frequently. Local politicians knew that when they needed a boost in their ratings, Domingo Peña was the man to call.

The South Texas legend died in 1983 but, nearly 40 years later, the show goes on. At first, Channel 3 kept the name "Domingo" — which translates to "Sunday" in Spanish. Later the show was renamed "Domingo Live", and it remains on air today.

Since his passing, other South Texans have taken on hosting duties, including Luis Alonso Muñoz, Mike Chávez, and the current hosts of the show Rudy Treviño and Barbi Leo.

The show is now in its 59th year, following a similar format developed in "El Show de Domingo Peña."

With each weekly airing of the show Peña's legacy lives on.

Cuentos Tejanos

Episode 18

The Lady in Black – Legendary Ghost Story Persists in South Texas

-By Manuel Flores

It was a brisk Saturday morning in the year 2010 and the two pick ups loaded with six Tejanos prepared to take off from Corpus Christi to the South Texas hamlet of Concepción, about 70 miles southwest.

It was a hunting trip and they were heading to José Salinas' ranch just a mile or two from the old Spanish land grant community. Myself, my sons Mario and Marcos and my friends Robert and Richard had "buck fever," as they call it 'round these parts. Deer hunting is a yearly ritual that perks up the spirit and gives one a chance to get back to nature. Besides, we had heard recent rains had made for some big bucks that year in Duval County. It was going to be a good day for hunting.

The weather was a brisk 37 degrees as we headed out dressed in our best hunting gear. The the wind chill made it feel colder and the heater in old Ford truck couldn't quite do the work of keeping us warm that morning. All us had a thermos full of hot coffee that seemed to be getting cooler by the minute as we traversed down the highway toward Alice and San Diego.

A light mist fell consistently as the windshield wipers kept time and the trucks made their way down U.S. 359 past Agua Dulce and Banquete, skirting through a quiet downtown Alice. At San Diego, the farm roads started. FM 339 was the route to Concepción.

It was cold. The wind whistled through the rear door windows that never shut right. The trucks were caravanning like a military unit on maneuvers. The passengers drank dark coffee and munched on tacos prepared especially for the trips. They were lukewarm, at best, by now.

"Are we almost there?" Marcos asked. "*Chingau* (darn it) Marcos you're not a kid anymore," Mario snapped back at his younger brother. "We're making good time. Besides, the road is wet and dangerous. We really can't see what's out there. A buck may pop in and front of us. We have to be careful."

Marcos answered, "Yeah. It's dark. But at least we would see a buck. You never know what may pop up on a dark night like this." Mario, Marcos, and Robert were in the rear truck. Myself and Richard were on the front truck. Mario and I were driving.

It was now almost 4 a.m. The goal was to make it to the ranch by 4:15 or 4:30 before daybreak so that the anxious hunters could take their shooting positions on deer blinds scattered throughout the 200-acre ranch.

The front truck slowed down as the vehicles approached FM 339 where an old *cantina* (bar) used to be located. It was gone now. Only the abandoned building stood. It seemed to glisten in the night as the light rain pilfered it with miniature droplets that seemed to turn to ice.

"It wasn't that cold," I thought.

The back truck slowed down, too.

The light rain mingled with a fog bank that seemed to float just over the road. By each side of the road was a blanket of small scraggly brush and grass area that seemed to sway like the waves of the Gulf of Mexico with the wind. The brush was waist-high to a hunter. It was mixed with buffelgrass. It would allow a deer to crouch down and hide under its wet camouflage.

"Not good," I thought.

Simply, it was hard to see.

"Watch out for deer," Richard said.

Deer had a habit of jumping out in front of cars and trucks these time of the morning. Blinded by the light, they just popped out of nowhere. But the hunters did not want to encounter a deer in that manner. They wanted to see the deer stride through the brush and thick grass and feel the excitement of the moment run through their veins as they put their finger on the trigger mechanism of their rifle and prepared for the moment of shot – *BANG!*

Suddenly we saw something. I stepped on the brakes to slow down. Mario, seeing my rear light flashub, did the same.

"Careful," Rudy told Mario.

The truck slowed down from the 30 mph it was going to maybe 15 mph. Mario followed suit.

"What's up?" Marcos asked.

"They slowed down," Mario answered.

"Did they see a deer?" Marcos asked, impatiently.

It was much worse, or perhaps much better than that. What the front truck with myself and Richard saw was something we would never forget for the rest of our lives.

It was frightening.

There, on the right side of the narrow road without shoulders was a young woman, whose dress would change in hues of black to white as she seemed to float by the road, the grass gently rubbing against her dress which stopped just above her knee. She wore high heels, black, and was wearing stockings, black. Her dress was skimpy, almost see-through and she was walking toward our ranch.

I stepped on the brakes to warn the pick-up truck behind us. I didn't want our trucks to hit her. She was that close. Slowing down, I kept going. We got a good look at her. She seemed translucent. If Richard had wanted, he could roll down the passenger side window and reach out to touch this mysterious young woman who should not be there.

Then, those in other truck got a glimpse of her and slowed down, too. This time she was walking toward them. They could see her face and Marcos uttered a familiar Mexican cuss word.

Mario later recalled her smile looked both inviting and menacing as he and she exchanged glances. With the pickup's lights illuminating her face, Marcos recalled that her eyes were pitch dark and didn't blink.

Essentially, we saw her walking west and the people in the back truck saw her walking east. She looked, in both cases, as if she was floating on air, just above the ground fog that kissed the tall grass.

We travelled to the ranch, which was now nearby, slowly in funeral procession style. In my truck, we didn't say word. In the back truck, even Marcos was quiet. We had a story to tell.

To this day, we don't know how she reversed her path. When the front truck saw her, she was dressed in black. When the second truck saw her she was totally clad in white and she had a dazed and anxious look, as if imploring for help, they said. Marcos, taken aback, just stared. They, too, felt she was floating. She was not wearing a coat or anything to keep her warm.

"We could almost reach out to touch her," Mario recalled later. But, just like that she blended into the mist and rains and vanished.

The trucks were near their destination now and continued, slowly. They stopped across the hunting ranch at the Salinas Ranch. José was waiting for them on the porch. It was 4:35 a.m. Plenty of time to get to the deer blinds or hunting positions for the morning hunt. But, first, there was the matter of the story. We got off the trucks and started sharing out tale with José.

"*No hombre, no es nada* (No man, it's nothing)," he said. "We're used to it. Yeah she appears every now and then. We talk about it here around "*La Chona,*" (what the locals call Concepción)." He stopped and sighed for a while and looked at the hunters, now wet with rain, mist, and fog and shivering. "There's all kinds of stories about her," José added. "Nothing ever happens. She just appears. You know, there used to be a *cantina* where she is usually spotted. There are stories . . ."

We, however, wanted to get ready to hunt. We trudged across the Salinas ranch to our hunting area where el Tío Lacho was waiting. "*Vámonos* (Let's go!)," he said excitedly. "*Se esta haciendo tarde y ustedes platicando* (It's getting late and you all are just talking)."

We explained to him what we saw.

"Well let's go find her," Tío Lacho, now an avowed bachelor, said.

"No Tío, she disappeared into the brush," I said.

"You all go on," he said. "You know where the blinds are. I'll go look for her."

We took off and got to our hunting areas, telling each other we would meet at 10 a.m. back where we met Tío Lacho.

Time passed. It was difficult concentrating. It was still colder than 40 degrees in the morning, especially by the "*laguna* (lagoon)" and by the pasture. Even our nice wool gloves and thick coats could not keep us warm. Our boots seemed useless to keep our feet warm. Hunting deer is not easy, but it is a passion, and we were there for the kill. We harvested two deer and would take them back to the front of the hunting area by 9:15 a.m. The job of skinning and salvaging the meat would start. It was time for refreshments. Coffee, beer, and Crown Royal were the drinks of choice. Satisfied with the hunt, we started to talk about our sighting. We talked about the white and the black dresses and Marcos asked, "Were there two of them?"

We laughed.

Robert, a retired refinery worker in his late 60s, added, "It was a ghost that we saw."

Well, that deserved a drink, even if it was lukewarm coffee.

Later that morning we were back at the Salinas ranch having a small breakfast he and his wife Laura had prepared. Tío Lacho was there, excited to ask us questions about the "ghost" we saw.

Jokingly, I asked.

?*Tío Lacho, la muchacha estaba muy bonita* (Was the girl was very pretty)¿"

He looked at me, disappointed, I thought.

? *La encontró* (Did you find her) ¿

He answered, "*No vide ni quellas,* (I didn't even see tracks)," he answered.

I could just picture him getting off his truck and walking in the tall grass and brush looking for tracks, high heels I might add.

 "Are you sure you saw her?" he asked us.

We had, indeed.

All of us had seen the young pretty woman with a translucent almost see-through dress, wearing high heels and black stockings walking on the side of the narrow road in the waist-high grass; she was walking in a light-rain just below a fog bank that seemed to turn to ice with the headlights of our truck beaming through the night.

Or, had we seen a ghost?

Later that week, we stopped at Club Latino a cantina in the westside of Corpus Christi. We were getting our numbers for Sunday's Dallas Cowboys game. Robert couldn't wait to tell the bar owner Raul what we had seen.

He looked at us and shook his head and asked, "So how long had you all been drinking?"

Out of self-defense, there was no answer.

But that wasn't the story. Deer were shot that day and we were there to boast.

Raul smiled and said, "You all have quite a story. I think, from now on, I'll call you all GhostBusters (after a movie and hit song by that name) 'cause you all ain't afraid of no ghost."

Oh, a sidenote, he later added the song to the juke box at the bar and would play it when we visited.

(Note: The story of "The Lady in Black" has been told and retold many times in South Texas. It also appeared simply as "Lady in Black" in the book "Stories That Must Not Die" by Texas A&I University professor Juan Sauvageau in the 1970s. Sauvageau, an expert in South Texas folklore, reported a sighting on highways 281 and 141 between Premont and Ben Bolt, not too far from *"La Chona."* Professor Sauvageau investigated the sightings, and as José Salinas had told us, it's an old legend. The professor determined the ghostly tale and legend dates back to the early 1800s when this area was part of the Spanish province of Nuevo Santander. Her name was Leonora Rodríguez de Ramos and she was killed by her husband Raul Ramos, who was a rich landowner in a jealous rage when he discovered the child she was carrying may not be his. Since those days, she has roamed the Brush Country of South Texas, perhaps in search of compassion. We saw her, but evidently she's modernized her look.)

Cuentos Tejanos

Episode 19

El Pájaro Gigante de Robe – The flight of a strange "Big Bird" terrorizes South Texas

-By Manuel Flores

People said it was a "*Lechuza*," a montorous and demonic bird that roamed the Brush County of South Texas at night in search of souls to take, or so the legend goes. That's what *lechuzas* do, you know?

It was in 1975 and into 1976 that the sightings of a "Big Bird" occurred, several of them.

At night, it would "hoot" like a barn owl.

"*Hoot!*"

Sometimes, an eerie squawk was heard.

"*Hoot!*"

Those who would look for it could see bright red eyes staring back at them and get chills down their spine. Some said it had the face of a human – man or woman. Evil was certainly present.

Hoot!

The people of South Texas and northern Mexico have always felt these sightings of *Lechuzas* represented an encounter with a witch and was an evil omen. Demons, "*Brujos*" and "*Brujas*" — warlocks and witches — embodied *Lechuzas*. At first glance, it was a common barn owl. But suddenly, People claimed demons transformed themselves into these creatures and at night would bring havoc to the population. Yes, *lechuzas* were and are very real to some.

Hoot!

South Texas folklorist Hernán Moreno-Hinojosa in his book "*Lechuza*" has several documented sightings and stories, *cuentos*, of a creature who roams the sky and whose plaintive cries echo through the darkness.

Hoot!

Folklorists say the *Hoot!* is really the way the Lechuza is warning you that it is nearby and "coming for you."

Hoot!

But what they saw in Robstown for several days in 1975 and through 1976 was different. It was more than a *Lechuza.* . This "bird" (*pajaro* in Spanish) was big and black and cast a large shadow as people felt it swoop down on them, its wings flapping furiously as it squawked sinisterly above. It too, had the face of a human and bright red eyes.

Hoot!

It was Scary, too, but different. Most agreed, it was a *Lechuza* for sure, the legendary creature from South Texas folklore whose presence was sometimes used to make children behave.

"Behave or the Lechuza will get you," parents told their noisy kids.

Hoot!

There were reported sightings in Robstown, Harlingen, Alice, Corpus Christi, San Diego, Laredo and throughout the Rio Grande Valley and even Austin. There and more than 20 documented case in newspapers and later Facebook postings of people relating their scary encounters or stories their parents or grandparents had told them can still be found. Police even got involved, answering to distress calls of people been disturbed after sighting a "Big Bird" swooping down on them from the sky.

Hoot!

It was dangerous. It was described as three to four feet tall with a wingspan 10 to 20 feet wide. Oh, and some said it had no feet.

Finally, the *legend of "El pajaro gigante de Robe* (the legend of the Big Bird from Robstown)" was born. A ballad, a corrido, by Tejano music group "Raul Ruiz y Los Campeones" soon was released and heard on the radio. Other Tejano groups also released the song making it a sure-fire South Texas legend. Most of the recordings were comical in nature and included a squawking sound that imitated a bird.

Hoot!

Whatever it was, it disappeared but lives on in the folklore of South Texas.

Hoot!

Cuentos Tejanos

Episode 20

Gregorio Cortez – "Tantos Pinche Gringos Para Un Pobre Mexicano"

-By Manuel Flores

South Texas has many legendary figures. One who has been immortalized in song poetry and film is Gregorio Cortez, a simple farmer and vaquero whose flight for justice has become inspirational and forever linked to South Texas folklore.

His legend dates to the start of the 20th century.

Books explaining his bravery and quest for freedom and justice have been written, a major motion picture and several documentaries have been produced to help reveal his story. Perhaps of more importance, a major academic study and book by Professor Américo Paredes of the University of Texas has been compiled to document his actions and the song and *corrido*, behind his legacy.

Parades' book, "With a Pistol in His Hand," is a folkloric study of "The Ballad of Gregorio Cortez (*El Corrido de Gregorio Cortez*)" and delves into the reasons for Cortez's fame, infamy to some, and lasting presence of the Tejano folk hero.

In a book written by renown Texas A&I University professor Juan Sauvageau, Cortez is referred to as "The Robin Hood of the Southwest." In "Stories That Must Not Die" Sauvageau writes that Cortez "could outdraw any (Texas) Ranger and disappear in front of a posse like Houdini." Nice stuff for a legend, but he was much more than that and he was no Robin Hood. He was one of a kind, a man named Gregorio Cortez. He was honest, head-strong and proud. He spoke a little English, but preferred Spanish. He was good with the gun and knew horses. He had three wives, two which he married while he was in prison, and four children. He was tried three times for the murder of two sheriffs, but was pardoned by the Governor of Texas. He fought in the Mexican Revolution and never regretted his actions which juries said were done in self-defense.

He was born in 1875 just south of the Texas-Mexico border, some say Matamoros, Mexico. His parents – Román Cortez Garza and Rosalía Lira Cortina - moved Manor, Texas, near Austin in 1887. Transient laborers, Gregorio and his brothers Romaldo and Tomás worked as ranch hands and vaqueros in nearby Karnes and Gonzales Counties. In 1900, at the age of 25, Gregorio, his wife Leonor and their small daughter Marianna, settled in a small ranch near Kenedy, Texas, in Karnes County.

It was there where the drama of Gregorio Cortez evolved. Seems like a horse was stolen and Sheriff W.T. (Brack) Morris, notorious for his shoot first and get this over with attitude, went out looking for a horse thief that was described as "...a medium- sized Mexican with a big red broad-brimmed hat." Deputies John Trimmell and Boone Choate accompanied Morris. They stopped at the Cortez's *ranchito* (small ranch) to investigate. Morris had heard that Gregorio had sold a horse to another rancher, Andrés Villarreal. Choate, who was supposed to be an expert on the Spanish language and spoke "Mexican," would serve as Morris' translator.

Therein would lie the problem.

It seems as if the Cortez had recently sold a mare, an adult female horse, to Villareal. In Spanish, an adult female horse has the distinct name of "*llegua* – (pronounced ye-gu-a)." It is different from a "*caballo* (horse)" and the terms are not interchangeable.

the lawmen first approached Romaldo, who called for Gregorio to come to the front of the ranch saying simply, "Gregorio, *te buscan* (Gregorio, they are looking for you."The Sheriff asked if any of them had recently sold a horse to Villarreal. "No!" came Gregorio's answer.

The Sheriff accused him of lying and said he was going to arrest him. Gregorio answered in Spanish that the sheriff could not arrest him because he had done nothing wrong and had not sold a horse to anyone. "*No me puede arrestar por nada. No le vendí un caballo a nadie* (You can't arrest me. I didn't sell a horse to anyone."

Clear enough.

Choate translated Cortez's words, telling Morris that Cortez had said, "No White Man will arrest me," or something to that effect. Angered, Morris shot at Gregorio and missed. Gregorio quickly returned fire and, according to some reports, hit Morris between the eyes. Morris fell dead in front of the Cortez ranch. Legend has it Romaldo was wounded in the exchange of gunfire. The deputies fled to inform the town. Soon, a chase would ensue.

After making sure his family was ok, Gregorio took off into the brush country, heading north at first. He soon learned from other rancheros along the way that there was a $1,000 price on his head.

A posse was formed. The Texas Rangers would get involved. There were reports that Gregorio was heading toward Gonzales, south of Austin. Indeed, he had walked 40 hours to gain distance from the posse. Soon, a friend gave him a horse and a pistol, south of San Antonio. Gregorio backtracked south. He crossed the Guadalupe River, riding through its shallow waters so as not to leave tracks. He was now headed south to the Rio Grande and Mexico.

He rode through Beeville and even was reported as far deep as Brownsville in the Rio Grande Valley, 150 miles away. Every hamlet, community and ranch heard about his story, reading about it in newspapers or hearing about Cortez's flight from their neighbors.

In *cantinas (Mexican bars)* from San Antonio to Laredo to Brownsville, word about Cortez's escapade grew stronger. Soon, songs were being written and sung in his honor. The *corridos* spread throughout Texas.

Among the most famous words in the lyrics were:

Decía Gregorio Cortez
Con su pistola en la mano:
"No corran rinches cobardes
Con un solo mexicano"

Translation:

Gregorio Cortez said,
with his pistol in his hand:
"Don't run you cowardly Rangers,
from one lone Mexican."

The song also proclaimed his innocence and that he acted in self-defense.

He was spotted on the way to Encinal, near Laredo. The newspapers reported he was still alone and on horseback. The posse and the Rangers had spotted him several times, but he would disappear in a gust of dusty wind. Newspapers reported the Rangers had said Gregorio Cortez was always a hillside or two in front the mounted lawmen. None of the Tejano or Mexicano ranchers or vaqueros would help the posse. The Rangers were despised in this area of Texas, where they had committed atrocities and crimes against the Mexicanos and Tejanos. In Encinal, there was another shootout and Cortez killed another sheriff.

Said the lyrics:

> *Decía Gregorio Cortez*
> *Con su pistola en la mano:*
> *"No siento haberlo matado*
> *Al que siento es a mi hermano"*

Translation:

> **Gregorio Cortez said,**
> **with his pistol in his hand:**
> **"I'm not sorry for killing him,**
> **my concern is for my brother."**

The Rangers and their posse talked to other lawmen along the way and were replaced with reinforcements and fresh mounts. By now all of Texas was aware of what some called Cortez's flight from justice. But how could one man evade capture with – as the song said - " more than 300 men chasing him." Figuring out where he was headed, the posees and Rangers took the railroad to get ahead of him. Other lawmen broke into the *chapparal* (brushy countryside) determined to catch him. Now, in the song, the price on Gregorio Cortez's head was up to $3,000.

In the song, a defiant Cortez says:

> *"¡Síganme rinches cobardes*
> *Yo soy Gregorio Cortez!"*

Translation:

> **"Follow me, you cowardly Rangers,**
> **I am Gregorio Cortez."**

Behind him were dozens of bloodhounds picking up his scent and barking loudly, their deep loud bays echoing off the hills near Laredo, as they hit on a trace of Cortez's trail.

One old Vaquero who was asked to help pick up Cortez's trail laughed at the Rangers. He figured out what Cortez was doing to escape capture. "*Les hizo on ocho* (He made the figure 8 with his trail), he laughed, drawing a figure on the hot Texas dirt. In other words, he had confused the lawmen and their bound by going around in circles. Once he was east of a hill, and then west or the top of it or to the left or right. Whatever plans the Rangers and their minds tried were not enough to subdue Cortez's jaunt through the South Texas brush.

And the song said:

> *Decía Gregorio Cortez:*
> *"¡Pa' qué se valen de planes*
> *Si no pueden agarrarme*
> *Ni con esos perros juanes!"*

Translation:

> **Gregorio Cortez said:**
> **"Why do you even make plans?**
> **You can't even catch me,**
> **with those hound dogs."**

The bloodhounds, too, were confused. Cortez would get off his horse and walk for hours. Again, the hounds and the Rangers lost the trial. Using the thick brush on the mesquite-laden landscape, Cortez was difficult to catch. His escape became known throughout South Texas and now rancheros and families along the way would offer him shelter and food. He was gaining hero status. After all, the corrido said he shot the sheriff, actually two, in self-defense.

The chase would last for weeks. Gregorio covered some 500 miles during his ride through South Texas. He was finally caught, near Laredo.

There are several versions of him finally being caught. The most credible one is the song's version which has survived for more than a century. The song says Cortez ended up in the Cypress Ranch and met up with ranch hand named Juan. There, he fought his way out, again.

> *En el redondel del rancho*
> *Lo alcanzaron a rodear*
> *Poquitos más de trescientos*
> *Y allí les brincó el corral*

Translation:

By the corral of the ranch
they surrounded him.
There were more than 300 men,
but he jumped over the corral.

Farther down the road, heading toward Laredo, Cortez finally gave up. With the help of an informant, the Rangers approached him cautiously. By now, he had heard his family had been sequestered or arrested illegally. Worried, he gave himself up. The song said:

Cuando llegan los cherifes
Gregorio se presentó:
"Por las buenas si me llevan
Porque de otro modo no"

Translation:

When the sheriffs arrived
Gregorio turned himself in.
"You can take me only on my terms,
no other way."

The movie version is the most popular among Tejanos. Desperate, the Rangers finally sequestered his wife and child. It was reported in the newspaper and soon Gregorio was aware. Afraid for his family's welfare, he got to the town of Cotulla, northwest of Laredo, and gave himself up at a sheep camp.

He was jailed in San Antonio. A famous photo of him was taken in front of the Bexar County jail. Gregorio, sitting on a wooden chair surrounded by approximately 50 lawmen. Here legend says and it was recorded in some newspaper, *"Tantos pinche rinches para un pobre Mexicano* (So many darned Rangers to take one poor Mexican)".

Gregorio was jailed in San Antonio and funds for his defense were collected through certain organizations and campaigns throughout South Texas. His first trial began on July 24, 1901. He was found innocent. There were several trials, in all the cases were dismissed for various reasons, including two hung juries. Finally, he was tried in Corpus Christi on April 25-30, 1902. The jury of Anglo farmers found Gregorio not guilty of the murder in the death of Sheriff Morris. The jury agreed that Gregorio had shot the sheriff in self-defense and in his brother's defense because Morris had attempted an unauthorized arrest. This verdict proved to be a victory not only for Gregorio Cortez, but for all Mexicans, Tejanos, in Texas who now could use self-defense as their proof of evidence. That is, if they got to trail. Many were lynched on the spot by vigilantes.

Gregorio Cortez, who had been accused of killing several people, was found guilty for the murder of Sheriff Robert M. Glover of Gonzalez County. This is when the posse was pursuing him. Gregorio was sentenced to life in prison. Gregorio entered the Huntsville Penitentiary on January 1, 1905. He was pardoned eight years later by Texas Governor O.B. Colquitt. When the Mexican Revolution gripped Mexico, Gregorio joined the Huerta forces but was wounded. He returned to Manor, Texas and later moved to Anson, Texas in 1916. There, he died at the home of a friend at the age of 41. Gregorio Cortez is buried in a small cemetery eight miles outside of Anson.

Gregorio Cortez's profound proclamation after he was arrested and put in jail in San Antonio stands as an act of courage at a time when Texas Rangers and other lawmen would shoot and kill a Mexican at will, on first sight. "*Tantos pinche rinches para un pobre Mexicano* (So many darned Rangers to take one poor Mexicano)".

Without a doubt, Gregorio Cortez captured the imagination of Texas and his legacy live on. He remains the man who taunted the Texas Rangers and dared them to arrest him, if they could. He told them "Catch me if you can."

Notes:

1. The lyrics for "El Corrido de Gregorio Cortez," were transcribed from a recording by Ramon Ayala. The essay uses only part of the lyrics in the song. For a full rendition please go to: https://genius.com/Ramon-ayala-y-sus-bravos-del-norte-el-corrido-de-gregorio-cortez-lyrics.

2. There are several versions. Others can be found on Americo Parades' book "With His Pistol in His Hand."

3. Some of the biographical information here was gathered from the University of Texas website http://www.laits.utexas.edu/jaime/jnicolopulos/cwp3/icg/cortez/index.html./

Cuentos Tejanos

Episode 21

Los Tequileros – Contraband and Treachery in South Texas

-By George T. Díaz

Tequileros [literally translated as *tequila people*] were smugglers of the U.S. Prohibition Era (1920-33) who transported liquor illegally from Mexico into the United States for profit. They typically operated through rural South Texas, navigating back trails, and making use of low water crossings along the Rio Grande that divides the two countries. These smugglers were usually male, ethnic Mexican (Tejano and Mexicanos), and often used donkeys and horses to transport their alcohol. *Tequileros* enjoyed a period of success, but were driven out of business before the end of Prohibition by Texas Rangers and U.S. Customs inspectors, with whom contact often ended violently.

Tequileros used horses, mules, and donkeys in their operations. Horses carried the smugglers, while mules and donkeys served to convey their contraband cargoes. *Tequileros* proved adept at packing their draft animals. A skilled packer could fit 50 or more protectively wrapped bottles on a mature mule or donkey. Layers of hay or grass helped prevent bottles from breaking and, with the twine bags that carried them, muffled the telltale clanking of glass. *Tequileros* trained their animals well and used them expertly. Mules and donkeys traveled single file and could journey without *tequileros'* guidance along familiar paths. Trained animals could also wait for their handlers at watering holes or home-in when separated from their masters. Texas Ranger Jesse Perez recounted that officers in the lower Rio Grande valley were continually frustrated by an animal they dubbed the "Lone Rum-Running Jackass of Starr County," whose special talent consisted of its ability to find its way home alone at night. During the day, the burro's handler guided the gifted animal across the river into Mexico where it would be loaded with liquor at nightfall. After loading, smugglers released the animal, confident it would make its way back home where its master waited. Officers' morning discoveries of a lone pair of donkey tracks emerging from the river provided silent testimony of the burro's success.

More discreet businessmen than violent brigands, *tequileros* tried to avoid conflict, going so far as to ride through scrubland for days to evade detection. Despite their prudence, U.S. law enforcement viewed *tequileros* as armed invaders and the successors of the *sedicisos* (seditionists) of the previous decade and actively sought them out.

Confrontations between horseback smugglers and County, State, and Federal law enforcement eventually ended *tequilero* operations. Mounted smugglers who did not lose their lives often lost their property, and this confiscation of equipment helped drive them out of business. The last five years of Prohibition saw only six reports of smugglers crossing through the brush in the counties south of Corpus Christi, (primarily Zapata County, Webb County (near Mirando City), Duval County in the San Diego area and Jim Hogg County in the Hebbronville-Randado zone.

Law enforcement's final skirmish with *tequileros* occurred in Jim Hogg County on February of 1927 when mounted Customs inspectors killed one smuggler and seized seven hundred bottles of alcohol and six horses. Future years would see the occasional horseback liquor smuggler, but mounted caravans came to an end six years before the repeal of national Prohibition in 1933. Because they limited their activity to evading unpopular laws and resisted institutionally racist Anglo authority in the process, ethnic Mexicans (Tejanos) often valorized tequileros despite their illegal acts. Folk admiration of *tequileros* endured in *corridos* (or romantic ballads) like "*Los Tequileros*," "*Dionisio Maldonado*," and "*Laredo*" that are still sung along the border and in the South Texas Brush Country.

Some, like Leandro Villarreal, have gained fame. Decades after his death at the hands of U.S. law enforcement, family members disinterred *tequilero* Leandro Villarreal from the unhallowed grave where Texas Rangers had left him. Rather than rebury him quietly, family members took pride in the legend that Leandro became in his last moments – a tequilero dying a violent death without due process at the hands of the Rangers. On Nov. 10, 2000, family members and locals celebrated Leandro's life in a memorial mass held at Our Lady of Lourdes Catholic Church in Zapata. Texas. Not only did information regarding Leandro's role in the song "Los Tequileros" appear in newspaper coverage of the event, family members chose to forever embrace Leandro's past as a liquor smuggler by literally chiseling it in the stone above his grave. The fact that the artisan who completed the headstone took no pay for his labor, but provided the monument at cost makes clear Leandro's reverence beyond his family and typifies *tequileros'* place of honor within the Tejano community of South Texas.

The song which helped add to the legendary status was recorded by Los Alegres de Teran. It's lyrics are:

El día tres de <u>Noviembre</u>
que día tan señalado
mataron tres <u>tequileros</u>
los <u>rinches</u> del otro lado.

Translation:
On November the 3rd,
A day of much consequence,
Three tequileros were killed
By the Texas Rangers in the U.S.

Salieron <u>desde</u> Guerrero
con <u>tequila</u> ya <u>anisado</u>
el <u>rumbo</u> que <u>ellos</u> llevaban
era San <u>Diego</u> mentado.

Translation:
They set out from Guerrero
With Tequila and anis,
They were headed toward
Notorious San Diego (Texas)

Al <u>llegar</u> al Río <u>Grande</u>
se <u>pusieron</u> a <u>pensar</u>
es <u>bueno</u> llevar a <u>Leandro</u>
porque <u>somos</u> dos nomás.

Translation:
When they arrived at the Río <u>Grande</u>
They started to discuss their trip,
It'll be good to take Leandro with us,
Because we are only two.

Fueron a <u>invitar</u> a <u>Leandro</u>
y les <u>contesto</u> que no,
miren que yo <u>estoy</u> enfermo
y así no <u>quisiera</u> ir yo.

Translation:

They went to invite Leandro
To join them on the trip,
Look I am not feeling well
And prefer not to join you.

Al fin de <u>tanto</u> rogarle
Leandro los acompaño
en las lomas de <u>Mirando</u>
fue el <u>primero</u> que murió.

Translation:

After imploring Leandro to join them,
He finally agreed,
By the hills of Mirando City
Leandro was the first to die.

Tumban el <u>caballo</u> a <u>Leandro</u>
y a él le <u>hieren</u> un <u>brazo</u>
ya no les podía <u>hacer</u> fuego
tenía <u>varios</u> balazos.

Translation:

Leondro's horse was also shot and fell.
Leandro was shot in an arm,
And could no longer fire back,
He had been shot several times.

Les <u>tiraron</u> a un <u>tiempo</u>
lo debían de <u>haber</u> sabido
calló Jerónimo <u>muerto</u>
Silvano muy mal herido.

Translation:

They shot at the lawmen several times,
They should have known that would happen,
Jerónimo fell dead, too
And Silvano was wounded badly.

Silvano muy mal <u>herido</u>
todavía les siguió <u>hablando</u>
mátenme <u>rinches</u> cobardes
ya no me estén preguntando.

Translation:

Silvano gravely wounded,
Continued to talk to the lawmen,
Kill me now cowardly Rangers
Stop asking me questions.

Le <u>preguntaban</u> de <u>donde</u> era,
su <u>nombre</u> y su dirección.
Me <u>llamo</u> Silvano <u>Gracia</u>
soy de <u>China</u> Nuevo León.

Translation:

They asked him where he was from,
His name and intended destination.
My name is Silvano Gracia
And I am from China, Nuevo Leon.

El capitán de los <u>rinches</u>
a <u>Silvano</u> se <u>acerco</u>
en unos <u>cuantos</u> segundos
Silvano <u>Gracia</u> murió.

Translation:

The captain of the Rangers
Approached Silvano,
In just a few seconds later,

Silvano was dead, too.

Ya con esta me <u>despido</u>
en mi <u>caballo</u> lucero,
mataron tres <u>gallos</u> finos
del <u>pueblito</u> de Guerrero.

Translation:

With this stanza I will ride away,
On my light colored sorrel.
They killed three fine men
From the town of Guerrero.

George T. Díaz is an Associate Professor of History at the University of Texas–Rio Grande Valley. He previously was an Assistant Professor at Sam Houston State University and a Visiting scholar and Visiting Assistant Professor of History at the Center for Mexican American Studies at the University of Houston. He also served on the faculty of the History and Philosophy Department South Texas College. He holds a Ph.D. in History from Southern Methodist University and master's and bachelor's degrees from Texas A&M International University. Excerpts for this article came from his book "Border Contraband: A History of Smuggling across the Rio Grande. (Austin: University of Texas Press, 2015).

Cuentos Tejanos

Episode 22

Scotus College Rises above horizon in Hebbronville.

-By Ramiro Molina and Manuel Flores

HEBBRONVILLE - As you drive west on HWY 359 toward Laredo or the Rio Grande, you will come across the community of Hebbronville. It has one of the most unique skylines in the Brush Country, and for that matter South Texas.

No, there isn't a high-rise hotel or bank building like in some areas of Texas.

Instead, in the horizon a surprising building appears. It seems out of place and seems to belong with ancient Spanish missions perhaps in San Antonio or California. But here, deep in the Brush Country in the Wild Horse Desert, it is as out of place as a sea gull roaming the sky.

Driving toward it is surprising, and more than one passenger has asked "What is that?" as they approach the sight nestled on a hilltop, adjacent to a beautiful Catholic church and an old-style Mexican *plaza* (town square) complete with a bandstand, gazebo and benches nestled neatly around the square.

On a cloudy day it seems to blink in and out of focus, hiding among the shadows of the clouds, like a mirage. At close range, it is surrounded by lush green carpet grass, statues of saints and angels, and well-trimmed date palms. It looks as if an oasis has suddenly appeared in the vacuum of the usually dry and arid South Texas landscape.

On a sunny day, it is magnificent, sparkling with its white stucco walls as its red tiled roof that rises majestically toward the cumulus clouds that buffer the South Texas sky.

The building is Scotus College, and its history is as interesting as its architecture. It rises magnificently into the South Texas sky. The four-story building is the tallest in the Brush Country south of San Antonio and north of McAllen. It has a unique history that touches two countries and speaks of the religious traditions of the town and Mexico.

Atop of the fourth floor is a mystical walkway that is reminiscent of European buildings during the Renaissance. If you're lucky, you will see one of the Franciscan priests assigned to the parish – Our Lady of Guadalupe Catholic Church in Hebbronville - walking to and fro as he recites his morning or evening prayers. Or, perhaps, he is up there just to admire the beautiful of view of ranch land and rugged but beautiful landscape that includes mesquite, huisache, sage, numerous cacti and abundant wildlife.

The Franciscan priests assigned to the Hebbronville parish have claimed the view is one of the best in Texas and Mexico. They welcome the assignment to the parish, and often ask to extend their stay.

So, why is it here? How did the Franciscan order from Mexico wind up in charge of the parish? The priests arrived here seeking shelter from a revolution that was determined to drive the Catholic church from the country.

An ugly war ensued in Mexico. It lasted from 1926 to 1929 persecuting the Catholic faith and especially its clergy. It was named the "Cristero War" or "*La Cristiada.*" The rebellion was set off when Mexican President Plutarco Elias Calles sought to eliminate the power of the Catholic Church and tried to enforce the anti-cleric articles of the Mexican Constitution of 1917. In some communities, Calles' soldiers ordered the removal of all priests and forbade them to wear their garments outside of the church. Many were rounded up, jailed or shot by firing squad, in the streets.

A refuge to continue training young Mexican men for the priesthood had to be found.

The Franciscan fathers found it in Hebbronville. In 1926, the Franciscan order arrived and took over a modest church completed in 1899 and called San Isidro.

Because of the Cristero War in Mexico, access to seminaries was limited or prohibited by law. In 1926, the Franciscan order based in Mexico chose Hebbronville for the site their seminary because of its remote location, 55 miles east of Laredo and the border, at its closest point. Several classes or cohorts of seminarians came to the Brush Country refuge on a lush hillside in Hebbronville. It is believed more than 250 priests completed their seminary education in the Hebbronville. Three went on to become bishops.

The building was originally made of wood. It was housed adjacent and around Hebbronville's first Catholic church and served its residents for more than 125 years. When young men began to train for the priesthood in the Hebbronville seminary, they were quickly introduced to the vaquero and Tejano culture of the area. They soon began opening missions in nearby ranch communities. The seminarians learned English and the parish became one of the first in Texas to offer Mass in English and Spanish.

The visiting priests had the support of the Hebbronville community, its faithful and working class from vaqueros to educators and merchants. But support, as if it came down from heaven, would come from a surprising and inspiring source.

South Texas philanthropist Marie Stella Kenedy was incredibly supportive of the Catholic Church's use of the seminary in Hebbronville. She had a vision of a grand seminary for the priests. A devout Catholic, she financed a new building starting in 1940. It was to be named for 14th century Franciscan philosopher John Duns Scotus.

John Dons Scotus was an inspirational Scottish Catholic priest and Franciscan friar whose role as a theologian was well-respected. He served as a university professor and philosopher. The namesake is appropriate for the building that housed young Franciscan brothers and priest escaping persecution and seeking to learn more about how the Catholic faith could regain it power in Mexico and spread throughout South Texas.

Plans for a beautiful multi-story building were made. Ironically, it was the people of Hebbronville who would build this beautiful seminary and not some big city architectural firm. Jose J. Alvarez, a local builder and carpenter, was named architect and oversaw construction. The Kennedy family provided the material he asked for, but always with the approval of Marie Stella Kenedy.

The building was completed in 1944. By that time, much of the religious training had returned to Mexico, but seminarians continued to arrive until 1960. Today the building is used for religious instruction by the parish and is being renovated.

Franciscan priests still complete some of their training at Scotus College. The Franciscan priests continue to celebrate Mass in English and Spanish and now have live streams of their services. In the meantime, their missions in the surrounding ranch communities continue to operate.

Scotus College has become a part of the fabric of Hebbronville, whose residents beam with pride when they are asked, "What is that big building on the outskirts of town?"

"It's Scotus College, a seminary for Catholic priests," they answer.

An interesting note about this story is that two movies were made about the Cristero War.

One, called "The Fugitive," (1947) was directed by the legendary John Ford and Emilio Fernández. It starred Pedro Armendariz, who was raised in Laredo, Henry Fonda and famed Mexican and American actress Dolores Del Rio. Like in real life, Anti-Catholic and anti-cleric policies in the Mexican state of Tabasco led the revolutionary government to persecute the state's last remaining priest. A battle to save him ensues as he fled for his life.

A more recent movie called "For Greater Glory," (2012) starred Corpus Christi's Eva Longoria, of "Desperate Housewives" fame. Also known as "*Cristiada,*" it was directed by Dean Wright and written by Michael Love. It is based on the events of the Cristero War. It also stars Andy García, , Rubén Blades, Peter O'Toole (in his last film appearance released in his lifetime), and Bruce Greenwood.

An added bonus is that Scotus College is located adjacent to Our Lady of Guadalupe Catholic Church, a three-steeple building with beautiful architecture and a hand-carved cedar altar donated by Mrs. Kenedy in memory of her husband John Gregory Kenedy in 1936, The altar was in San Isidro Catholic Church until it was move to the new church in the 1950s.

But, Scotus College is the focal point. With its unique architecture and sky walk, it is now embedded in South Texas lore.

Note: Ramiro Molina is a Tejano historian and has one of the state's largest collections of historical maps. He serves as a school board member for the Jim Hogg County Independent School District, was as an adviser to the construction of the Tejano Monument in Austin, is an advisory board member of the Tejano Civil Rights Museum and has served as an officer of the Hebbronville Museum and Jim Hogg County Historical Commission. He also did considerable work and research for the Jim Hogg County Centennial book published in 2014.

Cuentos Tejanos

Episode 23

The Bright Light from Realitos

-By Manuel Flores

Realitos is a small community founded in the 1880s about 88 miles southwest of Corpus Christi and 63 miles due east of Laredo. It is located in Duval Country 13 miles due east of Hebbronville. Realitos is on Macho Creek and the Texas-Mexican Railway twelve miles southwest of Benavides in south central Duval County. It was established on the former Santos García Spanish Land grant and in 1885 was described as "a settlement, also a ranch." Not much has changed since.

It has relied on ranching and agriculture to survive. Many talented people have come out of the little town in the heart of the South Texas chaparral. But all who have been there will always claim Realitos as their home and the place where they learned the values of life.

One such person was José de la Luz Sáenz, who perhaps should be dubbed, because of his name "Jose de la Luz", the *"La Luz Brillante de Realitos"* (The Bright Light from Realitos).

There is no other way to refer to this man who was a veteran of World War I, an author, educator and civic leader. Along the way he fought valiantly for the civil rights of his *"raza* (race or people)" always fighting for their honor and for their acceptance in his beloved country, the United States of America.

Sáenz was born on May 17, 1888 in Realitos, two years after a post office was established in the South Texas hamlet. He died in Corpus Christi on April 12, 1953. In between he was a political activist, an educator, an author and a political organizer. He was one of the first South Texans to get involved with the civil rights movement in the 20th century.

Growing up in South Texas, José de la Luz heard stories of his indigenous ancestry from his father, from whom he inherited a strong feeling of pride in his heritage. In 1900 the Sáenz family moved to Alice, Texas, where José de la Luz graduated high school in 1908. After attending business college in San Antonio, Sáenz obtained his teacher's certificate and began his lifelong vocation as an educator in South Texas. He and his wife María Petra Esparza married in 1917 and had nine children. When the U.S. entered World War I in 1917, Sáenz knew there was only one thing to do – join the military to fight for his country. He volunteered for service and served in the 360th Regiment Infantry of the 90th Division from Texas, stationed in France and occupied Germany.

It was during his military years the true measure of Sáenz was revealed.

He would become one of the chief chroniclers of the war effort. He would keep a diary of his experiences. An article by University of Texas professor Dr. Emilio Zamora in the *Corpus Christi Caller-Times* in 2019 shed light into Sáenz's book and character. "Sáenz began recording his observations from the moment he was inducted, through the fighting in France, and until he was released from military service in 1919," Zamora wrote. "He (Sáenz) wrote almost every day for well over a year. His entries written in any kind of paper that he could secure. After the war, he collated his notes — most of which he had sent his family—and published the 298-page diary in 1933 with Artes Gráficas in San Antonio," Zamora wrote.

The book was titled "*Los Mexico-Americanos en La Gran Guerra y Su Contingente en Pro de la Democracia, la Humanidad y La Justicia: Mi Diario Particular.*" Translated it stands for "The Mexican-Americans in the Great War and their Philosophy for Democracy, Humanity and Justice: My Diary." The book was published in Spanish. Dr. Zamora translated the book and published a new version in 2014 titled "The World War I Diary of José de la Luz Sáenz."

From this translation it is easier to see that Sáenz's linked the American World War I "rhetoric of democracy" with the Mexican American struggle for civil rights. Sáenz had described his experiences and sacrifices - and those of the many other American soldiers fighting for democracy – as part of the quest for Mexican American civil rights in Texas.

Sáenz's service, and that of other Tejanos during World War I, was a source of pride for him and countless others. After his discharge in 1919, Sáenz led an effort to build a monument in San Antonio to commemorate the contributions of Mexican American servicemen. He secured some donations, official support, and even a design for the structure. The plans were scrapped, however, when the fund for the monument was diverted to support the famous LULAC-backed desegregation fight against the Del Rio Independent School District. This was the Salvatierra case of 1930, the first legal challenge by Mexican Americans against school segregation in the United States which stands as a symbolic tribute to contributions of the Mexican American veterans of World War I.

His penchant for writing, however, continued. Sáenz penned numerous newspaper articles, especially for *La Prensa* (San Antonio), *El Latino-Americano* (Alice), *La Verdad* (Corpus Christi) and *La Voz* (Corpus Christi), the McAllen *Evening Monitor,* and *Texas Outlook* (Austin). According to family members, Sáenz was always on his typewriter commenting on the difficulties that Mexicans faced in highly segregated Texas settings.

Sáenz had an early involvement in the establishment of LULAC, the League of United Latin American Citizens. He was a member of the LULAC Board of Trustees between 1930 and 1932, and was president of the McAllen chapter in the 1930s. Through his numerous writings and his leadership in local activist organizations, Sáenz continued to battle discrimination.

During the Depression, Sáenz found work through the Federal Works Agency and continued his career as a teacher and school administrator in the South Texas towns of Moore, New Braunfels, Benavides, Premont, La Joya, Oilton, and Edinburg. United States involvement in World War II—and the participation of his own children in the war effort—brought renewed vigor to his belief that these contributions to the defense and promotion of American democracy made Mexican Americans deserving of equal legal and social treatment, and his writings and actions fighting discrimination demonstrate his continued leadership.

For instance, he noted Mexicans who had joined were more American than the segregationists were because they were fighting for the principles of democracy and justice despite anti-Mexican prejudice and discrimination.

Sáenz also elevated the Mexican cause for equal rights by analogizing it with the war against totalitarianism in Europe. His most moving and recurring observation was that Mexican Nationals and Mexican Americans had made the ultimate sacrifice on the battlefield so that descendants could invoke the memory to strengthen their call for equal rights.

While Sáenz's accomplishments were many. The writings in his diary remain a constant reminder of his patriotism and love for this people.

The following entry tells of Sáenz's motivations to go to war while passing by train through Dittlinger, where he once taught school, on his way from Camp Travis to France:

"At sundown, we passed by Dittlinger, a quarry worked by many men of my 'raza (race or people)'. This is where I taught or was in charge of their children's school for a year. That combination of work camp and community is another battlefield. I waged battles until I got the county to pay the teacher who taught our children. Those were the kinds of victories I sought in civilian life, opening the school doors for the workers' children. Now that I wear the warrior's uniform, I hope to win other battles and bring justice to our people as we join an afflicted humanity that is calling for the sacrifice of conscious and freethinking men. This is exactly where the idea to pick up my rifle occurred to me. I was moved by the bad treatment many members of my *raza* face in these places where the Teutonic or German people predominates. Ingrates, they deny us equality and forget the thousand and one guarantees given to their ancestors when they settled these lands."

The following is a letter he wrote his wife while preparing to enter the fighting:

"My dear wife: This is my last letter to you. The moment had to arrive sooner or later. It is here. Cry for me, I can understand this since we know how much you care for me and are recalling the difficult and happy times in our lives. You are also concerned about my children growing up as orphans. While you wait for the calm that is to come, know that my sacrifice was necessary and more than necessary, it was honorable. It was a thousand times honorable to have fallen for the inalienable rights of humankind and the future well-being of our children. You may think that they had everything with me there, but that is not the case. As long as the horrible and long-standing prejudice continues in Texas against our *raza*, our happiness will never be complete. I would not have been a man had I fled the draft to avoid the scorn where I was born and expected to die. The fight for the rights of the oppressed gives us the opportunity to claim justice for the humiliations and difficulties that we often face because we carry the indelible features of our *raza*. Our purpose is to demonstrate our dignity as a people before the whole world. It is necessary to fall where the best have died, and you can be sure that I will have fallen as a man of worth."

José de la Luz Sáenz was truly a credit to the Tejano legacy of South Texas. He was articulate, humble and respectful. He truly was. "*La Luz Brillante de Realitos* (The Brighjt Light from Realitos." His patriotism stands as an example of the pride he had in his country and belief that his "*raza* (people)" would some day be accepted as full citizens of the United States.

Some day.

(Note: Excerpts for this article used Dr. Emilio Zamora's articles on José de la Luz Sáenz that appeared in numerous academic journals and in the foreword and prologue to the translation of Sáenz book. Also used were excerpts from the Texas State Historical Association's "Handbook of Texas" online).

Cuentos Tejanos

Episode 24

"The Birth of Tejano Ranching"

-By José Antonio López

Chances are that if you asked Tejanas and Tejanos the one thing about Texas history that is uniquely Tejano, their answer would be *ranchos y vaqueros* (ranches and cowboys).

Truly, their belief stands on solid ground.

By the same token, ask Anglo Saxon and northern European-descent Texans to name a symbol that represents the beginning of Texas ranching and most likely they'll say the King Ranch. That's because U.S. mainstream historians have deliberately developed and continue to shape that make-believe myth.

In truth, the Anglo-slanted storyline is fundamentally, historically flawed. Generally, it follows one of two unsound assumptions. (1) Anglos migrating to the west brought ranching know-how with them. Or, (2) wrongly claim that ranching developed after the U.S. Civil War. Frankly, nothing could be farther from the truth.

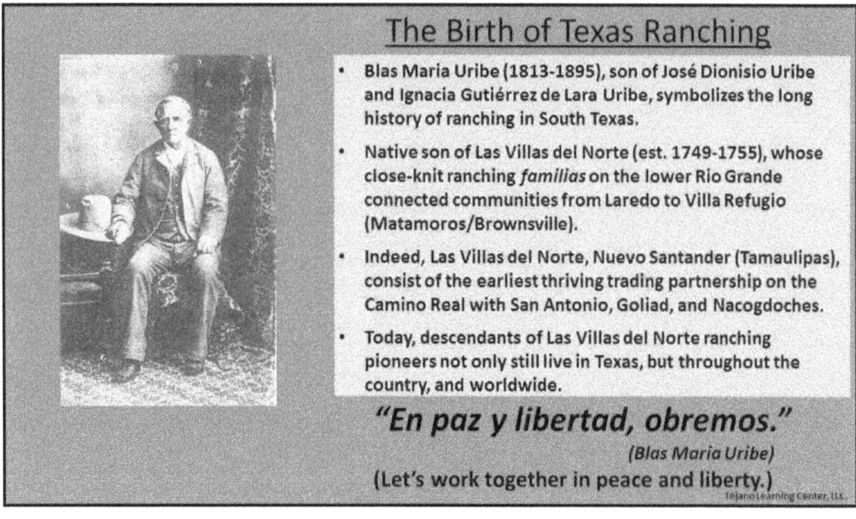

First, fifty years after the Spanish arrival in America, active cattle and horse ranches thrived in Central Mexico. As well, the cities of Saltillo, Querétaro, Monclova, and Monterrey began in the 1500s. Why is that important in Texas?

There's two reasons. (1) Today's Texas and southwest were part of the contiguous land mass encompassing Mexico's Northern provinces. (2) It was from established population centers that our pioneer ancestors were gradually moving to Texas and points north and northeast.

Most importantly, readers must clearly understand that the lower Rio Grande was not the unfriendly political boundary it is today. Rather, it was a local river in Nuevo Santander (Tamaulipas), where our ancestral close-knit families lived on both sides (*ambos lados*).

Besides, our Native American ancestors were accustomed to crossing the Rio unhindered for thousands of years. Likewise, Spanish Mexican pioneers traversed the Rio freely. Journeys on the Camino Real were designed to explore, trade, and/or visit thriving family ranchos as far north as beyond today's Austin and to the east, past the current Texas-Louisiana border.

Second, Marquis de Aguayo led the first cattle drive into Texas in 1721. Simultaneously, herds of cattle and horses introduced by Spanish Mexican pioneers as early as the 1690s substantially increased and freely roamed the state. Most folks today are surprised to learn that Spanish padres and their Native American parishioners nurtured those herds, becoming the first cowboys and cowgirls in Texas.

San Antonio, Los Adaes/Nacogdoches, La Bahia/Goliad, and Nuevo Santander's Las Villas del Norte in the Lower Rio Grande began in the early 1700s. They were the first regions to be settled and contained dozens of self-sustaining ranchos in between.

With skills they brought from Central and Northern Mexico, Spanish Mexican settlers established the original ranchos and perfected the cowboy way of life in the state. This is why basic cowboy terminology is of Spanish origin, as is the world-renowned cowboy demeanor.

Though, after Anglo- and Northern European-descent people took over the state in 1848, they intentionally created a false narrative. Doing so, they set out to repackage the cattle and horse raising industries in their own image.

A prime example of heritage-pirating is the persona mainstream historians have built around Richard King, a riverboat captain who was born in New York City. Said another way, all he knew about ranching, he learned from Tejanos.

However, try as they did, they couldn't make-over the *vaquero* (cowboy) character's origins. All attempts have failed — from mythical movies, farfetched paperback novels, and an exclusive Anglo viewpoint in school curriculum. That's why still today, cowboy attire & ranching traditional customs have Spanish Mexican Tejano roots.

Albeit, the newcomers eventually Anglicized Spanish words, such as: Ranch (Rancho); Cowboy/Buckaroo (*Vaquero*); Chaps (*Chaparreras*); Ten Gallon Hat (*Sombrero Galoneado*); Lasso (*Lazo*); Lariat (*La Riata*); Cinch (*Cincho/cincha*); Hackamore (*Jaquima*); and Mustang (*Mesteño*). Some terms retained the same spelling but Anglos changed the pronunciation, for instance, Corral and Rodeo.

In the words of historian Herbert E. Bolton, "…from the Spanish, the Anglo cowboy inherited his trade, his outfit, his vocabulary, and his methods". Not surprising, it's an inheritance that conventional Manifest Destiny-driven Anglo-descent historians reject.

In my view, the movie industry is the worst offender of the false narrative that diminishes Texas ranching origins. Why? Because Mexican-descent people are depicted as servants, low skill laborers, bandits, or minor actors with few or no respectable qualities.

Similarly, conventional historians continue to project the idea that Richard King was the first mega-rancher. There's no doubt that as a well-financed land speculator, he was able to buy land. Or, he heavy-handedly coerced Tejano rancheros into selling their properties, as their descendants today know very well.

In other words, all Mr. King brought was his money. Cattle raising and vaquero skills already existed in the working ranchos he acquired.

Incidentally, despite a popular illusion, the King Ranch is not one contiguous ranch. Rather, it's comprised of several large parcels of land that are not connected. Have there been Tejano and Tejana mega-ranchers? The answer is yes.

- In the 1760s, the Blas Maria de la Garza Falcón family owned all the land from the Rio Grande to the Nueces River.

- Rosa Maria Hinojosa de Balli was one of the first South Texas ranchers. A consummate entrepreneur, her vast estate at the time of her death in 1803 was over one million acres of land in today's Rio Grande Valley.

- Likewise, Captain José Vásquez Borrego, originally from Coahuila, once owned the land encompassing most of today's Zapata and Webb Counties.

Sufficient to say that these individuals represent only a fraction of a much larger list of Tejano/Tejana ranchers, most of whom lost their properties after 1848. Interestingly, here's an ironic twist to the story.

- 1. Our Spanish Mexican pioneer ancestors were successful in inviting the first Anglo immigrants from the U.S. to move to Texas.

- 2. Yet, once Anglos took over the state, our ancestors were unsuccessful in making their case that pre-1836 Texas is part of mainstream Texas history.

- 3. The result? Mexican-descent Texans grow up being treated as foreigners in their own homeland.

Nevertheless, giant steps have been taken within the last few years to correct the record. The 2012 unveiling of the Tejano Monument in Austin is a reminder that Mexican-descent pioneers founded the province (state) of Texas.

If you are of Mexican heritage and haven't visited the memorial yet, please do so and take your family. Hopefully, the trip will inspire you to share our rich pre-1836 Texas history with others. That's important today more than ever.

Also in 2012, Texas state officials finally recognized that there's more to the Álamo Plaza story than focusing only on the myth-based 1836 battle provoked by Anglo illegal immigrants seeking to reestablish slavery in Texas.

As well, the Tejano History Online website is another big step. Maybe one day, it will be merged with the state's official Handbook of Texas History Online.

Additionally, embracing the Mexican American Studies (MAS) program by many schools and universities allows Mexican-descent students to learn about their ancestors. It's a classroom benefit long denied to generations of their elders.

Obviously, we can't change the past. However, we can certainly make a difference by preserving our Spanish Mexican heritage, especially the origins of Texas ranching. Bluntly, we have no other choice.

Lastly, the Tejano Monument in Austin, Tejano History Online, and the MAS curricula are encouraging milestones leading us to our final destination – a seamless history of this great place we call Texas. To that end, Mahatma Gandhi's words light the torch that guides our path, *"Truth is by nature self-evident. As soon as you remove the cobwebs of ignorance that surrounds it, it shines clear"*.

Editor's Note: The above guest column was penned by historian José Antonio López. López is founder of the Tejano Learning Center, LLC, and www. tejanosunidos.org, a website dedicated to Spanish Mexican people and events in U.S. history that are mostly overlooked in mainstream history books. The column first appeared in the Rio Grande Guardian with the permission of the author. López can be reached via email at: jlopez8182@satx.rr.com.

Editor's Note: The main image accompanying this essay shows the Jesus Treviño-Blas Maria Uribe Rancho compound in San Ygnacio, Texas. The property is listed in the National Register of Historic Places and is now owned by a non-profit foundation that owns multiple historic properties in San Ygnacio.

Cuentos Tejanos

Episode 25

Juan "Johnny" Rocha – A reluctant hero

By Dr. Manuel Flores

Juan Rocha did not want to be a hero.

Yet, there he was on the campus Texas A&I University in Kingsville looking up at the strange sight hanging from one of the women dorms on College Blvd. It was him, no not him, but a figurine representing him hanging from the rafters of the picturesque building surrounding by palm trees and lush vegetation.

Someone had decided to "hang him in effigy."

His "crime", deciding to run for Student Government President of Texas A&I.

Of course, he did not step down. He did not win the election but the corner had been turned. The racist act against him would inspire others of Mexican American descent to run for student government positions and urge the campus be open for all.

Juan Rocha did not want to be a hero.

Yet, there he was bloody and beaten in the parking lot of the Holiday Inn off U.S. 77 in Kingsville after he was accosted by strangers who did not want him to be able to attend court the next day and defend the civil rights protestors who were jailed the night before after a rally at Gillette Junior High. Undeterred, he showed up in court with a black eye and bruises the next morning and bailed the students out. The protests led by the Mexican American Youth Organizations (MAYO) continued throughout the area. More than 70 walkouts asking for better quality education for Mexican American students at all levels followed. Juan Rocha was representing the protesting students as part of his job with the Mexican American Legal Defense Fund (MALDEF).

Juan Rocha did not want to be a hero.

Yet, there he was standing on carton of Pearl Beer in a San Antonio Eastside barrio gathering soliciting votes to be elected to city government. He was called an outsider but he stood his ground asking others to help him register others so they could vote and to change the politics of the Alamo City. He also encouraged them to run for city and county office and beyond and to encourage others to participate in the electoral process.

Soon, San Antonio would have its first Mexican American mayor, Henry Cisneros (1981-1989), since 1842. Another (Edward Garza, 2001-2005) and another (Julian Castro, 2009-2014) followed. The corner had been turned thanks to activism like that of Juan Rocha and others. In 2021, seven of the 11 city council members in San Antonio were of Mexican America descent.

Juan Rocha did not want to be a hero.

Yet, there he was sitting next to San Antonio (Mexican American Youth Organization) MAYO President José Ángel Gutiérrez on April 11, 1969 at a San Antonio press conference where the militant civil rights leader issued his famous "Eliminate the Gringo" speech. Rocha was there to represent Gutiérrez legally, just in case. Gutierrez's speech soon became known as "Kill the Gringo" speech and remains controversial. Rocha was asked what the civil right leader meant. His reply, "the words speak for themselves." Later, Gutiérrez explained the words when asked what he meant by "eliminate the gringo." Did he mean kill? "If worst comes to worst and we have to resort to that means, it would be self-defense."

Juan Rocha never started out to be a hero. And for some, he wasn't. But he was a fair and honest man who wanted the Mexican American citizens to be treated with class, dignity and respect and he would go out of the way to assure they were.

He was my "Tio (uncle)" through marriage to my aunt Clelia Chapa. He died October 24, 2011, after a distinguished career as a lawyer that took him all over the nation, including the halls of Congress and the White House in Washington, D.C. He left behind many memories . . .

A death in the family is something that is not easy to deal with, even when that family member is an in-law or related to you by marriage to someone in your immediate family. We learn to love and respect these people like members of our own family. Often, they bring joy and understanding to family issues and traditions.

Memories of the lost loved one flow through the minds of the surviving relatives like the waters of the Nueces River and Rio Grande heading toward the Gulf of Mexico. Like the rapid rush of that water, the memories fill one's consciousness like an overflowing bank at the edge of the bay and resonate into one's being with the fact that there is no stopping the obvious - just as the water will rush over the bank and into the Gulf - your relative will not be around anymore.

Yet, there he is. In our memories, fresh and resilient as ever. Smiling, questioning, observing . . .

Death does not negate the feelings one has about that lost relative. No rushing water can erase memories. Time will dim them but other family members, the younger ones, will pick up the flame.

Tía Clelia Chapa Rocha certainly has wonderful feelings about the relationship she had with her husband, Juan "Johnny" Rocha - my Tío Juan. More than 50 years of marriage and sharing a wonderful yet challenging life solidified those feelings into iconic family memories that will last generations.

Cuentos, tales, will be told about him forever. He was that kind of an individual. An articulate and personable man ready to talk about life or any issue that was brought up. Oh, he knew the answer, but he would only tell you when he was ready.

Juan Rocha passed away after a courageous battle with several illnesses. To the end, he was brilliant, vibrant and alive. Juan Rocha was and continues to be one of the most important persons of the 20th century in South Texas, Kingsville, Texas A&I, San Antonio, the state and nation. He had a brilliant mind and wrote a book of poetry titled *"Sin Nombre...Sin Cara* (Without a name or a face)" that chronicled his experiences and those of the Mexican American in South Texas. He loved reading books of all kinds - from philosophy to novels - and was as knowledgeable a person on the politics of South Texas, Texas and the nation. The friendships he forged during a political and legal career that spanned half a century were lasting and enduring and served as a beacon for his loving and caring character.

Juan Rocha, a.k.a. "Johnny". was a legend at Texas A&I (now Texas A&M University-Kingsville). He was involved in everything from student government to helping with the distribution of the *South Texan* student newspaper as its circulation manager. At A&I, he participated in the Little United Nations summit in Dallas. He was a member of the Alpha Chi national honor society, the Spanish Club, was named to Who's Who in American Colleges and Universities and was an officer in both his freshmen and senior classes.

Yet, all those accomplishments - like the water rushing toward the Gulf - may seem to be gone and, forgotten.

That's the feeling I got when I heard that my Tío Juan Rocha had passed away in the Rio Grande Valley. He was 74. Let me assure you, his legacy at Texas A&I, as a qualified and skilled attorney, as an advocate for civil rights for all and as a friend and family man will never be forgotten.

Tío Juan was an intellectual gentleman, *un caballero de primera clase,* who always seemed to be there with the wit and knowledge elders always bring to a conversation, dinner table, family gathering or *pachanga.* Thing is, he had this wit and knowledge even as a young man. As he grew older, his academic and Socratic way of thinking made you think twice before you spoke. If there was a riddle or a problem to be solved, no matter what the situation, Juan Rocha was there and back with an answer before any one got his or her cognitive motors (thinking caps) going.

Yes, Tío Juan was unique. He was an honest and God-fearing man who never once had an ill thought about people and always took the high road. Please, forgive me, but this is fact and not just lip service.

His career as a civil rights advocate and attorney would be as pristine as the fresh water streaming down from the Rocky Mountains and his valor reached heights few could imagine. He was a true advocate for civil liberties throughout his life. He participated in the Missouri civil rights movement calling for a museum to be built, the Chicano Movement in Texas and in multiple marches in support of the rights for migrant workers. He loved politics and held several offices in student government both in high school and college. While living in San Antonio in the 1960s, he ran an unsuccessful campaign for Bexar County Commissioner. There is an iconic campaign photo of him standing on top of a Pearl Beer case of beer placed on top of a pool table as he rallied for votes. He might not have won, but the message was not lost. Juan Rocha could communicate with any segment of the community and he was a true representative of the Mexican American people. He was - he always was - ready to lead.

Juan Rocha was married to my aunt, Clelia, my mom's sister. I first met him in the 1950s when he was a student at Texas A&I in Kingsville and he was dating my aunt. My grandfather, Pedro G. Chapa, and I went to Kingsville to visit them and to catch a Javelina football game. On the way from Hebbronville to Kingsville, my grandfather told me to not be surprised at the way I would be treated by the people in Kingsville. He warned me I could experience racism and discrimination from some. Then he told me, "But there are good people in Kingsville." I didn't know quite what to expect and said, *"Esta bien* (Well, okay grandpa), *'buelo."* Growing up in Hebbronville, I really didn't know what racism was. I thought they were just disagreements that could be settled.

Hispanics and Anglos got along fine, 'cause we all had to work for a living, including the rich land owners. I can only remember three instances of true discrimination in my lifetime in Hebbronville and one was against an Anglo kid who felt he didn't make the Little League All-Star team 'cause the coach wanted more *Mexicanos.* His father promptly told him to be quiet and stop crying.

I asked my grandfather why he was so hesitant about visiting A&I and he revealed an incident that happened to "Johnny" which has now become part of family lore and somewhat of an urban legend, a "Cutento Tejano (Tejano Tale)" that is chronicled in several history books about the Chicano civil rights movement.

Juan Rocha loved politics. The politics of the time were rife with words of civil rights. Several lawsuits had been filed in nearby Driscoll, Mathis and Bishop in South Texas and in Del Rio asking for civil rights and equal education and opportunity for Mexican Americans. In Corpus Christi, the headquarters for the League of United Latin American Citizens (LULAC) filed several lawsuits demanding equal education for Mexican American children. And, a new civil rights organization titled the American G.I. Forum and headed by a dynamic young doctor named Hector P. Garcia was making rumblings of organized demonstrations demanding equal rights, especially for veterans.

In the late 195os and '60s and onto the '70s, emotions on civil rights and equal opportunities for Mexican Americans were reaching a fever pitch. It was in this atmosphere that a young Juan Rocha decided to run for Student Government president at then Texas A&I. Things went well for a while, but when some of the Anglo students saw he had a chance to win, things got ugly. Name-calling, rude and crude signs demeaning Juan Rocha's ethnicity started to appear on campus. Some of the signs asked that he and his "witch" of a girlfriend (my Tia Clelia) drop out of college and go home (perhaps to Mexico?). College officials took down most of the signs, but the insults persisted as the election drew closer. The ultimate insult came when a mock-up of Juan Rocha was hung in effigy from one of the women's dorms. It had all the makings of a KKK activity. Yet, it was dismissed as a prank by co-eds. Juan lost that election, but he did not lose his dignity. In fact, the incident made him more determined to fight for the civil rights of all Americans.

He graduated from Texas A&I in 1959, did graduate work at the University of Missouri, and went on to get his law degree, graduating Magna Cum Laude from St. Mary's University in 1969. His law career would take him all over the nation. He would hold offices in Austin, San Antonio, Corpus Christi and McAllen in Texas. He would also have offices in Virginia, Chicago, Washington D.C. and Iowa. He would serve in both private practice and as a lobbyist. He would make his mark as a civil rights lawyer and worked for the Mexican American Legal Defense and Education Fund (MALDEF) for several years.

When MALDEF opened the Washington D.C. office in 1972 to keep abreast of federal policies, programs and grant funds, and be visible to federal policymakers, Juan Rocha was there. He was the organization's first associate counsel in Washington, D.C. Prior to that he had served as a staff attorney for the San Antonio office since 1968.

Ironically, it was Juan Rocha who defended the protesters in Kingsville in 1969 when some A&I students organized and joined students from Gillette Junior High School calling for better education opportunities. The A&I students were also demanding equal housing opportunities in Kingsville, more Mexican American teachers and professors, and bi-lingual education classes. Juan Rocha would advise the protesters not only on their civil rights, but also on how to peaceably conduct their protests within the law and not get arrested. Of course, they got arrested anyway. He worked with civil rights leader Carlos Guerra on the Kingsville protests. Guerra, who went on to be an award-winning columnist for the *San Antonio Express News,* was the president of the A&I chapter of the Mexican American Youth Organization (MAYO).

These were dark times in Kingsville. Threats of violence against Mexican Americans were everywhere. Retaliation by Mexicanos also was present. When students marched on Gillette Junior High School and were arrested, it was Juan Rocha who helped the students bond out of jail. They went home safely to their parents and home. Juan Rocha was not so lucky. He went to his room at the Holiday Inn and, in the parking lot with his brief case in hand, was physically assaulted and suffered minor injuries and bruises. No one found out who did it, but it was a message to not mess with the politics of his hometown of Kingsville. He came back stronger than ever and soon helped the student organizations ask for open housing ordinances from the university and the city of Kingsville.

Juan Rocha got involved with La Raza Unida Party and became the legal advisor for the founder of Raza Unida and president of the San Antonio chapter of MAYO, José Ángel Gutiérrez, who was going around the state demanding the gringo stop discriminating against Mexicanos and asking for people to rise up against their authority and vote them out of office and out of Texas, for that matter.

While Juan Rocha took on many cases during his 50-year career as an attorney, it was his early work with MALDEF that he was most proud of, he said just prior to his death. He felt he had a role in developing the philosophy and agenda for MALDEF. The Mexican American Legal Defense and Educational Fund (MALDEF) is a national non-profit civil rights organization formed in 1968 to protect the rights of Latinos in the United States. It was founded in San Antonio with the help of LULAC and funded by the Ford Foundation. It is now headquartered in Los Angeles, California and maintains regional offices in Sacramento, San Antonio, Houston, Chicago, Atlanta, and Washington, D.C.

In its first few years, the time when Juan Rocha was a lead attorney in San Antonio, MALDEF handled mostly legal-aid cases. Then MALDEF took part in employment discrimination and school funding cases, including Supreme Court cases through friend-of-the-court briefs. *Demetrio Rodriguez et al. v. San Antonio Independent School District* was a defeat, with the court ruling against equal financing of education.

White, et al. v. Regester, et al. was an important victory. The case created single-member districts for Texas county, city council, and school board districts, ending at-large voting that had weakened minority-voting power. In *White v. Regester*, the U.S. Supreme Court ruled that Texas's urban voting district in Bexar County, which covered more than 1,000 square miles and included nearly one million people, was unconstitutional because it diluted the Mexican American vote, which was concentrated in the Westside of San Antonio, and reduced Latino representation in the Texas House of Representatives.

In 1989 MALDEF won in Edgewood Independent School District v. State of Texas. The Texas Supreme Court found the state's financing of education unconstitutional and ordered the legislature to change it. This led to the "Robin Hood" funding system, where wealthier school districts had to give to a fund for poorer districts. This did not lead to educational equality, though, since wealthy districts could choose to spend even more on themselves. We are still fighting this issue in public education and, although it is not resolved, it was attorneys like Juan Rocha who brought it to light.

MALDEF also set up an education-litigation project, filed on behalf of undocumented parents' children barred from public schools. In *Plyler v. Doe,* the Supreme Court held these children are protected by the due-process clause of the Fourteenth Amendment. That meant schools across the nation have to educate the children of undocumented parents. It's still the law. Ironically, that decision is now being challenged by anti-Hispanic immigrant laws.

Then, in *LULAC et al. v. Richards et al.,* a 1987 class-action lawsuit charged the State of Texas with discrimination against Mexican Americans in South Texas because of inadequate funding of colleges and universities. In the University of Texas system, the UT campus in Austin (historically the campus attended by more children of the state's elites) actually received more funding than all other campuses combined, at the time. The jury did not find the state guilty of discrimination, but did find the legislature failed to establish "first-class" colleges and universities elsewhere in the state. Looking to avoid further embarrassing suits, the legislature passed the South Texas Border Initiative to give more financing to the University of Texas System schools in Brownsville, Edinburg, San Antonio and El Paso and Texas A&M University System branches in Corpus Christi, Laredo and Kingsville. That funding continued through 2018 but seems to be up for debate in every legislative session. It has received limited support the last two legislative sessions to keep programs forged from this initiative open.

MALDEF's early years were significant, and Juan Rocha was there. He was one of the "militant" young Texas lawyers the Ford Foundation donors did not like. In fact, they disliked the Texas "militants" so much they would move the headquarters from San Antonio to California before the organization's 10th anniversary. As they say, *"con dinero baila el chango,* (the monkey will dance for money)," but not Tío Juan. His last years with the organization were spent with him fighting for equal opportunity for higher education in South Texas.

One of the highlights of his stay in Washington was getting an invitation and attending the 1977 Inauguration Ball for President Jimmy Carter. He and his son, Mark Rocha, attended the ball that also was attended by John Lennon and his wife Yoko Ono.

Imagine.

Yes, ***imagine*** the life a young attorney from South Texas traveling the country in search of the truth and fighting for civil rights for all people of this great country. Impossible? Yet, Tío Juan in the shadows of all the wonderful monuments in Washington, D.C., looking up at the capitol or Lincoln's Memorial and realizing he, too, could make a difference.

Tío Juan came back to his South Texas roots and settled into a law career in the Rio Grande Valley where he could again serve his people with dignity and respect and continue to serve as an example of a life well lived and a role model for all.

As an elderly gentleman - 74, but with a wise and brilliant mind - reviewing the memories of a long and distinguished career and saying simply, *"Es tiempo* (It's time)." In the end, his illnesses may have betrayed his brilliant mind, but not his brilliant heart and soul. Even at the end, he could have outwitted us all. That sly smile he had would make you think twice about his life and yours as if to ask, "So you think this is the end?"

At his funeral in McAllen, State Sen. Carlos F. Truan delivered an eloquent eulogy praising Juan Rocha for his accomplishments and for living an extraordinary life quietly and with courage. "Some of us in politics love the attention. We love the publicity. Often it is those behind the scenes who prefer a quiet and honorable life that deserve the most credit for the accomplishments of others." Truan had been the Dean of the Texas Senate and often sought out Juan Rocha, his classmate at Kingsville High School and Texas A&I, for advice. 'Now he is gone and many of us never had a chance to say 'Thank you, Juan' for what he has done for many of us. Gracias (thank you) for your courage and wonderful life."

Juan Rocha did not want to be a hero, but there he was being praised for life well-lived and being thanked for all he did for South Texas. As Sen. Turan said later, "His actions speak for themselves."

Juan Rocha did not want to be a hero, but for his family, friends and those who knew him, he was.

Cuentos Tejanos

Episode 26

The Headless Horsemen of Ben Bolt and Duval County

-By Manuel Flores

We are all familiar with Washington Irving's iconic tale of the Headless Horseman of Sleepy Hollow. Ichabod Crane was the poor soul who was pursued by the macabre sight through the darkened woods of New York. The tale is now remembered in lore as "The Legend of Sleepy Hollow." The book and the legend still resonate and many believe it is "real" and not fiction.

It is, fiction.

What is real, however, is the story about the headless horseman from Ben Bolt. And, like all Texas stories, it seems, it has a tie to the Texas Rangers. In this case, the Ranger was the legendary Big Foot Wallace, whose traverses through the Lone Star State, many in South Texas, and Mexico are legendary. His real name was William Alexander Wallace. He became "Big Foot" when he was supposedly misidentified as a Comanche with the same moniker when he arrived in Texas. Suffice it to say that Big Foot originally came to Texas to avenge the slaying of his brother in the Goliad Massacre during the Texas Revolution in 1836. He was angry and looking for revenge against the Mexican government and all its people.

Back to Ben Bolt. During the mid-1860s, the area around what is now Alice, Texas, was a ruthless place where bandits, cattle rustlers, renegades, Indians, desperados, and opportunists roamed the thorny land. It was left up to the Texas Rangers to keep order.

Seems like one of the cattle rustlers gained notoriety for being elusive. Lawmen were unable to catch him and he would ride down to Mexico with his stolen cattle and horses to claim his loot and return to South Texas to pilfer more livestock, many of which had probably been stolen from Tejano ranchers in the first place.

The name of cattle rustler, according to Texas Rangers archives and books on Big Foot was simply "Vidal." It was he who would become the infamous "El Muerto" who rode around the South Texas Brush Country on his horse for many years. That was in the 1860s. Wallace and his Ranger compatriots caught up to Vidal and his compadres in a camp. They ambushed them before daybreak. Cattle rustling and stealing horses were major crimes and the Texas Rangers had authority to administer frontier justice. Something had to be done. According to a story in "LegendsofAmerica.com", Wallace took matters into his own hands. "In a dramatic example of frontier justice, Wallace beheaded Vidal then lashed him firmly into a saddle on the back of a wild mustang. Tying the outlaw's hands to the pommel and securing the torso to hold him upright, Big Foot then attached Vidal's head and sombrero to the saddle with a long strip of rawhide. He then turned the bucking horse loose."

The horse and rider wandered the Texas Brush Country for years and became a part of South Texas lore. For the record, Ben Bolt did not become a town until 1904, but even as a ranch community named after a 19th century love ballad, it inherited the reputation of the "Headless Horseman of Ben Bolt."

Vidal rode for many years, spooking settlers, vaqueros, Comanches and ranchers until his body fell off from decomposition.

There is another similar story. This one happened in Duval County early in the 20th century. Famed historian and author Juan Sauvageau from Texas A&I University wrote about it in his fabled book "Stories That Must Not Die."

This tale has a couple crisscrossing the South Texas brush around1917 and heading toward the man's uncle's home in the outskirts of San Diego. Tired from their dusty trip on a wagon pulled by two mules, they decided to stop by a lagoon which seemed to have friendly campfires and spend the night. As they approached the lagoon, the fires seemed to dimmish and burn out. Nevertheless, they camped for the night.

Suddenly, they hear a horse galloping toward them. It is gaining speed, racing faster as it approaches. A tall, gray horse is upon them before they know it and it has a headless rider on it. The wife faints. The husband watches the horse stride into the lagoon, and it seems to float, as if running on air, to the other side. A gust of wind gushed behind the headless rider and drowns the campfire. Only the mystic rhythm of the horse's hoofbeats can be heard now by the husband as the horse disappears into the chaparral.

Scared, the rancher and his wife pack up and headed to his uncle's home. It was still dark, but the moon suddenly came out and its rays lit the night enough for him to stay on the road with his mule-driven wagon.

When he arrived at his uncle's house, he was told that he had just passed through "Dead Man's Lagoon" or "La Laguna del Muerto."

"But, why the headless horseman?" he wondered.

He soon discovered that the legend of the Headless Horseman of Duval County was the body of a Mr. Dickinson and his horse Hercules. Seems like Mr. Dickinson was involved in a horse race with three other cowboys and he and his horse won the race handily. Angry, the other men killed him, cut his head off with a machete, and killed his horse. Ever since then, the ghostly appearance of a headless rider has been seen around the area, especially near the lagoon where he was killed.

This story was told to me frequently by my *abuela* (grandma) when my cousins and I would gather at our ranch house on the outskirts of my hometown and tell spooky stories at night before we went to bed. With crickets chirping, cigarras singing and owls hooting in the background, we tried to recite our scary tales to see who could scare the others more. My grandma would listen to us patiently and just smiled at our tall tales. Then, at the right moment, she would intercede, tell us to quiet down and listen and would recite one of her scary tales.

One night when she told the story about "La Laguna del Muerto," we almost lost our heads with fear.

Cuentos Tejanos

Episode 27

Jovita Idár –"The Fearless Tejana Journalist who Fought Racism, Sexism and the Texas Rangers and Never Blinked an Eye"

-By Manuel Flores

Jovita Idár was a fearless woman who fought for civil rights, women's suffrage, took on the Texas Rangers and the Hollywood movie industry volunteered as a nurse during the Mexican Revolution.

Oh, she was also an educator, believed in bi-lingual education and felt it was time for Texas to ensure that the children of its Tejano residents received and complete education.

Jovita Idár, however, was a journalist first and her pen was as mighty as any gun the Texas Rangers drew on her or rifle the Mexican Federales aimed at her.

This was the early 20th Century. Perhaps her most important fight was trying to convince authorities to stop the ruthless lynching of Mexican Americans, including children as young as 14-years-old. Lynching was rampant in South Texas during the early years of the 20th century and, at times, it seems that the only person in Texas with the courage to stand up to the horrendous practice and cry that it must stop, was Jovita Idár.

Hers is a marvelous and courageous story and she should be honored not only as a Texas hero but as a fighter for civil rights nationwide.

Jovita Idár came from a newspaper family. Her father Nicasio and brother Eduardo all worked for the family's newspaper and was one of the first women reporters and editors in the United States. She was one of eight children. She was born Sept. 7, 1885 in Laredo.

She attended Holding Institute in Laredo where she earned her teaching certificate. Her first job was in the ranch community of Los Ojuelos, 30 miles west of Laredo She later taught at her alma mater, but had a love for writing. When she found out that the books the state was providing her Mexican American students were inadequate, she wrote and published her own text book, called *"La Luz* (The Light)." Its subtitle was "*Revista de Instrucción Primaria* (Primary Instruction Book)" and she would be sure the education was in English and Spanish at a time when bi-lingual education had not even been heard about in education circles.

That love for writing would translate in writing columns, editorials and news stories on social issues such as discrimination and voting rights for her father's weekly newspaper in Laredo, As a young woman she filled the pages of her father's newspaper "*La Crónica*" with stories on discrimination toward Hispanics, lynching of Tejanos, oppression of the Hispanic/Mexicano culture and the often forbidden use of Spanish language in commerce, political and educational activities.

She was fearless, just as her father raised her, she once said. She loved politics and became one of the first females to be involved in the politics of Texas. Even at a young age, she focused on voting rights for women. She pioneered the formation of the first political organization for women in Texas.

Her writing inspired others to act and her passion for journalism convinced her father to encourage her to start her own newspaper, like her brother Eduardo. In 1916 she launched "*Evolución*" and it was success almost immediately. Her paper was "partisan" in the clearest sense of the word. It was full of political discourse, observations and opinions. But there was also room for news articles about meetings and society. Her columns were a litany of her feelings about society, including her distrust for the Texas Rangers.

She published her "mantra" about education in her father's newspaper, stating plainly and simply, "Mexican children in Texas need an education. There is no other means to do it but ourselves, so that we are not devalued and belittled." She encouraged the parents and community leaders not only in Laredo but in South Texas to take up the call for educating the children through high school and beyond.

She and others took educating the children of Laredo and South Texas into their own hands. At the Holding Institute, she noticed her students were lacking in the education of their Mexican and Tejano culture. They were lacking the resources and books. She published her own text books and found speakers on history, culture, morality and ethics.

Movies were starting to make an impact on society about this time. She helped pay for students to attend movies and there she noticed another crack in the foundation of education for children in Texas.

Turns out, the movies were racist and portraying Hispanics in a bad way. "The pictures that people see when motion pictures depict Mexicans in a bad way are not true and they are demeaning," she said. "This must change."

She also did not like how American Indians and Blacks were depicted and presented petitions to congressmen from Texas to help fight the Hollywood machine that seemed to produce film after film about the west, often portraying Mexicans in embarrassing roles such as bandids, harlot, thieves and criminals. "Greaser Films", movies depicting Mexicans in bad light, composed the most popular genre of the Silent Film Era. Jovita said they must stop. She at least brought attention to the problem and moved on to other goals.

For a while Jovita focused her attention on women's rights. She was a suffragette and worked to gain women the right to vote. But she was much more than that. In the pages of her newspaper and her family's newspapers she asked for women to not be afraid. She told them they could do more than cook, wash and raise children. She implored them, at various rallies she organized, to get involved with politics and especially with the education of their children. She formed the First Congress of Mexican Women and started sponsoring seminars in a variety of topics and issues to help educate and motivate the women to get involved. . Ironically, this confused some of the well-to-do residents of Laredo, because the organization was open to women from all walks of life. For the affluent residents of Laredo these people were the maids and servants and were not worthy of being treated with class, dignity and respect that Jovita demanded at these gatherings. And, if they couldn't read, she and others would teach them to have pride in themselves and their families.

She called for "working women to know their rights and proudly rise to face the struggle" and challenges that were tossed upon them. "The hour of their degradation is past," she wrote to women. "Women are no longer servants but the equals of men."

Later she turned her attention to the Texas Rangers and their actions, which she called "atrocities that must stop." Reporting on lynching after lynching, most of them of innocent people, angered her and she took not only to the pages of her newspaper but to the cooridors of city halls and counties and the legislature in Austin.

In an editorial/column in her father's newspaper, she challenged the need for Texas Rangers to be dispersed along the Rio Grande border.

She said their presence was intimidating and racist and asked for the organization to be dismantled. Ironically, a Texas legislator from South Texas, J.T. Canales, did the same. Canales petitioned the governor to disband the Ranged after a horrific massacre of Mexican American men in the Texas border community of El Porvenir. The governor listened to Canales and dissolved the Ranger units in West Texas. She claimed, that the Governor's actions "were not enough." Her battle with the Texas Rangers and their authority and brutality continued.

In 1916, in an editorial in *Evolución,* she wrote, "I challenge the need for the Texas Rangers to serve along the border." Shortly after she got a visit from a Texas Ranger unit stationed in South Texas. They shut down her paper, wrecking her equipment and presses.

Jovita had not yet begun to fight.

She believed her paper was the voice of the Hispano Americano. Headlines like "Hispanos Losing Land" were common. She used her paper to fight for women's rights and was one of the state's top suffragists. In a 2020 issue of *Texas Highways Magazine,* she was called a "game changer" for women's rights in Texas, one of five Texas Women to be so honored. Unlike male reporters and editors, Jovita wrote directy to women. In a column she encouraged women from both Laredos to unite and join *"La Liga Femenil Mexicanista"* (The League of Mexican Feminists) and later organized "The First Congress for Mexican Women."

When she wrote the article about *"La Liga Femenil Mexicanista"* she was so proud and excited that she wrote in her lead, the first paragraph of her story, "To be able to write this news article, the reporter wishes she had words that were like music and sublime thoughts full of expression and translated into stanzas of noble poetry." Even though many of the women in Laredo could not read, through the organization she organized leaders who would read the newspaper articles and opinion pieces to those who could not read. She was like an oasis of education and understanding and the women of both Laredos became active in all types of civic affairs from education, to service to the community and, yes, even politics.

She often wrote articles speaking out against racism and supporting the revolution in Mexico. She and her family organized The First Mexican Congress to unify Mexicans across the border to fight injustices. On Sept. 14, 1911, Jovita was elected president of The First Mexican Congress Women's League. Forming *"El Primer Congreso Mexicanista de Texas"* was a game-changer. All over South Texas, Tejanos in every small city and ranch town realized they had to organize to survive as American citizens. Organizations followed such as the Order of the Sons of American, the League of United Latin American Citizen and mutual societies (*Mutualistas*).

During this time, the Mexican Revolution was raging across the Rio Grande. Pancho Villa, Emiliano Zapata and their "*soldados* (soldiers)" were hell bent on overthrowing the government of Victoriano Huerta whose federalist troops were fighting to preserve the dictatorship he and others before him had forged. During the Mexican Revolution more than a million were killed and countless wounded. Jovita felt she must help. Undaunted she headed into the interior of Mexico, volunteering as a nurse for the White Cross, Mexico's equivalent to the Red Cross in the United States and helped Villa and his troops in northern Mexico.

After Pancho Villa and Emiliano Zapata took over Mexico City, the revolution was headed to its end around 1917-1918, although battles continued until 1920. The major fighting was over, Mexico had new leadership and it was time for Jovita to head back to Laredo and tend to her newspapering and other major issues. In the United States, major issues were evolving such as progressive movements on the length of the workday and laws against forced child labor, pollution, and standards for food. Most importantly, the women's suffrage movement had become a major national issue. The 19th amendment to the constitution was ratified by the states in 1920, guaranteeing all American women the right to vote. Jovita felt that was a major victory all people should celebrate.

Her pioneering efforts to involve women in the political and cultural cycles of the city continued. But she turned her attention more toward racism and racists groups. She would write about the Ku Klux Klan and lamented some chapters of the infamous organization had made their way into her beloved South Texas. With they came, they brought with them Jim Crow type attitudes and signs like "We Serve Whites Only – No Spanish or Mexican" began to appear.

Of course, the Texas Rangers, who as lawmen were charged with protecting the people of Texas were the worst, in Jovita's mind. The general population labelled them as "*Los Rinches Malditos* (The dreaded Rangers)" and she indeed felt they were horrible for Texas and for Tejanos and Mexicanos. She persisted in her attacks on the Rangers and expected others, in particular men who were in politics, to join her in her fight to disband the statewide unit.

Lynching of Mexicanos and Tejanos was becoming more frequent in South Texas, in particular in the Rio Grande Valley southeast of Laredo. She was particularly upset with a lynching that happened in Thorndale, Texas. She blamed the Rangers for not doing their job of protecting an American citizen, a young boy. The lynching of Antonio Gómez happened on June 19, 1911. He was 14 years old. He was accused of stabbing a man who chided him for littering the sidewalks with wood shavings he was carving from a shingle. Jovita wrote an article in *La Crónica*, that condemned the lynching death of Gómez as an act of cowardice. The writer was critical of the German community in Texas and stated that people in Mexico were boycotting stores owned by Germans. Thorndale is in Milam County about 40 miles southwest of Austin.

With this story, which gained nationwide publicity, *La Crónica's* and Jovita's fame spread. The Idár newspapers truly became a source for news and activism for Mexican American and Tejano civil rights.

Now with political motivation and a following, the Idár and Jovita took on President Woodrow Wilson. Historians claim she insulted Wilson after he send American troops to the border to quell a rebellion of vaqueros in the Rio Grande Valley. Jovita believed U.S. Federal troops should not be in the border region or anywhere in the United States for that matter. She felt that was the State's and local municipalities duties to protect us.

Soon, Texas politicians received word from Washington to do something about that crazy woman reporter down on the border. Perhaps, shut down her newspaper? Nothing was official, but the Texas Rangers got notice of Jovita's writings, something they were very familiar with and despicd. Jovita answered the threat with a simple *"Agui Estoy!* (I'm here!)" column and opinion piece. Soon, the Rangers showed up in front of *"El Progreso."*

When the Rangers arrived to close down *"El Progreso,"* Jovita Idár stood in the doorway to keep them from entering. The Rangers left, not willing to show aggressiveness toward a woman and a notable one like her. Jovita had told them they could not enter the newspaper because they would be violating the law, the First Amendment in particular. The Rangers left but returned under the cover of darkness and ransacked the print shop, smashing printers and spreading type and equipment everywhere in the small publishing site.

The next morning, Jovita returned to her paper and noticed it would be impossible to print her paper that week. Unperturbed, Jovita headed to Brownsville where her brother Eduardo had a newspaper and printing office. Within a day or two she was back in Laredo with a new issue of *"El Progreso"* and a new editorial condemning the Texas Rangers.

Jovita Idár had met the Texas Rangers face-to-face and did not blink an eye. She continued to call for their dismissal and the fervor of Tejanos against grew stronger.

Through it all she was working to keep her father's motto and goal alive. The motto appeared on the front page of every issue of *"La Crónica"* since her father opened it at the start of the century. That slogan said, *"Trabajamos por el progreso y Desarrollo industrial, moral e intelectual de los habitantes Mexicanos de Texas."* (We work for industrial, moral and intellectual progress and growth for the Mexican citizens of Texas). Jovita took over her father's paper when he died in 1914.

In 1920 Jovita married Bartolo Juarez and the couple soon moved to San Antonio. She became active in the Democratic Party of Texas and continued to strive and promote equal rights for women and Tejanos. By this time, she had her own motto. "When you educate a woman, you educate a family."

In San Antonio she also kept her passion for journalism alive. She became an editor of a Methodist publication called *"El Heraldo Cristiano (The Christian Herald)"*. She remained committed to her community work by volunteering as an interpreter at a San Antonio hospital to help Spanish-speaking patients with their medical needs. She also started a free kindergarten for children, with the idea of giving them a head start in their educational progress. She was, again, a pioneer in education.

Jovita Idár passed away in 1946 in San Antonio.

Her legacy as an American journalist, political activist, civil rights worker, education reformer, feminist, suffragist and voting rights activist lives on. Her defiance of the Texas Rangers and standing up against President Woodrow Wilson were heroic and inspirational because she was fighting for justice and doing things right. Confronted and with her life in danger, she did not blink. She stood up for justice.

Of course, she was a strong-willed and determined Tejana who deserves the respect of all who call Texas home and all who believe in justice and the American way.

Cuentos Tejanos

Episode 28

The Battle of Medina – An Emerald Green Flag once flew over independent Texas

-By Manuel Flores

How long have Tejanos been fighting for liberty and freedom in this land we call Texas?

Most of us are familiar with the battles at the Alamo and Goliad when hundres of Tejanos joined ranks with Gen. Sam Houston, William Travis, Jim Bowie and Davy Crockett to help oust the treacherous Mexican government of Gen. Santa Anna.

That was in 1836.

Few of us, however, are familiar with our battle for freedom against Spain, the country that controlled Texas and much of the American Southwest for several centuries. That struggle started in the late 18th century and reached its peak in the early 19th century. Tejanos - the first European settlers of Texas and the first to "mingle" with the indigenous population of the American southwest and what is now Mexico - wanted independence from Spanish tyranny.

Author and Tejano historian Dan Arrellano from San Antonio, has done an admirable job of reminding us that the Tejanos' quest for liberty and justice from oppression predates the Battle of the Alamo and the sovereignty of Mexico in Texas. Mexico won its independence from Spain in 1821. There were battles for freedom here in this land well before that date.

For a brief shining moment, Texas was a "republica" pre-dating the Republic of Texas of Gen. Sam Houston.

In 1812, Tejanos fed up with Spanish (not Mexican) rule rebelled. Arrellano's research reveals that on April 7, 1812 the Republican Army of the North crossed the Sabine River into Spanish Texas. Flying the Emerald Green Flag of Liberty, these Tejanos ensued in a journey across Texas that would see them claim victories over Spain in several key battles.

Don José Bernardo Gutiérrez de Lara and William Augustus Magee, supported by 142 American and 158 Tejano volunteers, invaded Spanish territory with the aim of forming a new government. The rag tag army would be successful in every battle and every skirmish against Spain, beginning with the capture of Nacogdoches, Trinidad, the four-month siege of the presidio in Goliad, the Battle of Rosillio, the capture of San Antonio and the Alamo and the Battle of Alazan. After victory in San Antonio, there was a declaration of independence for the State of Texas under the Republic of Mexico on April 6, 1813.

But Arrellano reminds us that, unfortunately, Spain was still a superpower in the early 19th century and it would only be a matter of time before it squashed the upstart rebellion. Spain would send an army of its best soldiers to take on the Tejano rebels. Gen. Joaquín de Arredondo, commandant-general of the *Provincias Internas* (Internal Provinces of Spain) of the Spanish government, organized an army of 1,838 men and marched them early in August from Laredo toward San Antonio to quell the rebellion.

On August 18, 1813, the Tejano Republican Army of the North set out to fight in what would become the biggest and bloodiest battle ever fought on Texas soil - "The Battle of Medina."

The upstart army, consisting now of approximately 300 Americans, one to two hundred Native Americans and eight to nine hundred Tejanos were tired from the continuous skirmishes against the Spanish, but willing to stand up and fight for freedom. The Tejanos - in particular - were determined.

They would encounter a well-trained and disciplined Spanish Royalist Army. The Tejano Republicans were ambushed and, out of the 1,400 of its soldiers, only one hundred would survive. The bodies of soldiers killed in battle were left where they fell. It would be nine years before their bones were gathered and buried in a communal grave.

Ninety of the survivors would be Americans, which proves beyond any shadow of a doubt that the ones with the most to lose would fight the hardest for freedom were the Tejanos and their Native American allies. The Tejanos and their indigenous brothers stood and fought to the last man. "This battle raged on for about four hours with our Tejanos who, like Leonidas at Thermopylae, were determined to achieve victory or die trying," Arrellano writes on the research of the account of the battle. Little did anyone realize the sacrifice these men would pay would be the ultimate.

After the battle, the victorious Spanish Army marched into San Antonio where 500 additional Tejanos would be arrested and crammed into a makeshift prison. The Spanish were furious and wanted to not only quell the revolt but send a message to the residents of Texas that Spanish rule was supreme. Spanish military records show that 17 of those jailed, suffocated in the scorching heat of night. The next day several would be released, as a show of leniency from the Spanish crown, but to also spread the word that there would be consequences if another rebellion occurred. Soon, 327 Tejanos who remained in jail would be executed. Three a day would be taken out and shot, beheaded then their heads were placed on spikes and displayed around the square (what is now Market Square in San Antonio) for all to see as a lesson to those who dared rise up against Spanish rule.

Arrellano writes that no one would be spared the wrath of General Arredondo, not even the women and children. Ironically, one of the Spanish Royalist officers was a young lieutenant named Antonio López de Santa Anna. Of course, he would return to San Antonio in 1836 with his Mexican Army to quell yet another rebellion by Texans and Tejanos.

Spanish military records show, according to Arrellano, that approximately 300 of the wives, mothers and daughters of the Tejanos would be imprisoned. He reports that many of them would be brutally and repeatedly raped, several dying as a result of the brutality. The women were forced on their knees from 4 in the morning till 10 at night to grind the corn to make the tortillas to feed the despised Spanish Army. And through the windows of their makeshift prison, the mothers could see their children searching for food and shelter on the street which legend holds became Dolorosa St. in San Antonio.

The Battle of Medina is historic.

It showed that these new settlers of Texas were people of courage, foresight and discipline. They were a special breed, whose descendants would survive this and other atrocities the world would throw at them in the 19th and 20th centuries. It showed that this new breed of settler - The Tejano - would not stand still and allow to be ruled by despots and cowards who did not value human life or freedom. In short, their sacrifice - both men and women - in the Battle of Medina and in the streets of San Antonio would foreshadow the downfall of Spain in the new world and eventually lead to the formation of Texas.

Arrellano writes, "Short-lived as it may have been, this Republic was a real Republic and this was a real revolution, a revolution of the people, by the people, and for the people and these were our ancestors, and to this day they have remained unknown and unrecognized by many for their ultimate sacrifice."

In the San Antonio area, several associations celebrate the Battle of Medina. The celebration is usually around what is now the community of Medina Valley, south of San Antonio. Re-enactments of the battle are common. Words are spoken about valor and roots. This is wonderful, but we should do more.

This battle is an important part of Texas history and should be taught to our children. It cannot be found in the history books. It is the "bloodiest battle" ever fought on Texas soil. It represented a struggle for freedom that is still with us today. It's time we recognize this battle and make it part of our every day conversations about the Lone Star State.

Texas history did not start with Davy Crockett (John Wayne) and the Alamo. It started with the indigenous who were here, the Tejanos who helped tame the land and their ancestors who survived atrocity after atrocity to make sure they could stay and live in the land we call Texas.

Cuentos Tejanos

Episode 29

*The Seventh Flag Over Texas – The Republic of the Rio Grande
rose to promince in the 1840s*

-By Manuel Flores

We are all familiar with the flags of the six independent nations that have flown over Texas. The United States, Spanish and French flags are certainly prominent in that memory of the evolution of the Lone Star State. The flags of Confederate States of America and Mexico are in the mix as is Texas' own standard-bearer – the tri-colored red, white and blue Lone Star flag.

That makes 6 official flags that have flown over Texas. But, did you know there was a 7th?

History shows there was a seventh flag – the flag of the Republic of the Rio Grande.

Texas had just become a republic in 1836, but Mexico still laid claim to the land south of the Nueces River. Mexico still laid claim to the Nueces Strip. In the meantime, the battle of who would lead Mexico continued. A series of disputes between the Centralist government, under the control of Gen. Santa Anna and his cronies, and the Federalists, who wanted stronger local authority, lingered.

The Federalists organized a core of leaders and supporters and met in Laredo, Texas, for a convention on Jan. 17, 1840. The convention declared independence from Mexico and claimed for its territory the Mexican States of Tamaulipas and Coahuila north to the Nueces and Medina rivers, respectively, and Nuevo León, Zacatecas, Durango, Chihuahua, and New Mexico. Coahuila was basically what is now South Texas south of San Antonio and down to the Rio Grande.

Soon, the residents of the Brush Country, what is now the Rio Grande Valley and those in the Del Rio and Eagle Pass area were saluting the tri-starred and tri-colored red, white and black emblem of a fledgling Republic of the Rio Grande – an independent country in what is now South Texas and parts of Northern Mexico.

A building adjacent to what is now La Posada Hotel in the historic San Agustin downtown area of Laredo served as the capitol. It has been restored and serves as a museum open to the public.

Mexico, which had just lost half of its territory to Texas, was not going to let the upstart republic continue without a struggle. War ensued.

Antonio Canales was named commander-in-chief of the Republic of the Rio Grande's army, composed mainly of large landowners and their vaqueros from northeast Mexico and South Texas. Canales was joined by legendary freedom fighter Antonio Zapata, a charismatic "mulatto (of African and Indian blood)" from Guerrero. Among the Volant were Republic of Texas Colonel Reuben Rossas, Samuel Jordan under Zapata's command was his friend Captain José María Benavides, a three-term mayor of Revilla and captain of the garrison there. Benavides was from the Hebbronville area and his descendants Isidro B. Gutierrez and Marta Gutierrez still live there.

Early on, Canales and Zapata proved to be a formidable force, winning several scrimmages over the Centralists. Soon, however, the Mexican Army of the North led by Gen. Mariano Artista repelled them. Canales and Zapata were forced to retreat their troops as far north of Espantosa Lake (near what is now Carrizo Springs) and Fort Lipantitlan (located between Orange Grove and what is now the Calallen area in northwest Corpus Christi).

The ill-fated republic and its army fought on for approximately a year. In the spring of 1840, the Republic of the Rio Grande's demise started. Gen. Artista captured Zapata in the Battle of Santa Rita in Morelos. Zapata was offered amnesty, but chose death.

In doing so, he became a legend. The City of Zapata – originally named Carrizo - is named for him. Canales was also captured and the Republic of the Rio Grande faded into history. At the end, the Federalist army retreated as far north as San Antonio and Victoria, ending the rebellion. The rebellion lasted from January 17 to November 6, 1840.

Historians in both Mexican and the United States have never formally declared the Republic of the Rio Grande as an independent nation. They see it instead as a political uprising against the Mexican Centralists and an opportunity to seek aid from Texas and the United States.

Perhaps, but the lasting legacy of those freedom fighters still lingers in a little building in Laredo which proudly proclaims itself the Capitol of the Republic of the Rio Grande and flies all seven flags over its doors to proclaim that the flags of seven republics have flown over Texas.

(Note: Information for this article came from various sources, including the Texas State Historical Association a May 2010 articles on Texas Co-Op Power Magazine by Gene Fowler titled "Seven Flags Over Texas?")

Dr. Manuel Flores is a professor of journalism/communications at Texas A&M University-Kingsville and is a member of the advisory board of the Tejano Civil Rights Museum.

Cuentos Tejanos

Episode 30

The Blue and the Gray Fought Here – The Civil Was came to South Texas and the Rio Grande Valley

-By Manuel Flores

The role of Texas, in particular South Texas and the Rio Grande Valley, in the Civil War has mainly been ignored by historians, educators and the general public.

Ask any one in the Lone Star State if Texas was involved in the Civil War and most will answer with an emphatic "no." The Civil War they believe, rightfully so, was fought in Virginia, Georgia, Alabama and other southern states. Well, Texas was part of the Confederacy and it too was involved with countless battles between the Blue and Gray.

Texas had been part of the United States just 15 years when secessionists prevailed in a statewide election. Each county voted. Ironically, some chose to remain in the Union, but the vast majority decided to secede. Texas formally seceded on March 2, 1861 to become the seventh state in the new Confederacy. Sam Houston was governor when Texas seceded from the United States but refused to declare any loyalty to the new Confederacy.

Several historians like Dr. Jerry Thompson at Texas A&M International University in Laredo have written brilliant books, essays and historical accounts of the battles and heroes of the turbulent era.

Dr. Thompson's book – *"Vaqueros in Blue and Gray"* - was surprising to many when it came out in 1976. For the first time, someone, this time a noted historian, was claiming he had evidence that South Texas was involved in the Civil War. Thompson claim that as many as 9,500 men of Hispanic heritage fought in the United States' Civil War. He also showed list of 2,500 Tejano confederate soldiers from South Texas and another list of at least 500 Tejano Union soldiers. The book was reprinted in the year 2000 and again caused a stir. Since then, Dr. Thompson has written a follow up book with more statics titled *"Tejanos in Gray."* Both Thompson books show that the bitter conflict that deeply divided the nation also affected Tejanos (Texans of Mexican heritage). The books reveal the story of these Tejanos who participated in the Civil War. Thompson's books and numerous essays reveal the history of these vaqueros and contain the first comprehensive list, containing almost 4,000 names, ever compiled of the Confederate and Union Hispanics from Texas who served in the war. "*Vaqueros in Blue & Gray*" presents a stirring saga of these brave people, their land, and their epic role in the Civil War and in the history of Texas.

"*Vaqueros in Gray,*" published in 2011, features letters sent by Tejano Civil War soldiers, again solid proof that they were involved in the thick of the conflict. The book features the letters of two Tejano Confederate captains – Manuel Yturri and Joseph Rafael de la Garza. "The experiences and impressions reflected in the letters of these two young members of the Tejano elite from San Antonio, related by marriage, provide fascinating glimpses of a Texas that had displaced many Mexican-descent families after the (Texas) Revolution, yet could still inspire their loyalty to the Confederate flag. De la Garza, in fact, would go on to give his life for the Southern cause," a news release on the book notes. The letters are magnificent and reveal the passion these men had for the cause they were fighting for.

More recently, a historical essay by Paul Garza published in St. Mary's "STMU History Media" research journal showed the Union also had soldiers in South Texas. Titled "Adrian Vidal: A Tejano Caught Between Two Wars," it reflects the anguish and pain one of South Texas' most prominent families had to face when their son departed the Confederacy and joined the Union. Vidal and his men fled to Mexico where they hoped to get help from the Union. He was captured and imprisoned and was executed in Mexico. Vidal came from a well-known family in South Texas, the Kenedy family. He was the son of Petra Vela and adopted son of steamboat captain and entrepreneur Mifflin Kenedy. The family had one of the biggest ranches in Texas. They had become famous. They operated the Laureles Ranch in South Texas. But it did not matter. Even after his father tried valiantly to buy back his freedom, Petra Vela Kenedy and her husband Mifflin Kenedy felt the pain of losing a son to a war that divided the country, even those in Texas.

Perhaps the most comprehensive book or review is "*Blue and Gray on the Border: The Rio Grande Valley Civil War Trail*" by historians at the University of Texas-Rio Grande Valley. The book led to added recognition of the Civil War and the scores of battles between the Blue and the Gray along the Rio Grande. The book helped inaugurate the Rio Grande Valley Civil War Trail.

The project took five years to complete with researchers, historians, librarians, archaeologists, artists, museum officials, sociologists and officials from cities and counties from the area — not to mention scores of university students — all pitching in to make the Rio Grande Valley Civil War Trail a reality.

The book takes the reader in a magnificent journey that can be taken on the highways and farm roads of South Texas or on a virtual website that brings the trail to life. After reading the book or experiencing the virtual website, no one will doubt that the Civil War was here.

The Rio Grande Valley Civil War Trail traverses five counties bordering the Rio Grande and Mexico. The counties covered by the trail are Cameron, Hidalgo, Starr, Zapata and Webb. The book's central focus is the Civil War years (1861-1865) in South Texas, but it also encompasses the history of the area and includes important sites associated with the Texas Revolution (1836) and the U.S.-Mexico War (1846-1848).

All the battles are listed. During the Civil War, the Rio Grande served as a significant point of contention as skirmishes between both Union and Confederate forces erupted along the border between the military forts of Fort McIntosh in Laredo, Ringgold Barracks in Rio Grande City and Fort Brown in Brownsville. The original Spanish names of villages and towns and the important battle sites can be found in the book. And, if reading is not your pleasure, take a "virtual" trip online at "utrgv.edu/civilwar-trail." Here you can learn about those sites that interest you and listen to a description.

John L. Nau III, chair of the National Park Foundation Board of Trustees, said in his foreword, "When it comes to Civil War history, the Rio Grande Valley is often overlooked . . . the importance of the Rio Grande Valley to the Confederate economy or of the troop buildup along the Texas-Mexico border is rarely addressed."

This book does that.

It is a marvelous tour guide with excellent research and wonderful descriptions of the battles and heroes. It is also one of the few books with a detailed description of the African American troops who served with the Union during the Civil War and were stationed at the forts along the Rio Grande for several years after the war's end. An entire chapter is devoted to "US Colored Troops."

The book and website are excellent resources for middle or high school teachers and students, and a wonderful research site for historians and students at the university or graduate level. The information is compelling and proves the Civil War was fought in Texas.

Photos, maps, diagrams, illustrations, pictures of buildings dating back to the 1840s and shots of Civil War cemeteries in South Texas and the Rio Grande Valley all help to authenticate the book.

From the mustering of Confederate troops along the border in 1861, to the arrival of 7,000 Union troops in Brownsville in 1863 and the last battle of the Civil War in Palmito Ranch near Brownsville in 1865, it is all here. The info about the RGV's role in the Civil War is presented eloquently and with pride and it should continue to be part of the lore of South Texas and the Rio Grande Valley..

Along the way, you will become familiar with the magical names of heroes, entrepreneurs, bandits and fortune hunters who used the Civil War to become legendary, rich or just to make a name for themselves.

Among the names you will here are Juan Cortina, John McAllen, "Rip" Ford, Santos Benavides, Gen. H.P. Bee, Mifflin Kenedy, Richard King, Henry Davis, Antonio Zapata and many others.

You will learn about battle sites that are still in plain view and the men who gave their lives while fighting for the cause they believed in. You will learn about the importance of the lighthouse at now Port Isabel and see remnants of the bridge built by Gen. Zachary Taylor. You will learn about all the great Army forts along the border from Brownsville to Eagle Pass and be amazed that more than 170 years later, many of those structures have survived.

This book (and website) are enough to make you get in your ol' red pickup truck or fancy sedan and head down the very important and historic Rio Grande Valley Civil War Trail.

Among the important stories about personalities in South Texas who were involved in the Civile War are those of Santos Benavides, Mifflin Kenedy and Richard King.

Colonel Santos Benavides became the highest-ranking Tejano to serve the Confederacy. Born in Laredo in 1823, he was a descendant of Tomás Sánchez de la Barrera y Garza, the founder of Laredo in 1755. As a political and military leader in Laredo, Benavides brought a traditionally isolated region closer to the mainstream of Texas politics while preserving a sense of local independence. Assigned by the Confederacy to the Rio Grande Military District at the beginning of the war, Benavides drove his rival Juan Cortina into Mexico at the battle of Carrizo in May 1861. He crushed other local revolts against Confederate authority on the Rio Grande. In November 1863 Benavides was authorized to raise his own force that became known simply as Benavides' Regiment. Perhaps his greatest triumph came on March 19, 1864 when he drove back more than two hundred soldiers from the Texas Union Cavalry. More importantly, Benavides helped make possible the safe passage of cotton and other goods across the Rio Grande to Mexico during the Union occupation of the Lower Rio Grande Valley in 1863-64. During Reconstruction, Benavides remained active in his mercantile and ranching activities along with his brother Cristobal. He served three times in the Texas House of Representatives from 1879 to 1884, the only Tejano in the legislature at time, and twice served as alderman in Laredo. He died at his home in Laredo in 1891.

Mifflin Kenedy and Richard King kept the confederacy going by traversing steamboats on the Rio Grande. These steamboats were the lifeblood of the confederacy. The sale of the cotton the steamboats were loaded with help fund the Confederate war effort and, indeed, feed the south as well. King and Kenedy Kenedy 's company-controlled shipping along the Rio Grande River during the Civil War. The Mifflin Kenedy Warehouse in Starr County, where the company stored cotton and other goods, is a last reminder of that era. Rio Grande City later became an official Confederate port of entry and customhouse. Remnants of those buildings still exist. The ships would bring back leather, clothing, blankets, guns, ammunition, and medical supplies. In 1864 the 1st U.S. Texas Cavalry reoccupied Ringgold Barracks and seized the cotton that was stored in this warehouse.

John Salmon "RIP" Ford was a Texas Ranger who was given a command with Confederacy during the Civil War in South Texas. He was elected colonel of the Second Texas Cavalry, with a command in the Rio Grande District. In May of 1865 he led the Confederate troops in the Battle of Palmito Ranch, the last battle of the Civil War. The war had been over, but word did not get down to South Texas as Ford led his confederate troops to a pyrrhic victory in the last battle of the Civil War.

The book also reveals there are several cemeteries with headstones from soldiers who participated in the Civil War.

It is important to note that battles were fought throughout the 40,000 square mile area of South Texas from south of San Antonio, Houston and

Del Rio to the banks for the Rio Grande. Some were minor skirmishes, but all were important.

The Battle of Corpus Christi was one of those. The Battle of Corpus Christi was fought between August 12 and August 18, 1862, during the American Civil War. United States Navy forces blockading Texas fought a small land and sea engagement with Confederate forces in and around Corpus Christi Bay and bombarded Corpus Christi while anchored in the Bay. This was the start of the Union Blockade of South Texas which made travel in the Rio Grande more important. The goods on the ship were then sent into the Port of Bagdad south of Brownsville in Mexico where they found eager merchants from all over the world.

Cuentos Tejanos

Episode 31

Juan Seguín – "A True Texas Legend"

-By Dr. Manuel Flores

Juan Nepomuceno Seguín is a Tejano hero, Texas legend and one of the fiercest fighters and patriots ever in the history of the United States.

But his legacy of heroism and love for Texas is clouded. So, how did this Tejano patriot run afoul of those whom he helped gain independence for Texas? Simply, it was his last name and his Spanish-Mexican heritage. He or his troops were at Battle of the Alamo and San Jacinto. In San Jacinto, he and his *soldados* (soldiers) played a pivotal role in Sam Houston's Texas Army defeating the Mexican Army of Santa Anna.

Seguín went from a hero of the Texas Revolution of independence from Mexico to a despised person and outcast never to return to Texas until his death. Seguín envisioned a "free" Texas ready to become a powerful nation alongside the growing United States of America to the east and Mexico to the south.

Seguín was fighting the Mexican dictatorship of Santa Anna long before the Battle of San Jacinto. His anger against Santa Anna and his brutal techniques of leadership compelled him to organize Tejanos and join sides with the arriving Americans who would help define Texas' future.

His family was well-established in Texas and lived in the area adjacent to San Antonio for many years. His father Erasmo Seguín had been instrumental in helping the new American settlers move into the San Antonio and now Austin area. They greeted Stephen F. Austin, Jim Bowie, Davy Crockett and others and implored them to join the fight for Texas independence.

The Texas Revolution could not have happened and may not have been won without the aid of Seguin's family and his *Soldados*. It was in large measure because of Seguín that Tejanos fought for Texas at every stage of the struggle for independence from Mexico.

There were Tejanos in the Battles of Agua Dulce, Refugio and San Patricio where vaqueros from Benavides and ranchers from nearby Refugio and other ranching areas joined forces to stall Mexican General Urrea's forces heading north to help Santa Anna in San Jacinto where Sam Houston and Seguín were waiting for the perfect opportunity to attack. Urrea's troops arrived too late, assuring a Texas victory. It was from these battles that Placido Benavides, the Paul Revere of Texas, emerged and rode north to warn Fannin in Goliad and Gen. Sam Houston that another Mexican army was on its way.

Prior to the main battles of the Alamo and San Jacinto, Seguín had organized a formidable Tejano Army that Sam Houston used as scouts and spies throughout Texas. His soldados were the predecessors to the Texas Rangers. They were a mounted cavalry unit in the tradition of the Spanish *"companías volantes"* – quick and dashing mounted units that could get from one battle or emergency in a matter of minutes. Seguín was the leader of the Tejanos' role in the revolution for Texas independence, without a doubt.

Reviewing the names of a list of Seguin's *Soldados* is like looking over a list of football players from a South Texas high school football team, today. There were more than 700, the majority of whom participated in the Battle of San Jacinto. Among the last names were Benavides, Bueno, Bustillos, Camarillo, Cantú, Carbajal, Cárdenas, Castillo, Cavazos, Chaves, Díaz, Coy, Delgado, Enriques, Esparza, Estrada, Flores, Fuentes, Galán, García, Garza, Gómez, Gaytán, González, Guerra, Guerrero, Hernández, Herrera, Huizar, Jaimes, Jiménez, Landera, Lazo, Losoya, Maldonado, Mancha, Martínez, Miranda, Montalvo, Moran, Morelos, Nava, Navarro, Palacios, Peña, Pineda, Ramírez, Ramos, Rio, Rivas, Rocha, Rodríguez, Rubio, Ruiz, Salinas, Sambrano, Sánchez, Silva, Soto, Treviño, Valdez, Villanueva, Zepeda, and Zúñiga to mention a few.

These men were valiant and were as much as part of Texas Independence as anyone.

Seguín was also in command to the Tejano troops in the Alamo, the Alamo defenders. In the final analysis, only 10 Tejanos fought at famous battle, but there were originally 30 Tejanos. Seguín was sent out by Travis to apprise Sam Houston about the situation. Another 20 or so were out as scouts throughout the chapparal and brush of the San Antonio area serving as spies to keep the Texas Army up-do-date of the approaching Mexican troops.

Seguín's Soldados flew the flag of the Mexican state of Coahuila y Tejas during the siege of the Alamo. It features green, white and red stripes with two stars centered in the middle white bar. The only other flag to fly on the Alamo during the 13-day siege by the Mexican Army was the powder blue flag of the First Company of Texas Volunteers from New Orleans. Ironically, the "1824 Flag" which called for implementation to the Constitution of 1824, which most Tejanos and Texans agreed with, did not fly over the Alamo during the siege. The Constitution of 1824 called for statehood in Mexico for Texas.

Eight of Seguín's Tejanos died at the Alamo. Those soldados were:

1. Juan Abamillo
2. Juan Antonio Badillo
3. Carlos Espalier
4. José María "Gregorio" Esparza
5. Antonio Fuentes
6. Damacio Jiménez
7. José Toribio Losoya and
8. Andrés Nava

After the battle, Santa Anna ordered the execution of the surviving male rebels. After that, the Mexican Army gathered the dead and set them on fire. Seguín returned to San Antonio, gathered the ashes and gave the heroes a proper burial. Many believe the ashes are inside San Fernando Cathedral in downtown San Antonio. A crypt in San Fernando Cathedral purports to hold the ashes of the Alamo heroes.

At the Battle of San Jacinto, legend holds Seguín and his Tejanos wore American playing cards on their hats or uniforms to distinguish them from the Mexican soldiers. Sam Houston had just over 700 men in his Texas Army. More than 250 of those were Tejanos assigned to Seguin. They were referred to as Seguín's Soldados. In a very short, 18-minute battle, the war was over. Santa Anna's Mexican Army was defeated and headed back to Mexico in defeat past the Nueces and the Rio Grande rivers. After the Battle of San Jacinto, Seguín's men became among the first Texas Rangers in the new, independent Republic of Texas.

Without a doubt, Seguín had proved himself to be a Texas hero. Always the politician and well-educated, Juan Seguín's place in one of San Antonio's elite families put him on the road to politics. He served at the age of 22 as one of the city's two *regidors,* or city council members, and later as *alcalde*, or mayor and chief executive of San Antonio. Politics suited him and his family well. After Texas declared independence from Mexico, Seguín was elected to the Texas Senate in 1837, the only Tejano to serve in that body. He later served two more terms as mayor of San Antonio.

Soon, however, politics got the best of him. A land speculation deal and the subsequent recapture of San Antonio by Mexico in 1840 led to people to not trust Seguín. San Antonio fell for two days into Mexican hands, again, while Seguín was mayor and did not fight back. He would be called a traitor, to Texas this time, by some.

The citizens of San Antonio were angered by his lack of action and his questionable land dealings. Seguín decided to flee with his family for safety. He ended up in Mexico, where he was imprisoned and forced, Seguín said, to choose between remaining in prison or joining the Mexican army. He chose the army. He served for Mexico in the U.S.-Mexico War from 1846-1848. Once consider a traitor to Mexico, he was now an officer in the Mexican Army.

Indeed, Seguín had always been a soldier and a fighter. It was in his blood and family's DNA. He longed for freedom and the wide-open spaces of his beloved Texas and tried several times to regain his Texas citizenship.

As the Mexican War wound down in 1848, Seguín was allowed to return to Texas with his family, living at his father's ranch, Casa Blanca, near Floresville. He had a chance to redeem his value to Texas and his status as a Texas hero. But, the reception was icy and he could tell he was not welcomed.

In the late 1860s, he settled in Nuevo Laredo on the Texas-Mexico border. One of his sons served as mayor of the city at the time and offered him protection. He died in 1890 and was buried in Nuevo Laredo at the age of 83. His sons and relatives wanted him to be buried in the sacred grounds of Texas, perhaps in San Antonio or even Austin. It was not to be, yet.

Nearly 85 years later, the city of Seguin, which changed its name to honor Juan Seguín in 1838, won permission from Mexico to transfer Seguín's remains there in 1974. The town was originally known as Walnut Springs. It was the perfect resting place of the Tejano hero.

Two years later, the remains were laid to rest in an oak-shaded Seguin park, which has been the site of annual celebrations honoring the war hero. A marble statue of Seguín was added downtown in 2000.

At long last Seguín came to rest in his beloved Texas.

Cuentos Tejanos

Episode 32

Rancho Santa Petronila – A Way Station for Spanish Explorers

-By Manuel Flores

On the Corpus Christi Bayfront down Shoreline Ave. and just south of the well-visited Queen of Tejano Music Selena Monument rests another statue that most do not pay attention to as they pass by the scenic route.

Known as the Friendship Monument, it depicts South Texas Spanish Colonizer Captain Blás María de la Garza Falcón, who sits on a Spanish mustang majestically raising his colonial era hat on high as if greeting all to the area.

The gesture is appropriate, for it was Captain Falcón who created the first Spanish settlement in what is now Nueces County and it was Captain Falcón and his Spanish soldiers and settlers who first encountered the Karankawa Indians and who populated the Texas coast. Falcón had quite a reputation as a colonizer and was the founder of Camargo and seven other colonies in Nuevo Santander, a province of New Spain that included much of South Texas and northern Mexico at that time.

The statue, located on the Lawrence St. crossover adjacent to Corpus Christi Bay, was dedicated in 1992. It was a collaborative effort led by the Westside Business Association, Dr. Clotilde García and the DeVary Durrill Foundation and many other civic leaders. Dr. Sherman Coleman was the sculptor of the majestic figure that sits on a granite slab weighing more than 2,500 pounds. It honors the friendship and link between the United States and people of Spain and Mexico.

Falcón, who is credited to be Texas' "first ranchero," was among the first colonizers of Texas. He was sent by José de Escandón to explore and settle the coastal plains of South Texas.

In 1762, Captain Falcón founded Rancho Santa Petronila, about 18 miles southwest of Corpus Christi. In 1764 Falcón received the first land grant issued by the Spanish Governor. By 1766, the ranch was settled. It became the largest cattle and horse ranch in the hemisphere and its thousands of cattle and mustangs roamed the Wildhorse Desert from Padre Island to the Brush County. The ranch became a way station for other Spanish explorers who would stop to get fresh mounts and cattle for food to fortify their journeys across Texas and beyond.

Captain Falcón established a garrison and a mission to Christianize the Karankawa. Falcón later brought the first longhorn cattle to South Texas and to what is known now at the Coastal Bend. His herd of Spanish cattle grew to more than 20,000. In the meantime, his stock of Spanish mustangs *(mesteños* as they were known at the time) grew to more than 5,000.

Legend holds that the ranch was founded on May 31, the feast day of the Spanish saint Santa Petronila, thus the name of the ranch and the now small community of 2,000 on Farm-to-Market Roads 665 and 892 between Corpus Christi and Driscoll. Today, there are few signs left of the ranch as most of it has become farmland. Only pastures and farmland that yields mostly cotton and sorghum can be seen as cars zoom by the small city of Petronila, population estimated at 125-150. A small store, an elementary school, a church and a grain elevator are all that is left.

But, nearby rests a cemetery with graves dating back to the mid-1700s. It is neglected and only whirlwinds of dust and dead weed serve as a reminder of the once great cattle and horse ranch that dominated the grassy plains of Coastal Texas in the 18th century.

The monument on the Corpus Christi Bayfront was dedicated in 1992 and it too is a remembrance of Spanish Texas and its courageous explorers who paved the way for others to come and settle South Texas.

Known as the Friendship Monument, it depicts South Texas Spanish Colonizer Captain Blás María de la Garza Falcón who sits on a Spanish mustang majestically raising his colonial-era hat on high as if greeting all to the area. It is situated on the Corpus Christi Bayfront. (The Friendship Monument, **www.visitcorpuschristi.com).**

Cuentos Tejanos

Episode 33

The Battle for Civil Rights for Tejanos – South Texas has produced its share of activities

-By Nick Adame

South Texas, in particular Corpus Christi, has produced several leaders in the battle for civil rights for Mexican Americans and Tejanos. It also was the birthplace of the two top Mexican American civil rights organizations in the nation – The League of United Latin American Citizens (LULAC) and the American G.I. Forum (AGIF).

The area's legacy in the civil rights movement reflects a deep commitment to equality for all and for the right of all to seek the American dream. Often people put aside the struggle for civil rights for Mexican Americans and Tejano as not as important as other national movement. Truth is, the Mexican American civil rights movement happened here, in South Texas, and it too went nationwide. Without some leaders who helped spur and define the movement, progress would hav been slower.

We've been fighting for civil rights for a long time, but often the struggle of the Mexican American's quest for civil rights is left out of the history pages.

After the Alamo, Tejanos quickly became second-class citizens in their own land.

Tejanos, American citizens, were treated like animals, shot and dragged by Texas Rangers. Brutal lynching, theft of property and outright discrimination was rampant. Vigilantes ran settled Tejano families from their homes and ranches. Tejano children were not allowed in schools.

Someone had to step up. Many did.

Trailblazing Hispanics fought for their civil rights and without this, Texas and our nation would not have prospered. The Tejanos who stepped up were fighting to preserve the American dream of equality for all and they were fighting to preserve the Texas they helped settle and fought for its freedom from the dictatorial government of Santa Anna.

Here are some heroes everyone should know.

In South Texas, it started in the late 19th century when Tejano journalist and activist Catarino Garza travelled from community-to-community urging the ranchers and farmers to organize or risk losing their culture and way of life. He ran a newspaper in Corpus Christi and three others throughout South Texas. A scholar and a tremendous orator, he organized Garza's Raiders to ensure Tejanos were not denied their civil rights. So impressive were his exploits that *Harper's Weekly* magazine ran an article about him and his men in the late 1892. Garza's men would head into the Brush Country of South Texas to ensure that Tejano ranchers would not lose their farms and land. If need be, they would fight to get it back to the rightful owner. In his newspaper, Garza advocated action to stop the take over of Tejano property and land by the new Anglo settlers who dominated the banks and politics. He implored them to organize or lose their way of life forever. Many did.

The struggle continued into the 20th century. Jesús de la Luz Sáenz from Realitos and Alonso Perales, from Alice, stepped to the forefront. Perales, a civil rights lawyer and diplomat for the United States, served as one of the founding leaders of LULAC. In 1930 Perales testified before a United States Congressional hearing on Mexican immigration. A Democrat, he helped found the Independent Voters Association, a Mexican-American political club in San Antonio in the early 1930s.

Sáenz an educator and activist decided he would join the military during World War I to prove that Tejanos were ready to fight for America and were unafraid of anything. He wrote a book about his experiences in the big war. It was in diary form and it showed the love for his country with a patriotic fervor few had seen. Sáenz remains an icon of service to country.

In the 20th century a journalism family, the Idár, surfaced as an intelligent and courageous advocates for civil rights. Their father, Nicolas, started a newspaper in Laredo. His children, Jovita and Eduardo Idár, followed his journalistic footsteps and joined him in the fight against discrimination in their columns and editorials. They, too, would start their own newspaper. They had newspapers in Laredo and Brownsville and immediately took up the battle cry against discrimination of Tejanos. His daughter Jovita had her own newspaper in Laredo and, when she was confronted by the Texas Rangers, she met them face-to-face and refused to back down. The Rangers tore up her printing and newspaper office, but she drove to Brownsville and published her paper at her brother Eduardo's newspaper shop. Jovita even took on Hollywood and went all the way to Washington, D.C., to fight the often unfair and stereotypical portrayal of Mexican Americans in movies.

Meanwhile, south of San Antonio, Emma Tenayuca was a labor organizer and civil rights leader. She is perhaps best remembered for her role in organizing the largest strike in San Antonio history, the Pecan Shellers Strike in 1938.

Among the most courageous pioneers was J.T. Canales, a state legislator and a superintendent of schools in the Rio Grande Valley. He, too, helped found LULAC, but he is best known for taking on the Texas Rangers in the legislature in Austin. As a state representative, he stood up against discrimination and racism and had the courage to take on the Texas Ranger. Upset with the atrocities committed by the Rangers against his fellow Tejanos, he filed 19 charges against the Texas Rangers in January 1918 and demanded a legislative investigation and the reorganization of the force. This came after the brutal massacre of all the men and boys in the village of El Porvenir, Texas, on the edge of the Texas-Mexico border. His demands then went to Gov. Jim Hogg who surprisingly agreed with Canales' request and disbanded the West Texas unit of the Texas Rangers. For this and other actions, Canales became known as "The Most Dangerous Man in Texas." He was a Tejano with political clout. It didn't get more dangerous than that at that time.

In 1929 the first LULAC convention was held in Corpus Christi, uniting chapters from throughout Texas in one solid, united civil rights organization. Ben Garza from Corpus Christi was elected the organization's president on the now national organization. Garza lobbied for voting rights and represented the organization several times in Congressional hearings in Washington. LULAC also adopted a motto. "One for All, and All for One" proposed by Canales. Civil rights and access to education became the central objectives for LULAC. Today LULAC has more than 132,000 members in more than 1,000 councils nationwide. Corpus Christi had the first council. I'm proud to be the current president (2021) of LULAC Council No. 1 and I will continue to work diligently to ensure that the rights of Mexican Americans, Tejanos and all of the people of Texas and the United States are not violated. We have a legacy here in Corpus Christi and South Texas to stand up for what is right and I and all of the members of this and other LULAC Councils will not shrink from that duty.

But there's more.

Dr. Hector P. Perez Garcia founded the American G.I. Forum in Corpus Christi in 1948. Garcia, whose hometown is Mercedes in the Rio Grande Valley, settled in Corpus Christi and started his medical practice here after serving as a Captain during World War II. When he got here he noticed that Tejano veterans were not treated with respect and often denied the benefits they had earned while serving in the military. Many were in ill health and denied VA benefits. Their paperwork was just "lost" or "delayed." Garcia also noticed the that the healthcare of the residents of the city and South Texas were lacking. He rallied the troops, so to say, and formed the American G.I. Forum in Corpus Christi to ensure that Tejano veterans would have a voice that was represented at every level of government and before any institution that would deny them benefits or failed to honor them for their service. The first chapter was in Corpus Christi. Soon, other chapters spread throughout Texas and the nation. Protecting rights of veterans and fighting for justice in the education system were the main goals of the organization. "Education is our freedom, and freedom should be everybody's business" became Dr. Garcia's rallying cry. Initially formed to request services for World War II veterans of Mexican descent who were denied medical services by the United States Department of Veterans Affairs, the AGIF soon entered into non-veteran's issues such as voting rights, jury selection, and educational desegregation, advocating for the civil rights of all Mexican Americans. Today the organization has chapters in 40 states and is headquartered in Washington, D.C.

Dr. Garcia's sister – Dr. Clotilde Garcia – was on the Del Mar College board and was a leader in Spanish Genealogy research. Simply known as "Dr. Cleo" by her friends and adoring patients, Garcia was a physician, writer, historian, avid researcher. and community activist. She studied and promoted South Texas history and Hispanic genealogy securing important genealogical records that are now open to the public at the Corpus Christi Public Library main office and online. In recognition of her efforts, in 1990 she was awarded the Royal American Order of Isabella the Catholic by Juan Carlos I of Spain. García published a translated account of the 1812 Siege of Camargo, and eight other books on local historical figures such as José Nicolás Ballí, Blas María de la Garza Falcón and Enrique Villareal. In 1987 she co-founded and served as the first president of the Spanish American Genealogical Association. She also is primarily responsible for the Friendship Monument depicting Falcón and the impact of Spanish settlers in Texas located on the Corpus Christi Bayfront. She not only followed in her brother's footsteps, she went in new directions and carved her own legacy and civil rights leader in South Texas.

In Corpus Christi the Bonilla family became prominent leaders in civil rights and community organizations and gained statewide and national office positions with LULAC. All earned law degrees. Tony became a state legislator. His sister Mary Helen Bonilla Berlanga was elected to the State Board of Education. Tony and Ruben were state and national leaders in LULAC. William founded the law firm Bonilla & Chapa. Ruben was also the city's representative to the Port Commission, an important and vital economic position in South Texas. The Bonilla are one of the most distinguished families in South Texas and their law firm in the heart of the Corpus Christi barrio and Mexican American section in the westside of Corpus Christi continues to be a beacon of hope for man.

Kingsville state representative Irma Rangel became a powerhouse in the Legislature, the first Mexican American woman to serve in that capacity, and was instrumental in establishing the Texas A&M College of Pharmacy in Kingsville, the building now bears her name.

State Sen. Carlos F. Truan wrote the Texas Bilingual Education Act of 1969. At the time, the state had an English-only law and an 80 percent dropout rate among Hispanics. He also championed upper-level degrees at universities and doctoral programs were soon part of the curricula at Texas A&M-Kingsville, Texas A&M-Corpus Christi and other universities in South Texas.

Carlos Guerra from Robstown and José Ángel Gutiérrez from Crystal City, both former students at Texas A&I in Kingsville, were leaders of the Chicano political movement in the late 1960s and in the 1970s. Guerra led the Mexican American Youth Organization(MAYO) in several protests and school walkouts throughout South Texas and the Rio Grande Valley. Gutierrez founded La Raza Unida Party and formed it into a statewide force, supporting candidates for local offices from county judge to the governor. Ramsey Muñiz from Corpus Christi ran for governor under the flag of La Raza Unida Party in the 1970s and garnered 7% of the statewide vote. He is the first Hispanic whose name appeared on a Texas gubernatorial general election ballot. A football player at Baylor University in Waco after a stellar prep career at Miller High School in Corpus Christ, he joined the MAYO chapter at Baylor. The passion for civil rights he learned from his South Texas roots stirred his interest in fighting discrimination. He once organized a protest by Baylor athletes on behalf of the first African

American seeking to join the cheerleading squad. Muniz, too, was a part of the South Texas struggle for civil rights.

There are many more who deserve mention, but it is important to note that there are civil rights heroes right here in South Texas. The struggle for civil rights also included Tejanos and a good portion of that battle occurred right in our backyard.

Those who have succeed them continue the struggle.

Dr. Nick Adame is chairman of the executive board of the Tejano Civil Rights Museum and Resource Center in Corpus Christi. He also serves as president for LULAC Council #1 and is on the Del Mar College Board of Regents.

Cuentos Tejanos

Episode 34

A Penny for Your Thoughts

The saga of newspaperman Pedro G. Chapa

- By Manuel Flores
And Lynda Lee Sáenz Soliz

The proverb "A penny for your thoughts" played a big role in the life of a South Texas pioneer journalist Pedro G. Chapa, a.k.a. "Chapita." He remains the only man in Texas who purchased a newspaper for 1 cent and went on to become one of the few Mexican Americans who served as editor and publisher of a weekly newspaper.

The newspaper was the *Jim Hogg County Enterprise,* a weekly English publication, in Hebbronville, Texas, 50 miles east of Laredo, in the Brush Country area of South Texas. The profession served him and his community well.

Chapita was a thinker and avid reader of books in both English and Spanish. He loved the feel of a book in his hands and often would just sit in a living room chair or rocker in the front porch or back patio and just read.

He didn't have a formal education, but was self-taught. Born in Agualeguas, Nuevo Leon, Mexico[1]. on Jan. 31, 1901, he read newspapers religiously as a teen-ager growing up close to the U.S.-Mexico border. From reading newspapers, he picked up a sense of community and current affairs. In the early 20th century, South Texas and Northern Mexico were replete with newspapers reporting on Texas, Mexico and International affairs. Frankly, it was exciting reading about the revolution in Mexico and the civil rights movement in South Texas with the incursion of the "*Rinches Malditos* (Texas Rangers)" in the area. He fantasized about being a reporter and writing about those escapades of revolutionaries and freedom fighters.

---

1 *Note: Agualuegas, N.L., Mexico was settled by the indigenous tribe Gualuegas and has nothing to do with "agua (water)" Nuevo Leon borders the U.S. Mexico border. It became a city in 1821. Mexico.pueblosamerica.com.*

Chapita" decided at a young age he would become a printer, or maybe a reporter or editor.

Agualuegas, N.L. was a small town of about four thousand people and there were not many opportunities there, not even for a good education. His father, Cenobio, had emigrated to the United States and had taken a job with the post office in Laredo, Texas. Agualuegas was connected to Nuevo Laredo, Tamaulipas – across the border from Laredo, Texas, via railroad.

"Chapita" yearned to have the freedom to write. In Laredo, the Idar family had become legendary journalists, operating a controversial newspaper who stood up against the Texas Rangers" atrocities, U.S. President Woodrow Wilson's military incursion into South Texas and calling for Tejanos to organize or perish and lose their civil rights. When the Texas Rangers destroyed Jovita Idar's print shop and newspaper office in Laredo,[2] he was determined more than ever to join the quest for equality and civil rights for Tejanos and Mexicanos on the border.

At the age of 14, he decided to cross the U.S. Mexico border and join his father in Laredo.[3] He boarded the train to Nuevo Laredo where he waited for the opportune time to cross, without any legal documentation. He didn't want to go through the main international bridge or cross the Rio Grande. He decided instead to walk over the railroad bridge connecting the two cities.

After crossing the railroad bridge, he found himself in downtown Laredo close to the newspaper and print shop of the Idar. It was getting rebuilt and had a job posting in front of it. It was in English and Spanish and simply said "*se busca ayuda* (help wanted) ayudante de imprenta (print shop helper; essentially a printer's devil in English)."[4]

He went to his father's house and joined other family members. Almost immediately his father told him to find a job. He wanted him to study business at a local business school.[5] Chapita told him he liked to be a printer and reporter. Chapita hurriedly explained that the Idar were

---

2 *Note: The Idar were journalists in South Texas with newspapers in Laredo and Brownsville. They reported on social and political issues relevant to the Tejano population of Texas. (The Idar. www.tshaonline.org)*

3 *Use genealogy source here.*

4 A printer's devil is typically a young boy serving at or below the level of apprentice in a print shop or newspaper office. (Printer's Devil/https://poetry.arizona.edu)

5 Hylton, Hillary, "A Man and His Newspaper," Sept. 11, 1977, p. H1.

looking for help. Cenobio told him he would go with him in the morning to inquire about the job.

Thus began Chapita's journey in journalism. He began his career as a printer's devil for the Spanish-language newspaper *Evolución* in 1916, working for the controversial Idar family. Soon, he was doing reports, news stories, about events in Laredo. He would later work for the *Laredo Times* as a printer and reporter.[6] Chapita loved it. He loved the printing equipment and wanted to find out more about it. A trip to Louisiana to enroll in a printing school followed and there he became a master printer and certified journalist.

He would return to Laredo to continue his career as a printer and journalist. He married María Marta Sáenz in 1921 and they had a daughter, María Lucia Chapa on Dec. 13, 1923. Unfortunately, María Marta died at childbirth.

He later married Beatriz Salas and they had two children, Clelia in 1936 and Pedro Jr. in 1938.

In 1935, Chapita had moved to Hebbronville, Texas, and became a printer at *The Enterprise*.[7] In 1942, he was named assistant editor. His reputation was getting solid and several job offers were made, including one in Mercedes, Texas, in the Rio Grand Valley.[8] But Chapita wanted his own paper so he asked the publisher and owner W.A. Dannelley if he would sell it to him and for how much? According to family lore, Dannelley answered "Chapita, I'll sell it to you for a penny." In 1947, Chapita became the editor and publisher of the now "Jim Hogg County Enterprise"[9] He paid Mr. Dannelly $9,000.[10]

Chapita quickly worked to get his mark and character on the newspaper. He like to brag, "I write most of the stories, take all the pictures, print it on the old flat-bed press and sweep up, too."10 An avid sports fan, in particular baseball, he started his own column titled "Listen This One's On Me." In it he reviewed many local and social issues and implored politicians to become involved in state and national business. His columns called for a sewage system, new roads, a memorial monument for the town's fallen soldiers of World War II and for the development of Little League

---

6 Sáenz, Lynda Lee, "The Enterprise," The Hebbronville Story, Hebbronville High School, Hebbronville, Texas.

7 Sáenz.

8 Hylton.

9 Sáenz.

10 Interview with Pedro G. Chapa, Dec. 24, 1992, by Manuel Flores

baseball, to mention a few. He also called for more community events and published the Jim Hogg County 50th Year Anniversary book with the Chamber of Commerce.[11]

But it wasn't always smooth sailing. Between the 1950s an 1970s South Texas was consumed with the politics of the *"Patrón System"* - an oligarchy and feudal society where big land-owners make the majority of the decisions in the area. Frank Anders, in his book "Boss Rule in South Texas," covers the topic brilliantly.[12] On Oct. 26, 1956, Chapita discovered he was right in the middle of the "Patrón System" when Jim Hogg County Judge Francisco Barrera Guerra was shot in front of a Hebbronville barbershop close to town's post office.[13] Chapita reported only the facts and worked hard to keep his newspaper independent while many others in the area took sides. In his column he called for quick justice and the perpetrator was sentenced to life in prison. Years later, he received a full pardon from the President of the United States.

He was not always liked, especially by politicians in the area who often wore holstered pistols around towns in South Texas. One day, an area county political group came to his office and told him flatly they were not going to print any government documents any more at his shop. He was just, "too expensive." Besides the newspaper ads, Chapita's income came from printing wedding invitations, graduation announcements and government documents. They were going to take their business to the big city, Laredo. Chapita was just too expensive, they kept saying. Chapita thanked them for their visit and asked them to leave. All advertisements and legal notices were also stopped for the newspaper. Area printers and other newspapers stepped in to help him. The following year, with new county leadership in charge, they contacted Chapita again. They asked if the county could do business with him again. He said, "yes," and added, "but it's going to cost you. The cost of business has gone up."[14]

Chapita was a humble man with a sense of humor. For example, the byline in all of his columns said they were written by *"Chaparral,"* a distinct reference to the thick and thorny Brush Country of the area.[15] But, did

---

11 Flores, Mauel. "Hispanics in the Media: 200 Years of Spanish-language communication in U.S. Media, Kendell-Hunt, Dubuque, Iowa, 2008. P. 64.
12 Anders, Evan. "Boss Rule in South Texas," University of Texas Press, 1982, pp. vii-xii.
13 George B. Parr, Texas Handbook Online, www.tshaonline
14 ersonal Observation, July 22, 1979.
15 Franklin, Benjamin. "Silence Dogood-Busy Body-Early Writings," Library of America, 2005.

he have guest columnists to tackle some of the thorny issues surrounding Hebbronville and Jim Hogg County? Also, his use of the pseudonym speaks well of his knowledge of journalism history and copies the work of Ben Franklin who used the moniker Silence Dogood for his column during the American Revolutionary days. But, of course, he had ghost writers and plenty of friends like Thomas Jefferson, George Washington and even Thomas Paine to use from. Did Chapita have ghost writers? No one will ever know.

Chapita was a humble man pleased with the auspiciousness of his work and profession. He loved the old printing machines – the flat-bed press with its roots back to Gutenberg in the 1400s and the rackety Lin-0-Type machine that set the type for every column inch of the newspaper, every ad and every wedding or graduation announcement.

He was no Ben Franklin or Thomas Paine nor even an Idar, but he had his own style of reporting and caring for his community that made him a legend and key part of South Texas. He was one of the first Tejanos in charge of a newspaper in Texas and one of the first Hispanics in the nation to operate, own and publish his own newspaper.

One thing for sure, he was a newspaperman in every sense of the word. He wrote the news, set the type, made up the pages, and printed the newspaper. He sold ads, bought the ink, melted the lead, operated the type-setting machine, and cleaned up the place.

And he did it all for his hometown – Hebbronville. He had a favorite Spanish adage he used to describe his work to his employees who must of have realized the importance of Chapita's profession "He would tell them, "*Los nombres que publicamos son la comunidad.* (The names we publish are our community."[16]

Chapita retired when it was 88 and died on Sept. 20, 1994 at the age of 93.[17]

He reached his dream of being a true newspaperman.

I know, I (Manuel Flores) was a printer's devil at The *Jim Hogg County Enterprise.* He is my grandfather.

------

16 Flores, p. 64.
17 Flores, p. 64.

Cuentos Tejanos

Fotos y Recuerdos de el Sur de Tejas

Pedro Chapa at Linotype

Pedro G. Chapa while he was a printer and journalist in Laredo, Texas.

Bobby Cavazos from the King Ranch starred at Texas Tech University in the 1950s.
(From Texas Tech Sports Information)

Catarino Garza, Tejano newspaperman, editor and publisher.
(From Personal Collection and Archives of Dr. Manuel Flores)

Bobby Cavazos Chicago Cards trading card.
(From Personal Collection and Archives of Dr. Manuel Flores)

Dr. Manuel Flores served 12 years as a captain in the Texas Army
National Guard.

(From Personal Collection and Archives of Dr. Manuel Flores)

Flag of Coahuilla and Texas that flew at the Alamo. It was (l to r) green, white and red with two stars in the center of the white middle stripe.

The Domingo Peña Show onLife KIII-TV Channel 3 in Corpus Christi circa 1978.

(From Personal Collection and Archives of Dr. Manuel Flores)

Dr. Hector P, Garcia, founder of the American G.I. Forum.
(Published with permission from Garcia family)

Emma Tenayuca, Civil Rights Leader from San Antonio led Pecan
Shellers' Strike in 1930s.
(From Personal Collection and Archives of Dr. Manuel Flores)

Life in a South Texas Rancho shows Marcos and Mario Flores playing with a fawn. Their "abuelo" Lupe Acevedo is in background.
(From Personal Collection and Archives of Dr. Manuel Flores)

Marcos and Mario Flores in the early morning of a buck-hunting trip in South Texas.

Lt. Gen. Ricardo Sanchez from Rio Grande City is one of 10 South Texas generals featured in this book. Sanchez is a graduate of Texas A&I University (now Texas A&M-Kingsville).

(From Personal Collection and Archives of Dr. Manuel Flores)

State Rep. J.T. Canales petitioned the Texas Legislature to reorganize the Texas Rangers.

(Printed with permission from the family)

Sisters in a South Texas orange grove.
(From Personal Collection and Archives of Dr. Manuel Flores)

Rendering of South Texas artist Servando Hinojosa's "Ameramorfosis."
(Printed with permission from the artist.)

"Historia de Tejas," art work by South Texas artist Servando Hinojosa.
(Printed with permission from the artist)

Idar Paper Collage

Saenz family photo Oilton, Texas, circa 1895
(From Personal Collection and Archives of Dr. Manuel Flores)

Jose Navarro Tombstone

Jovita Idar, Laredo journalist and newspaper owner.
(From Personal Collection and Archives of Dr. Manuel Flores)

Statue of Juan Seguín in Seguin, Texas
(From Personal Collection and Archives of Dr. Manuel Flores)

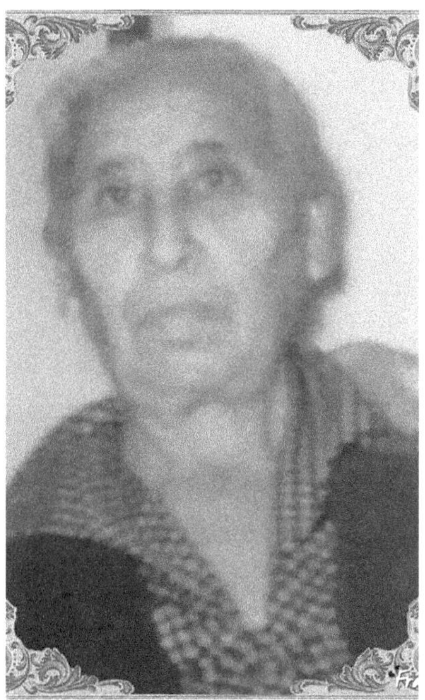

Julia Flores, "Nana", grandmother of author,
(From Personal Collection and Archives of Dr. Manuel Flores)

Mario and Marcos Flores ready to ride at the Balderas Ranchito in
Hebbronville.
(From Personal Collection and Archives of Dr. Manuel Flores)

Maria Marta Saenz with pet burro circa 1890.
(From Personal Collection and Archives of Dr. Manuel Flores)

Dan Arrellano, Tejano historian and expert on the historic "Battle of
Medina" where more than 1,000 Tejanos were killed by the Spanish army
in 1813.

Mario Flores with buck he shot in Jim Hogg County.
(From Personal Collection and Archives of Dr. Manuel Flores)

A "Pachanga" at La Parrita Ranch in Jim Hogg County. Oh, the *cuentos*
they told.
(From Personal Collection and Archives of Dr. Manuel Flores)

Pachanga at La Parrita Ranch. This time "let's take a picture before the Panchanga starts,"
(From Personal Collection and Archives of Dr. Manuel Flores)

Saenz family portrait circa 1886,
(From Personal Collection and Archives of Dr. Manuel Flores)

Ramsey Muniz for Governor. Campaign poster from 1972 Texas gubernatorial election during La Raza Unida's candidate Ramsey Muniz swing through Jim Hogg County.
(From Personal Collection and Archives of Dr. Manuel Flores)

Rene Ramirez playing for the Texas Longhorns circa 1959.
(From Personal Collection and Archives of Amando Saenz family)

Ramsey Muniz collage featuring him playing football at Baylor, in front of State Capitol in Austin, and on campaign poster for Governor. (From Personal Collection and Archives of Dr. Manuel Flores)

Rene Ramires playing for Texas Longhorns publicity photo and running the ball in Sugar Bowl 1959.

"Historia de Tejas" art work by South Texas artist Servando Hinojosa.
(Printed with permission from the artist)

Josquin Barraza in World War II uniform. He is the father of South
Texas Chicano artist Santa Barraza.

(Printed with permission from the Barraza family)

Jose de Escandon

Simón Gómez was the first Spanish-surnamed student-athlete at Texas A&I (now Texas A&M-Kingsville. He was a first baseman for the Javelinas in 1928.

Engagement photo of Maria Marta Saenz (center) pictured with her mother Francisca Leon de Saenz and father Transito Saenz.

Marcos Flores by the windmill at La Parrita Ranch near Hebbronville.
Once run by his grandfather Guadalupe Acevedo it is now operated by
the Flores brothers Marcos and Mario and their sister Teresa Marisol
Flores Lentz.

(From Personal Collection and Archives of Dr. Manuel Flores)

Friendship Monument

State Sen. Carlos F. Truan was known as "The Dean of the Texas Senate" and was responsible for many civil rights social legislation designed to help the people of South Texas, including the bill to create the College of Pharmacy on the campus of Texas A&M-Kingsville. Sen. Truan also spoke at the funeral of Juan Rocha.

Irma Rangel Closeup

Statue of Irma Rangel in front of the Rangel College of Pharmacy on the campus of Texas A&M University-Kingsville
(From Personal Collection and Archives of Dr. Manuel Flores)

Rancho Soliz – Humberto and Lynda Lee Soliz with sons Ivan and Javier.

Emilio Saenz circa 1900.

Cattle Branding still goes on in South Texas ranchos.

Scotus College in Hebbronville, Texas.

Bri at the rancho

Ivan at rancho

Toro and JD Soliz

Cuentos Tejanos

Episode 35

The Galloping Gaucho & Other Gridiron Tales – South Texas has had its share of Tejano college football legends

-By Manuel Flores

There have been many excellent athletes in South Texas throughout the years. Here are some who were trailblazers in college football at a time when Mexican Americans were not allowed to play collegiate sports, much less football.

The Galloping Gaucho from Hebbronville

Rene Ramirez, the "Galloping Gaucho" from Hebbronville, Texas, was one of the first Tejano to play Division I football, as a halfback on the Texas Longhorns squads of 1956–59.

He had a unique running style taking the ball and running with a fury of a man on horse, a vaquero perhaps or a gaucho. Thus, his nickname "Galloping Gaucho." Ramirez was a combination of power and finesse. His powerful legs would fend off defenders as his zigged and zagged his way through the defense. He was also a powerful runner crashing his body into would be tacklers by lunging forward right into their chest.

The first time he touched the football for Texas, he returned a kickoff 86 yards for a touchdown. His Cinderella career would last four years and in 2013 he was elected to the Texas Sports Hall of Fame.

It was a fitting tribute to Ramirez who helped lead Hebbronville to the Class 2A regional championship and the state quarterfinals as an end (receiver) in 1955. He was an All-State receiver for the Hebbronville Longhorns.

At Texas, he was a two-way player, starring as a halfback and throwing passes on offense and as a defensive back on special situations. Here are some of his accomplishments.

- As a sophomore in 1957, he led the team in all-purpose yards (567) and touchdowns (5). Texas went 6-3-1 in '57 after a dismal 1-9 campaign the year before.

- Texas earned a berth in the Sugar Bowl that year against the University of Mississippi (Ole Miss).

- One year later, Ramirez tied for the team lead in touchdowns (5) and had significant plays in Texas' 15-14 victory over Oklahoma that ended the Sooners' six-year series winning streak. He also had a 52-yard TD run in the 24-6 victory over Arkansas, and in 1958 scored three touchdowns in the season finale, a 27-0 win over Texas A&M.

- Ramirez brought a unique aspect to Coach Royal's offensive attack. Originally a receiver in his hometown of Hebbronville and a power rusher on end sweeps when he got to Texas, he was also used as a left-handed passer on sweeps around the left end.

- As a senior, he earned first team All-Southwest Conference honors on a team which finished the year No. 4 in both national polls, posted a 9-2 record and finished tied for first in the league, giving Coach Darrell Royal his first conference title while still in the cut-throat Southwest Conference.

- In 1959, he helped lead Texas to the 1960 Cotton Bowl.

- Also, a solid defensive player, he posted four career interceptions

- Ramirez earned a mechanical engineering degree from UT and spent his in the insurance business in Austin and Rio Grande Valley.

(Source: texassports.com)

The Three Rs from Hebbronville

Ramirez was of three football players from Hebbronville to go on to play college football during the 1950s. The others were Rodemiro Gonzales and Rene Medellin.

The three became known as "The Three Rs from Hebbronville" in later years as fans realized the unique quality of play they and others brought to the small Brush Country town in deep South Texas.

Under Coach Milton Hild, the Longhorns won five consecutive district titles and posted a 46-4-2 record with two trips to regional championship and on to the State Quarterfinals between 1953 and1957,

Gonzales, was the quarterback for the 1955 Hebbronville Longhorns team and earned All-State honors passing for 1,993 yards at a time when football was primarily used a "three-yards and a cloud of dust" offensive philosophy. He was among Texas' all-time leading passers for several years setting season and career records for passing yards and touchdowns. Some of his records stood for more than 25 years. At TCU Gonzales earned three letters and was a defensive back. He also was a pitcher for to the Horned Frogs baseball team. After graduating from TCU he became a coach in the San Antonio area and later an administrator.

A 1955 Hebbronville High School graduate, Gonzales played football and baseball at TCU. He was one of the first Hispanics to attend the Fort Worth university on an athletic scholarship, making him a pioneer on and off the field.

He died in 2012 at the age of 75.

He talked about those tough, early days at TCU in a 2006 interview.

"Coming from Hebbronville, I had culture shock at the beginning because there were no Mexicanos at TCU," Gonzales said. "I'd look around and think to myself, 'What am I doing here?' But you gradually adjust to all those things."

At TCU, he started at safety as a senior in 1959, and lettered as a pitcher on the TCU baseball team in 1957 and 1958.

Medellin was a three-year lettermen for Hebbronville and played halfback and quarterback, earning All-District honors each year he played high school football. He too, led South Texas and the state in several passing statistics that year. He went to play football for the Southern Methodist University Mustangs. At SMU he played wide receiver, started on defense and was the team's place kicker. "The Jim Hogg County 100th Anniversary" book relates a story about Medellin's college days. Seems like the Hebbronville product went up to his coach John Cudmore before a game and told him he was having problems with his foreign language course. When the coach asked him what the course was, Medellin answered "English."

Medellin earned a business degree from SMU and went into a very successful restaurant business.

Ocoha captained the Texas Longhorns in the 1953 Cotton Bowl

Some mistakenly label Ramirez as the first Mexican American to play football at the University of Texas. He may have had a little more notoriety because of his nickname, but the first was a powerful running back and defensive standout from Laredo Martin High School

Richard "Dickie" Ochoa came to the University of Texas as a 6-foot-2, 200-pound full back and lettered three years (1950-52). He was tri-captain of the 1952 Southwest Conference (SWC) championship team. He switched from defense to offense after helping 1950 Texas team to SWC title.

In 1952 he was All-SWC selection after leading conference in rushing.

A true leader, UT was 25-7 during his career

Ochoa was named the "Outstanding Back "of 1953 Cotton Bowl a 16-0 win over Tennessee, when he ran for 108 yards. He was drafted by the New York Giants in 1953.

King Ranch brothers star for the Raiders

Richard and Bobby Cavazos were "Kiñenos," the name given to Cowboys/Vaqueros in the fabled King Ranch. But they were also football players, good ones. Their quest for education and to play football led them to Texas Tech University in Lubbock. They were among the first Mexican Americans in Texas and nationwide to play college football, and the first at Texas Tech.

Older brother Richard was the first Mexican American to don a Red Raiders uniform, distinguishing himself in 1949 and 1950. Getting on the football field at first was a difficult situation for him. It seems like the team's equipment manager, apparently surprised that a "Mexican" wanted to play football, refused to issue him a uniform until the coach told him to. He later made history as the first Hispanic four-star general in the United States Army, serving in Korea and Vietnam. From 1989 to 1995, he also served on the Texas Tech Board of Regents.

At Texas Tech, Richard Cavazos opened the door of others to follow. But, as Texas Tech historians like to brag, if Richard opened the door, Bobby kicked it in.

Simply, Bobby Cavazos is a Red Raiders legend and one of the best to play football at the university and the state.

At Tech. Bobby Cavazos helped lead the Red Raiders to three conference titles in four seasons. Back then Tech played in the Border Intercollegiate Athletic Association with the likes of Hardin Simmons, Texas Western, Arizona, Arizona State, West Texas A&M, and New Mexico State.

In his first start, Cavazos ran for 103 yards in a loss to Houston. He followed that up with 100-yard performances against SWC members TCU and Baylor. Cavazos earned honorable mention All-American recognition and All-BIAA merit every year of his collegiate career. In 1951 the Red Raiders finished 7-4, won the BIAA and beat Pacific in the Sun Bowl, the school's first-ever postseason win.

His best season was his last in Lubbock as the Red Raider football team reached unprecedented heights and finally draw the attention of the juggernaut Southwest Conference. The Red Raiders finished 11-1 with the lone loss coming to Texas A&M.

Bobby Cavazos in recap:

- Also, a solid defensive player, Bobby Cavazos posted four career interceptions

- He starred as a senior on the team that went 11-1 and beat Auburn 35-13 in the Gator Bowl. Cavazos was the game's most valuable player, rushing for 141 yards and three touchdowns. That capped a season in which he finished among the nation's leaders in points (80) and rushing yards (757).

- As a sophomore in 1951, he was Honorable Mention All-America for a team that beat Pacific in the Sun Bowl for Tech's first bowl victory. He had 706 yards and nine touchdowns that season and 674 yards and 10 TDs the next.

- In each of Cavazos' last three seasons, he led the Red Raiders in rushing and was named all-Border Conference. A few years later, Tech received a long-awaited invitation into the SWC.

- The Chicago Cardinals drafted Cavazos in the third round of the 1954 amateur draft, but a shoulder injury prevented him from continuing his football career.

Another Cavazos brother, Lauro Cavazos, became the first and only Hispanic President of Texas Tech. He also served as Secretary of Education in the United States, serving under Presidents Ronald Reagan and George H.W. Bush.

They were the sons of Lauro Cavazos who was the "*Caporal(foreman)*" of the King Ranch which prides itself in developing good Texas stock. Certainly, the Cavazos brothers were "*Good Texas Stock*".

The "C" stood for courage

His name was E.C. Lerma. Some said the "C" stood for courage.

He was a trailblazing football player and coach who starred in football at the high school and college level and went on to a stellar coaching career.

His real name was Everardo Carlos Lerma. In life, he would simply be known as "E.C." Both of his parents were born in Mexico, and they came to the Lone Star State seeking a better life for themselves and (what would eventually be) their one dozen children. He was the youngest and was raised by his siblings, after his parents' deaths.

"E.C" was born in Bishop and later moved to Kingsville with his family. His goal was to play football for the Brahmas. When he took to the field in Kingsville High School, he was the only Spanish-surnamed player on the team. Mexicans simply did not do this - play football – or so some people claimed. Lerma survived his high school football trial and was the only Brahma to earn All-District honors his senior year. He was an end.

Except for some small Texas towns, it was a rarity to see a Mexican American play on varsity, much less start and star. His play attracted the attention of then Southwest Conference powerhouse, Texas Christian University. Of course, *familia* (family) was important to "E.C." so he turned down a scholarship offer from TCU and elected to play for Texas A&I in Kingsville.

Jorge Iber, who wrote the book "More than Just *Peloteros* (More than Just ballplayers)" interviewed Lerma before his death in1998 and wrote, "Circumstances were little different at the higher level of competition and the racism Lerma faced while in (Kingsville) high school continued (at the collegiate level). E.C. "endured taunts, cheap shots and discriminatory practices while on the squad; and that was from his teammates;"

Iber, who served as an Associate Dean in the Student Division and Professor of History at Texas Tech University, was impressed by E.C.'s courage.

He wrote that the taunts continued on the road from opposing players. By that time, however, the Javelinas football team had bonded with Lerma. Players soon found out that Lerma was a hard-working player whose grit and talent would help the Javelinas win.

Lerma lettered for A&I between 1935 and 1937. The Javelinas were co-champions and champs of the Alamo Conference in 1936 and 1937.

Iber noted that "E.C." praised Javelina Coach Bud McCallum for allowing him the opportunity to play. In a post in "Sports in American History" online blog, "E.C." called McCallum "a fair, tough, honest football coach that demanded 100% effort at all times. He cared not what the color of your skin was."

Lerma became an integral part of A&I's legendary football teams. As the first Mexican American to letter for Javelina football, he became a legend himself. At A&I he was a member of the legendary "T" Association reserved for lettermen. He was inducted into the Javelina Hall of Fame in 1977.

In 1940 he became one of the first Mexican American high school football coaches in the nation, not to mention just Texas, when he was hired at Benavides as Head Football Coach. "Mexican Americans," Lerma said in an interview, "just didn't become head coaches 'cause some felt they weren't intelligent enough." But, there was "E.C." looking all the bit like Knute Rockne of Notre Dame fame donning a fedora hat and overcoat while coaching on the sidelines.

Lerma's Benavides teams were some of the all-time best in South Texas. The Eagles earned four district titles, were bi-district champs three times and earned two regional titles (the farthest small classification teams could advance at the time). The Eagles had undefeated seasons in 1943 and 1949. Lerma also coached Benavides to the regional championship in basketball in 1944. He left Benavides in 1955 and went to Rio Grande City where he continued his legacy of producing champions in the field and in life.

At Rio Grande City, Lerma revived the Rattlers football program. RGC became a Rio Grande Valley and Laredo area powerhouse. Lerma retired from coaching with a 154-98 record and 13 championships.

"The football stadium in Benavides is named in his honor, " 'E.C.' Lerma Stadium. It was dedicated in 1991. "E.C." died in 1998.

(Note: This short essay focused on football standouts from South Texas. Of course, many followed in the second half of the 20th century. And, there were others in other sports.)

Homero T. Martinez was an All-Southwest Conference pitcher for Texas A&M from 1933 to 1936. Simon Gomez was the first Spanish-surnamed student athlete at Texas A&I (now Texas A&M-Kingsville). Simon played baseball in 1928. Dozens of other white and black athletes were also trailblazers in their own right. This, however, is an essay about the Tejano student-athletes who led the way for many others.

Cuentos Tejanos

Episode 36

"El Colegio Altamirano"
Pioneering education in the Tejano ranch country of South Texas

There is a myth that has permeated in South Texas and the American Southwest that has been most damaging to the character and culture of the Tejano. That myth is that Tejanos and Mexican Americans, in grnrtsl, do not care about their children's education.

From the beginning of Spanish colonization in the 18th century there were schools available in the missions and *presidios* (forts). When Spain fell to Mexico, that tradition continued. When Mexico fell to Texas, the education of the Tejano children stopped being a priority. Since then, Tejano and Mexican American children have historically been marginalized by the denial of access to educational opportunities.

In the latter part of the 19th century this oppression and marginalization became the norm. However, research shows Tejanos started to resist this trend in the latter part of the 19th century and into the 20th century by establishing their own schools and filing discrimination lawsuits.

The first elements of this movement in South Texas were the schools in ranchos designed to educate the children of the Tejano landowners and those of the vaqueros. Examples of these were found in the Benavides, San Diego, and Randado areas. The King Ranch, too, started its own schools.

It must be remembered that the majority of the population in South Texas in the 19th century and even the 20th century lived in isolated areas sprinkled from the border area of Brownsville-McAllen and Laredo to the Brush Country of South Texas and the Coastal Plains.

Civilization, much less education, was a far cry from reaching these people.

The South Texas town of Hebbronville known as "The Vaquero Capital of Texas," stands as a symbol for the struggle to get education to its area, in particular its children.

Located in Jim Hogg County 100 miles southwest of Corpus Christi and 50 miles southeast of Laredo, the early settlers of the area understood the value of education. Other small communities like San Diego, Benavides, Falfurrias, Sinton and those in the Rio Grande Valley and Laredo area have similar stories about pioneering education to tell.

Families in this area trace their roots back to the Spanish and Mexican land grants of the 18th and 19th centuries. The settlers were educated and understood the need for books, schools, and libraries. They also understood the need to study culture, history and language – including English.

There was a problem. Educating Mexicano or Tejano children was not a priority for the educational system of the state. Many Mexicano and Tejano children dropped out school at early grades, learning the rudimentary skills of writing their name and reading not to extend past the 3rd grade level. There were also cultural pressures. The family often needed the children to work on the fields to help the family make a living and plain old survive.

But, out of the South Texas chapparal and mesquital and dusty cow and horse trails, leaders arose. They would build their own schools, hire educated teachers with a background in the arts and social graces. They were on the way to create their own legacy and prove Tejanos cared about the education of their children.

The ranch community stepped up and dismissed the myth that Tejanos did not care about education. Realizing the importance of education, Tejano ranch owners opened schools for their children and those of their vaqueros. Among the examples from that area were children of Rancho El Colorado, owned by the Guerra family, who hired teachers and started teaching the basics. Degreed educators were sought to teach children in English and Spanish at La Violeta Ranch. The students of Rancho Nuevo owned by the Martinez family were an example of that commitment to education held by the Tejanos. At the Los Ojuellos ranch community, the leaders hired Jovita Idar, journalist and civil rights leader from Laredo, to teach their children. Idar, when she discovered the school was lacking textbooks, printed her own version so that the students would not miss out on a proper education. She later did the same in Laredo.

All children were expected to attend school and they did. Scholars were soon created at this ranches. They would continue their education in high school and some into college at a time when that seemed impossible for many.

The first general school in the ranch country of South Texas was founded in Hebbronville when "*El Colegio Altamirano*" was opened in 1897. Hebbronville, founded in 1883, is a hundred miles southwest of Corpus

Christi and 50 miles southeast of Laredo, had the education tradition from the ranches, but needed something in the town - something better. "El Colegio Altamirano" fit their needs.

An article by Dr. Cinthia Salinas, profesor at the University of Texas, identified the founders as Dionicio Peña, Francisco Barrera Guerra, Tomas Barrera, José Ángel Garza and Ascensión Martínez. They lent their financial support and quickly earned the support of the community. The school taught art, music, discipline, the social graces as well reading, writing and arithmetic.

The school was opened to all children and not limited to children who lived within the town's boundaries. Ranch children and those in town were treated equally. Some families moved into town and others sent their children to live with relatives. Those in the ranch would ride their horses to school. Soon, enrollment averaged about 100 students annually. Its students transferred successfully into the Jim Hogg County public school system which opened in the 1920s.

The first class had 12 boys and four girls. Enrollment grew quickly and hovered around 100 students until it closed in 1958. The building still stands on East Santa Clara Street across from Our Lady of Guadalupe Catholic Church and Scotus College, once a seminary for Franciscan priests.

"El Colegio Altamirano" was called "*La Escuelita* (little school)" by the residents. Rigor was the word for their curriculum and expectations. Final exams consisted of students in each grade presenting an oral and written report in front of their peers and the board of education. Rigor was the norm.

The first "*profesor*" was *Don* (pronounced in Spanish and denotes a well-respected person) Rosendo Barrera. Señorita Emilia Dávila , became his assistant and later took over as the headmistress of the school.

What is also important to remember is that these education pioneers used their own economic means to ensure their children's education and to keep the school open and functioning.

The Tejanos of Jim Hogg County instilled in their children the values and beliefs of their ancestors. Simultaneously, they provided their children with educational opportunities that would ensure their place in mainstream Anglo society and public schools.

Dr. Salinas explained the formation of "*El Colegio Altamirano*" in a scholarly article for the academic journal "Educational Forum" in 1998.

She noted it is important to emphasize that "*El Colegio Altamirano*" was established by a group of Mexican-American middle class citizens. "In founding the Colegio Altamirano, the Tejanos of the community were providing access and equity to their children,'" Salinas wrote.

As time progressed and the area became part of Jim Hogg County, the school added the goal to "prepare every Mexican child with the knowledge of their mother tongue to facilitate the learning of the English language," Salinas noted. By the 1920s, the school was preparing its students to transfer into the public school system. "An undated document from the 1920s by Harvey Edds, president of the Hebbronville Independent School District (Board), praised '*Colegio Altamirano*' students for being 'more regular in their attendance, more obedient, and more capable of grasping the English language than those who have not had this training,'" Salinas wrote.

Salinas concludes, "Using their own economic means and community association, the Chicanos of Jim Hogg County instilled in their children the values and beliefs of their ancestors. Simultaneously, they provided their children with educational opportunities that would ensure their place in mainstream Anglo society and public schools."

"El Colegio Altamirano" stands as a model for educational opportunities for Tejanos and should erase the notion that Tejanos, Mexican Americans, did not care about their children's education.

"El Colegio Altamirano" officially closed as a school in 1958, but it kept its name and stands as a model for educational opportunities for Tejanos and should erase the notion that Tejanos, Mexican Americans, did not care about the education of their children.

The building is located on E. Santa Clara Street, its original location, across from Our Lady of Guadalupe Catholic Church and Scotus College, once a seminary for Franciscan priests. It continues to be used for various social and educational functions. As of 2021 it was serving as the headquarters for the HeadStart Program in Jim Hogg County.

(Note: Information for this article came from various sources, including the 50th and 100th anniversary editions of the History of Jim Hogg County and the article by Dr. Cinthia Salinas, a former resident of Hebbronville: Cinthia Salinas (2001) El Colegio Altamirano (1897–1958): New Histories of Chicano Education in the Southwest, The Educational Forum, 65:1, 80-86.)

Closing Thoughts

The term _Tejano_, pronounced te-ha-no, means "Texan" in Spanish and is significant because it refers to the native Spanish and Mexican settlers who founded Texas initially as a province of New Spain and later as a state of the Republic of Mexico Later, Texas became it's on country, rebelling against Mexico. Although the term refers specifically to the original Tejanos, the term lends itself also to Hispanics of various national origins who can relate to a common heritage as modern Texans, even though they may come from diverse national origins.

The Tejano Monument is one of the largest monuments on the grounds of the Texas state Capitol in Austin and features a 20-foot granite base with 10 statues and five bronze-relief plaques. It was proposed by the Tejano Monument, Inc., a private fundraising committee of Mexican American leaders. On May 17, 2001, the Seventy-seventh Texas Legislature adopted House Concurrent Resolution (HCR) 38 authorizing the committee to erect the monument, created by Laredo sculptor Armando Hinojosa, on the Texas <u>Capitol</u> grounds to pay tribute to the contributions of Tejanos—the founding Spanish and Mexican settlers—to the state of Texas. It was erected on The board members of the Tejano Monument, Inc., raised approximately $2 million to fund and erect the monument on March 29, 2012, in an elaborate unveiling ceremony which featured speeches by Governor Rick Perry and other officials, a parade, and a history symposium.

Tejano Monument, (Tejano Monument, www.tshaonline.org/handbook)

Tejano Soy

Tejano Soy – A poem of culture and destiny

(Editor's Note: The following poem was written by Dr. Manuel Flores to depict the struggle and story of the Tejano in Texas. It is bilingual (in English and Spanish) because the majority of Tejanos use both languages in their everyday life and a little bit of a mix called TexMex.)

Tejano Monument, www.tshaonline.org/handbook

El sol caliente la sangre que corre dentro de mi

The sun warms the blood that runs inside of me

¡Soy Tejano, Americano, Latino, Mexicano y Mestizo, Si!

I'm Texan, American, Spanish, Latin, Mexican and Mestizo, Yes!

Amanse la tierra de los muertos y el desierto abandonado

I tamed the land of the dead and the lonely desert

cuando otra gente decía que no valía un centavo.

When some people claimed it wasn't worth a cent.

Llegue aquí con los Españoles, y vine con Escandón,

I arrived in this land with the Spaniards and I came with Escandon,

por la tierra firme y extraña que gano mi corazón.

Through this bold and strange land that won my heart.

Establecimos los ranchos y fuimos los primeros ganaderos,

We established ranching and we were the first cattlemen,

Porque en este mundo no había ni para los perros.

Because in this Word there were not even scraps to feed the dogs.

Paleamos por nuestra libertad una, dos, tres y cuatro veces.

We fought for our Liberty once, twice, three and four times.

Primero contra España, luego con Santa Anna y ortos imbéciles.

First against Spain, then Santa Anna and other imbeciles.

**¡Por fin, nos juntamos con los indígenas y hicimos una raza nueva –
Mestizos!**

Finally, we joined the Indigenous and created a new breed- Mestizos!

**Juntos hemos peleado más de dos siglos por el derecho de estar en esta
tierra.**

Together we have fought more than two centuries for the right to be in
this land.

También peleamos por Tejas, pero no lo reconocen,
We also fought for Texas, but it is not acknowledged,

por esa gente malcriada que robo y nos mató pero no nos dominó.
by those poorly raised people who robbed and killed us but failed to dominate us.

También somos Americanos y peleamos por esta tierra Americana,
We are also Americans, and we fought for this land we call America,

que nos dio oportunidad, por fin, para vivir y para volar.
that gave us opportunity, finally, to live and to thrive.

Somos hombres y mujeres listos para sobrevivir,
We are men and women ready to survive,

cualquier cosa quo nos tira esta vida infeliz.
whatever obstacles this hard life puts in our paths.

El sol caliente la sangre que corre dentro de mi.
The sun warms the blood that runs inside of me.

¡Soy Tejano, Americano, Latino, Mexicano y Mestizo, Si!
I'm Texan, American, Spanish, Latin, Mexican and Mestizo, Yes!

¡Soy Tejano, si Señor! ¡Aquí estoy y no ve voy!
Yes sir, I am a Tejano! I'm here and I'm not going anywhere!

Esta tierra en un día fue de mi bisabuelos, y ellos me la heredaron.
This land once belonged to my great-grandfathers and it was willed to me.

Yo también hoy soy su dueño, y les hago una promesa.

Today, I too own this land, and I will make you a promise.

 El día que yo me muera, mis hijos se quedan con esta,

The day I die, this land will belong to my children.

¡Soy Tejano, Americano, Latino, Mexicano y Mestizo, Si!

I'm Texan, American, Spanish, Latin, Mexican and Mestizo, Yes!

¡Tengo orgullo, soy feliz, y nadie me corre de aquí!

I'm proud, happy and no one will run me from this land!

Epilogue: Tejano Soy, "Flores, Manuel, "Hispanics in the Media: More Than 200 Years of Spanish-Language Influence in U.S. Communications," Kenall/Hunt, Dubuque, Iowa, p. 215

Acknowledgements

On the cover: The photo on the cover features the Transito Sáenz family circa 1888 at their home in Oilton, Texas. He is the basis for the first "cuento" in the introduction. They are Francisca and Transito Sáenz and their niece María Marta. (Marcos M. Flores collection)

This book would not have been possible without the tales and cuentos handed down generation-to-generation by my family and friends. Much thanks goes to my mother María Lucia Chapa Flores Sáenz, my grandfather Pedro G. Chapa, my stepdad Amando Saenz, my sons Mario and Marcos Flores, and friend Ramiro Molina for sharing these stories with me and keeping the storytelling tradition alive in South Texas. ¡Gracias! They were the basis for this book.

In addition, this book is an anthology, a collection of stories. Nine other noted Tejano and Texas historians or community leaders contributed pieces for this book. They helped add substance, credibility and authenticity to the book. I list them here with a short bio. ¡Gracias!

Dr. Cynthia Orozco: Dr. Cynthia E. Orozco is an award-winning best-selling author, public historian, and educator. She earned degrees at the University of Texas at Austin and UCLA. She is the author of *No Mexicans, Women or Dogs Allowed: The Rise of the Mexican American Civil Rights Movement; Agent of Change: Adela Sloss-Vento: Mexican American Civil Rights Activist and Texas Feminist; and Pioneer of Mexican American Civil Rights: Alonso S. Perales. She is the co-editor of Mexican Americans in Texas History,* an associate editor of Latinas in the United States: An Historical Encyclopedia and served as Research Associate at the Texas State Historical Association where she wrote 80 articles on Texas history for the *New Handbook of Texas.* Her contribution to this work as *"Ben Garza – Corpus Christi Leader and First President of LULAC."*

The Hon. Juan E. Escobar: Juan Escobar served as Judge of Kleberg County, Texas, and on the Texas legislature as a state representative. He was elected to the Texas House of Representatives replacing the late Irma

Rangel in May 2003. He served in that capacity until January 2009. In 2010 he was elected as Kleberg County Judge and served until December 2014. He is Vietnam War veteran and recipient of the Purple Heart. He achieved the rank of Staff Sergeant before retiring from the U.S. Marine. He was stationed in Washington D.C. assigned to United States Marine Barracks 8th & I, where he served as a pall bearer for Presidents Lyndon B. Johnson and Harry S. Truman. With He retired from the Department of Homeland Security in 2003.[He later served in the U.S. Border Patrol (1978-2003) where he rose to the rank of Senior Special Agent with the Organized Crime Drug Enforcement Task Force. A native of Roma, Texas, he was an excellent basketball player and has been inducted into several athletics halls of honor. He is a graduate of the University of Pan American (now the University of Texas- Rio Grande Valley. He has two selections in this book: "Don Martin de Leon: Founder of Victoria, Texas" and "Cinco de Mayo and the Texas Connection – Gen. Zaragoza saves Mexico and the U.S."

Servando Hinojosa: Servando Hinojosa is a noted Tejano artist who has made it his life quest to make sure the contributions of the Tejano are recognized in Texas and beyond. He has done several public artwork projects and illustrated several historical books. He is a retired educator from Alice. Texas, and earned his bachelor's and master's degree from Texas A&I University (now Texas A&M University-Kingsville). His metal sculpture in downtown Alice "Mario Y Jose" is one of the most recognized pieces of art in South Texas. Academically, He has been commissioned to illustrate books such as the fourth volume of *"Stories That Must Not Die"*, bilingual (Spanish/English) novel *"Across the River"* in black and white by Dr. Juan Sauvageau. Other books he has illustrated are the award-winning book by Dr. Andres Tijerina *"Tejano Empire, "and "Healing By Hand"* by Drs. Oths and Hinojosa. He also designed the book jacket for "Llanos Mesteños" by Agnes Grimm, and the cover for the Goliad, Texas pamphlet *"Two Hundred Years At La Bahia."* and a children's book by Mary Dru Burns. Other illustrations have been for Texas archeologists and anthropologists. He has two pieces in this book. One is autobiographical about his life as a South Texas Tejano artist and the other is the "Epilogue" on why this book is important.

Ramiro Molina: Ramiro Molina is a Tejano historian and has one of the state's largest collections of historical maps, which are on display at the Tejano Civil Rights Museum and Resource Center in Heritage Park in

Corpus Christi, Texas. He served as an adviser to the construction of the Tejano Monument in Austin, is an advisory board member of the Tejano Civil Rights Museum and has served as an officer of the Hebbronville Museum and Jim Hogg County Historical Commission. He also served as a board member of the Jim Hogg County (Hebbronville) school district and is involved in many community projects. He attended the University of Texas. He is a free-lance writer contributing articles on South Texas history. His contributions in this book include *"La Matanza (The Massacre) – A Dark Time in the History of Texas." And "Scotus College Rises Above the Horizon in Hebbronville (Texas)."*

Rosa Canales Pérez: Rosa Canales Pérez and her husband José O. Pérez are part of a musical group that performs music from the border of Mexico and the U.S. Natives of Premont, Texas, they have lived in the Rio Grande Valley since 1980, relocating from Austin to accept teaching jobs in the border area, first in McAllen and then in Brownsville. The couple produced and hosted "North of the Border," an audio/ radio program of Mexican roots music presented with socio-historical commentary in English for the NPR affiliate in the Lower Rio Grande Valley from 2002 - 2007.They are graduates of Texas A&I University (now Texas A&M University-Kingsville). Rosa and Joe are founding members of the Narciso Martínez Writers' Forum, which provides a venue for Valley writers to express their bi-lingual/bi-cultural literary interpretations of the region. Rosa taught English and Mexican American Studies at Hanna High School in Brownsville from 1984 until her retirement in 2001. She is a former Board Member of the Narciso Martínez Cultural Arts Center. Rosa is also a songwriter and Tejano historian. Her selection in this book is *"Américo Paredes – A Texas–Mexican Cancionero."*

Dr. Ricardo Romo: Dr. Ricardo Romo was the fifth president of the University of Texas-San Antonio. He earned a B.S. degree from the University of Texas Austin; a M.A. degree in American History from Loyola University Los Angeles; and a Ph.D. in American History from the University of California Los Angeles. At Texas he was a track star earning several medals and recognition. Academically, he is a recognized urban historian, art and Mexican American civil rights expert. Romo has taught and published in the field of civil rights, Mexican American history, and urban history. His book, *"East Los Angeles: History of a Barrio,"* is in its 9th edition. He served as president of UTSA from 1999 to 2017. Romo currently serves as a member of the Board of Directors for Southwest Research Institute, Board of Directors for the Brackenridge Park Conservancy, and Board of Directors for Humanities Texas. He is a member and past Vice President for The Philosophical Society of Texas. He is also active as the cultural and political writer as well as editorial board member for *La Prensa Texas*, a bilingual newspaper in San Antonio and writes a weekly online column on Texas and Chicano art. Among the awards and recognition that Romo has received are: Fellow at the Center for Advanced Studies at Stanford; the Clark Kerr Award for Distinguished Leadership in Higher Education from the University of California-Berkeley; the Outstanding Civilian Service Medal from the United States Army North; the Distinguished Alumnus Award from the Texas Exes. Dr. Romo's piece in this book is *"My Mestizo Family Crossed the Rio Grande in 1752."*

Dr. George T. Díaz: - Dr. George T. Díaz is the Director of the Center for Mexican American Studies at the University of Texas Río Grande Valley where he serves as an Associate Professor of History. He teaches U.S. History, Borderlands, and Mexican American History. His award-winning book, *"Border Contraband: A History of Smuggling across the Rio Grande"* is a social history of smuggling in the borderlands. Díaz is co-editor of the collection *Border Policing: A History of Enforcement and Evasion in North America* (University of Texas Press, 2020). His current book project, Mañana Land: Life and Death in a Mexican Prison in Texas, examines everyday life on Texas prison farms and how ethnic Mexican prisoners utilized their cultural practices as a means of resilience and resistance. Dr. Díaz's research is informed by investigations in Mexican and U.S. archives, as well as a lifetime of living on the border. His contribution to this book was the scholarly essay *"Los Tequileros – Contraband and Treachery in South Texas."*

José Antonio López: José Antonio López was born and raised in Laredo, Texas. He is a Tejano History columnist for the *Rio Grande Guardian* online newspaper and has written five books on Tejano history and genealogy . His books are dedicated to Spanish Mexican people and events in U.S. history that are mostly overlooked in mainstream history books. His latest book is *"Preserving Early Texas History (Essays of an Eighth-Generation South Texan),* Volume 3".. He is a USAF Veteran. He has college degrees from Laredo Jr. College and Southwest Texas State University (SWTSU), San Marcos, Texas. He also earned a Master's Degree in Education from SWTSU (now Texas State University). His piece in this book is "The Birth of Tejano Ranching."

Dr. Nick Adame: Dr. Nick Adame is a community advocate active in education and civil rights. He has served as president for the League of United Latin American Citizens (LULAC) for the past 15 years and has been a regent for Del Mar College in Corpus Christi, Texas, since 2008. A graduate from Parker College, Dr. Adame has been a chiropractor for over 20 years. Born and raised in Corpus Christi he is actively involved in the community and is a U.S. Navy Vietnam War veteran. His forte is community service and has served as a member City of Corpus Christi Ethics Commission and the Texas Jazz Festival Society. Dr. Adame wrote *"The Battle for Civil Rights for Tejanos – South Texas Has Produced its Share of Activities."*

Epilogue

By Servando Hinojosa

All of us have stories to tell. Dr. Manuel Flores tells his in books, essays and lectures. They are like old-fashioned "*cuentos* (tales)" reminding us of historic and significant events that have occurred during our lives or just, as Texas A&I professor Juan Sauvageau used to say in his classic Tejano Folklore book, are "stories that must not die"

I believe Dr. Flores has penned another Tejano classic that will help us remember our past with pride and understanding that we had some interesting stories to tell. We all have stories to tell. Dr. Flores chose the printed word.

I choose to tell my stories through art.

Since I was in elementary school, I was fascinated with Spanish Explorers - *Los Conquistadores.* Later on, in Junior High School I learned about Texas history and its fabulous stories. Spain, and later Mexico, seemed to be at the center of all these tales and legends.

At one point, after reading how bad the Mexican people were portrayed and treated since the battle of the Alamo in 1836, I started to question what I read in the Texas History books. I was disappointed in how we, people of Spanish and Mexican origin but also Tejanos who had been in Texas since the 18th century, were portrayed. Mexicans killed everyone at the Alamo in 1836 in a brutal way – etc. It was as if we were never forgiven and as Tejanos bore that original sin of infamy in Texas.

While in college at Texas A&I University in Kingsville, Texas, I learned, in Texas history class, new facts about our Lone Star State. We had a marvelous history that led back to the indigenous populations of the area. Strong Spanish, Mexican and then other European pioneers would settle the land. Still, Mexicans were portrayed historically as bandidos, not too intelligent and they were seen as lazy. We're not lazy!

In the classroom, many of us were regarded as "not smart enough" to be studying at this level of higher education. On campus, we were not allowed in certain dorms or to join some student organizations like fraternities and sororities. A Tejano could not run, for example, for Homecoming royalty or even student government at one point. And, some of the rent houses around campus were off limits to minorities. It hurt. It left me angry.

So, as an artist, I made it my goal to study more Texas history and portray the more truthful view of my people - *la raza*. Through art, I began to portray Hispanics, Tejanos, Mexicanos in a more truthful, positive way. I wanted to show that there was value in the role Tejanos played in developing the ranching and cattle industry of the 18th and 19th centuries and of working in the farms under the hot Texas sun and picking crops for low wages all over the nation. My vision of our story had to be told. I began creating more art such as paintings, prints, drawings that were going to become murals, sculptures and portraits that were more positive. I also illustrated Texas history books such as "Stories the Must Not Die" by Dr. Juan Sauvageau and other scholarly works like Andres Tijerina's "Tejano Empire." I also illustrated works for books and text books for anthropology like that of Dr. Servando Z. Hinojosa, a professor of anthropology at UT-RGV (The University of Texas Rio Grande Valley). I did work on academic journals and designed art for scholarly essays, power points and films and delved into public art and museum exhibits. My metal sculpture titled "*Alicia y Juan*", depicting a young Tejano couple dancing at a fandango, in Alice Texas on Hwy 44 is a tribute to the Tejano who came to this land, settled it and has strived to make it better every day. But we were fun-loving people, too, and loved our music and our dances. Still do.

You see, I believe that everyone should do his or her part to promote our Spanish, Mexican, Indigenous, American and Texas culture. We are a mix of people. Mestizos, we are called. We have the blood of the Spanish conquistador and the Indigenous of Mexico and Texas running through our veins and we can be proud of that because we have survived in spite of many obstacles.

And, so, all of us must tell our story. They are tales of love, sorrow and perseverance. The more we tell our story the more the real story of Texas will unfold. And, if we don't tell our story, others will. Chances are it won't be honest or truthful.

There are stories and art work of us working in the farm fields, tending cattle, working on an oil rig, teaching, practicing law, being politicians, oh my God, there are so many. So, tell them! Paint them. Do a film or documentary. But, tell our stories – our "*Cuentos Teajnos.*"

Don't be silent. If we stay silent, our stories will fade into the sunset and be blown away by the winds of time. 19th century civil rights advocate and revolutionary Catarino Garza, in the late 1800s, used to warn the people of South Texas that if they did not unite, our way of life would perish. Jovita Idar said all of us, even women, should have a voice. She and educator/politician J.T. Canales asked for the Texas Rangers to be dismantled. Ben Garza and Dr. Hector P. Garcia saw our hope in organizations like LULAC and the American G.I. Form. Dr. Manuel Flores and many other scholars like Emilio Zamora of the University of Texas write books. They are and were not silent.

So, it is with honor that I write this epilogue for *"Cuentos Tejanos – Tejano Tales"*. May it help explain our way of life, our story and our fortitude to ensure that it is never forgotten.

(Metal sculpture designed by Alice, Texas, artist Servando Hinojosa and metal artist Juan Farias in downtown Alice on Sept 5, 2008.)

Pilón - Extra

The Cadillac Bar

A Personal Story about the

Legendary Restaurant in Nuevo Laredo

-By Dr. Manuel Flores

(Editor's Note: The Cadillac Bar was a popular romantic and eclectic Mexican restaurant that opened in 1924 in Nuevo Laredo, Mexico. It was the "go to" place to savor good Mexican cuisine with a New Orleans flavor. Its favorite dish was ("Cabrito asado" – roasted goat kid) and its favorite beverage was the Ramos Gin Fizz. Of course, it had all of the other favorite Mexican dishes. Its atmosphere was unique and looked like a scene from a 1950s black and white movie set with waiters in white tuxedo jackets, a black bow tie and black pants. Often, there was a piano playing and, at times, an occasional mariachi or trio. It opened on Vicente Guerrero Avenue, Nuevo Laredo's main thoroughfare, in 1924. It had a dirt floor at the time. It moved to Calle Belden and Avenida Ocampo on July 4, 1929 and stayed there until 2010.)

(Source, Walsh, Robb. "The Tex-Mex Cookbook", P. 232-233). This is a personal family a story and a "cuento" that has been in the family for decades.

Here's the "Cuento."

My "abuelita" (grandma) was busy making migas (an eggs and fried corn tortillas dish) for our *almuerzo* (brunch). It was a very humid but cool and foggy March day and dew was still dripping from the mesquite tree outside in our backyard. My sisters, Lynda and Judy, would soon be arriving from college at Texas A&I University in Kingsville and would be hungry.

It was already 8:30 and the morning was fading quickly. Besides, we had to get ready for our annual Lenten trip to the Cadillac Bar in Nuevo Laredo, Mexico, that afternoon. Oh, it wasn't religious. It was just fun.

"Maria," my grandma asked my mom, " *¿Le ponemos tocino?* (Do we add bacon?)

Mom answered flustered with a quick "No" in Spanish and explained it was Lent, and no meat should be eaten. Mom was a member of the Guadalupanas (Our Lady of Guadalupe organization) at our Catholic church and my step-dad Amando was a member of the Knights of Columbus. My grandfather had been a Grand Knight. So, there was a religious atmosphere around at that time.

My grandmother just shook her head, fully realizing the whole family would be eating *cabrito* (a Mexican dish made with a roasted kid goat as the main course) later that day at the restaurant in Nuevo Laredo.

Shortly, my sisters arrived and all the usual *Mexicano abrazos* (hugs) and kisses and slaps in the back ensued.

"Ay mama what smells so good?" Lynda asked.

"I'm starving," Judy remarked. "*Tengo mucho hambre* (I'm very hungry)."

Just then my stepdad Amando arrived. "¿Cuando nos vamos para Laredo? (When are we leaving for Laredo)? He asked."

Mom flustered added that as soon as the girls ate we could start preparing to leave.

My sisters were excited as they enjoyed their meatless breakfast with eggs, diced corn tortillas and *pico de gallo* (Mexican salsa) along with a side of refried beans with Mexican cheese as a topping. And, of course there were steamy hot fresh flour tortillas grandma had just made.

"I'm ready now," Judy said. "Besides we do this for mom every year. It's a family tradition."

Lynda added, "Yes we know how much you love this trip mom," hugging her lovingly.

Mom just looked into the air and went to get dressed. Amando and I sat down to watch a baseball game on TV. It was almost noon and the "Game of t he Week" was about to come on with Dizzy Dean and Pee Wee Reese. The hustle and bustle in the house was exciting. We couldn't wait for the delicacy of the food we were to eat at the famous restaurant. "It's just the best place on the border," my step-dad said.

The family had been going to the Cadillac Bar every year since the girls were in elementary school. This was our 15th year of this family ritual, or so we thought. But, who's counting?

I had arrived the previous night from the Dallas area where I was doing graduate work at the University of North Texas in Denton. I was fully aware that this was a trip we did to make "mom" happy, and we knew she enjoyed it very much – or so we thought.

Mom looked somewhat irritated, but that's how moms are at times. Easter Sunday was *mañana* (tomorrow) and there were religious obligations to attend (maybe Midnight mass that night?) and food to prepare. There was lots to do and mom was getting up in age. She looked tired and somewhat agitated, too.

But the plans to go to the Cadillac Bar in Nuevo Laredo, Mexico, continued.

My sisters sped into their bedrooms to change and get ready. My *abuelita* (grandma Nana) started to clean up and would stay to take care of the dogs and cats saying briskly, "*Que las vaya bien y vayan con Díos* (Basically, have a good trip and go with God), and then made the sign of the cross blessing all of us and said "Amen." By instinct, all of us did the sign of the cross.

 My step-dad had just gassed up the car and washed it and was wearing his light blue Guayabera (Mexican wedding shirt), dress slacks and black cowboy boots for the occasion. I was wearing jeans and my University of North Texas sweatshirt. It was still somewhat cool out there for March.

"So, I want to leave by 3," my stepdad exclaimed. "That way we can get there in time so we can have a Ramos Gin Fizz (a cocktail with dry gin, powdered sugar, heavy cream, fresh lemon juice, lime juice, an egg white, and orange flower water made famous in New Orleans) or two, or maybe a couple of "*cervezas*" (beers)."

Mom looked at him incredulously. "We're going to eat, not drink," she told him.

My stepdad ignored her point and shouted to the girls, "Your mom likes those Gin Fizzes so much and your brother and I can have a couple of Carta Blancas (the favorite Mexican beer at the time)."

The Cadillac Bar was a fancy place. It was "the place" to be in the Laredo area and even had Mexican revolutionary Pancho Villa's saddle (the real one) on display. My sisters and I had all taken photos on the saddle that my mom proudly displayed in our living room. We would probably take another picture or two with the saddle later that day.

By 3 p.m., the sun was out, and it was hot, South Texas hot. The air conditioning in the car hardly worked. We had just gotten it installed. But, the one-hour trip was quick from our hometown of Hebbronville to the Mexican border. . At the border checkpoint, the traffic was heavy as we crossed the international bridge. We got to Nuevo Laredo and meandered through the narrow streets and parked at the restaurant's gated parking lot. We were lucky.

An attendant came to help, and my step-dad gave him a $5 tip "to watch the car." We felt safe and anxious for our meal.

Mom looked tired.

The restaurant was packed with scores of people eating and enjoying the music of a *trio* (a Mexican musical group composed of three guitarists and singers). The aroma of Mexican cuisine and roasted goat filled the air. The restaurant bar was also known for frog legs they got from the nearby Rio Grande. With beer or a *margarita* or a Gin Fizz, they were awesome.

The waiters were dressed in white tuxedo-like sports coats with black bow ties and impeccably pressed black slacks. Some carried the food to the tables, balancing them with one hand in the air as they rushed toward the customers. The Pancho Villa saddle display had a line with children of all ages waiting to take their pictures.

It was crowded.

My step-dad signaled to one of the waiters and handed him a $10 bill. Amazingly, we found a table, quick.

My step-dad and I had beers, Carta Blancas, and mom and my sisters ordered the traditional Gin Fizz drink everyone had at the Cadillac Bar. We ordered cabrito for the table so that we all could share the succulent dish prepared expertly at the restaurant. We also ordered individual platters of enchiladas, tacos, refried beans and tortillas and a variety of *salsas* to accentuate our dishes.

The musical trio came over and played "*Cuando Caliente el Sol aquí en la playa* (When the sun warms here on the beach) and later the very romantic *"Amor Eterno* (Eternal Love)," They were good. Stepdad gave them $20 for their efforts.

Suddenly, mom started to cry.

We were baffled, and at first we thought she was reacting to the songs.

"*Ama* (mom) are you okay?" I asked and more tears came down.

It was sort of embarrassing, but now my sisters went into full Mexican-daughter mode and walked her to the bathroom. My stepdad and I sat there and ordered another Carta Blanca.

Ten minutes later, they came back.

"She wants to go home, now," Lynda, my older sister said emphatically as Judy put her arms around her and tried to calm her down. We had been there maybe an hour at the most, but it was time to go. It would be dark soon. No midnight Mass tonight, I thought. We left, got into the car and headed back, foregoing our usual shopping trip to the *mercado* (marketplace) in Nuevo Laredo.

The trip back was silent. Judy then asked mom if she was alright. More tears and then came her testimony. My step-dad slowed down to maybe 55 mph.

Mom spoke, between sobs.

"I don't know why you all insist on coming here on Easter Saturday. I have too much to do for tomorrow and I'm worried I won't have time. I should have stayed at home. I have so much food to prepare for our Easter Sunday gathering. I only do this trip for you all, but it's too much for me now, I'm getting old."

More sobs. And then my sisters started to sob. My step-dad looked back at them and said. "*Ya vamos a llegar,* (We're almost home)." My sisters, almost in unison, said they would help her prepare for the Easter Dinner and gathering. At least 15 people were coming Sunday evening for the dinner. Sunday morning would mean Mass at Our Lady of Guadalupe Catholic Church.

Amando promised to grill some meat and I would help him and bring some beer for the men.

"Don't worry," he said, "*Te vamos ayudar* (We're going to help you)."

Then he asked her, "Well did you enjoy the *cabrito*, Maria?"

The girls laughed at his timing or lack of it. I just shook my head. And, my mom started to cry again. I kept my eye on the road. So, she had been doing this trip for us and we had been doing the trip for her.

Thus, the paradigm of our trips to the Cadillac Bar.

That was the last time we took that trip. But, oh, the memories persist. The Cadillac Bar restaurant was legendary and, evidently, so were our trips to Nuevo Laredo.

Cadillac Bar, Nuevo Laredo, Mexico.

(Amando Sáenz cooking "pan de campo" (a.k.a. cowboy bread) at a Pachanga
(party, gathering) at La Parrita Ranch near Hebbronville, Texas, in 2005

The Tejano Tradition survives in many South Texas families as it does for the Flores family. Here Elena Marisol Lentz walks toward the main house of La Parrita Ranch in Jim Hogg County near Hebbronville, Texas. She is two years old but is ready for the Tejano tradition. She's got her boots on. La Parrita Ranch was first operated by her great-grandfather Guadalupe Acevedo and grandfather Manuel C. Flores Jr. It is now operated by her mother Teresa Marisol Flores Lentz and her uncles Mario and Marcos Flores.

www.ingramcontent.com/pod-product-compliance
Lightning Source LLC
Chambersburg PA
CBHW040902010826
48978CB00013BB/1113